# *Cruise* BRITANNIA

*Oriana*, being passed by a hovercraft in the late 1960s.

# *Cruise* BRITANNIA

## THE STORY OF
## THE BRITISH CRUISE SHIP

### ROGER CARTWRIGHT
### & CLIVE HARVEY

TEMPUS

# ACKNOWLEDGEMENTS

We are indebted to the countless cruise passengers and cruise-line staff who have helped us in the pleasurable task of cataloguing those ships that have operated in the UK cruise market. We are very appreciative of the assistance and advice (and photographs) provided by Campbell McCutcheon, our editor at Tempus.

First published 2004

Tempus Publishing Ltd
The Mill, Brimscombe Port
Stroud, Gloucestershire GL5 2QG
www.tempus-publishing.com

© Roger Cartwright and Clive Harvey, 2004

British Library Cataloguing in Publication Data.
A catalogue record for this book is available from the British Library.

ISBN 0 7524 2989 2

Typesetting and origination by Tempus Publishing.
Printed and bound in Great Britain.

# CONTENTS

# FOREWORD

Beginning in August 1979, I was very fortunate to have made no less than eight cruises from Southampton aboard three great P&O liners. The *Canberra* and the *Oriana* were still together, built for the final years of the UK-Australia service, but then running mostly two- and three-week cruises to warm weather or resort-like, sometimes quite exotic ports. The *Sea Princess*, the third of these P&O liners, was in fact a cruise ship for almost all of her days, having begun her life as Sweden's *Kungsholm*.

Each ship provided a wonderful voyage. There were, of course, great shipboard amenities: the food, the service, games, lectures, the after-dinner shows and, not to be forgotten, quiet afternoons in a deck chair. Then there were the fascinating itineraries: the cool waters of the Baltic, the majestic Fjordlands, the historic Mediterranean and those sun-drenched Atlantic Isles. But possibly most of all for me, there were the other passengers and the crews. Being a guest lecturer, I had something of a quick, easy access to many of them. This created something of an onboard treasure chest of stories and anecdotes.

Many of the passengers tended to be older, usually retired, often veterans of the Depression, the Second World War, the era of George V and Queen Mary. A few had cruised in the 1920s and '30s, on ships such as P&O's *Rawalpindi*, White Star's *Doric* and Cunard's *Lancastria*. They spoke of pound-a-day fares, minimal on-board entertainment, but also escapism from the harsh, Depression-era realities back home. Others, perhaps slightly younger, spoke of cruises in the 1950s, as British travellers re-emerged from the cruel, bleak, threadbare days of the Second World War. Now, there were leisure voyages on a new generation of ships such as P&O's *Chusan*, Royal Mail's *Andes* and those Fyffes 'banana boats'. There were cheerful, often detailed, certainly nostalgic comments about these and many other ships.

The British had been, after all, cruising for a century by the mid-1950s. They perfected it, expanded it, set shipboard standards and made it very popular. P&O's *Ceylon* made the first recorded cruise back in 1858. Of course, it was all rather primitive, well before the days of umbrella-lined lido decks and thermostatically adjustable air-conditioning, hotel-like staterooms with private bathrooms and cushioned comfortable coaches waiting on the quayside.

By the 1930s, there were more cruises than ever before: One-day cruises, week-long jaunts to Madeira and Oslo, two and three weeks around the Mediterranean and up to the likes of eight weeks around continental Africa and four months around-the-world. Fabled Atlantic luxury liners such as the *Aquitania*, *Mauretania* and *Homeric* 'sailed to the sun' and went cruising from Britain. The British also had two of the most popular, standard-setting cruise liners of that era, the *Arandora Star* and the *Atlantis*.

In 1948, Cunard added the 34,000grt *Caronia*, painted in various shades of green and so also becoming the illustrious 'Green Goddess'. She ranked as the largest, most luxurious liner built in Britain since the War. More floating club than floating hotel, with loyal guests served by a handpicked staff, the *Caronia* was appraised almost from the start as the finest cruise ship afloat. For well over a decade, she was unsurpassed.

By the 1960s, cruises from British ports onboard British ships were richly and diversely abundant. A sample listing might include the *Uganda* and *Nevasa*, the *Carmania* and *Sylvania* and even the legendary *Queen Mary* and *Queen Elizabeth*, the *Orsova*, *Arcadia*, *Iberia* and *Himalaya*, the *Southern Cross* and the *Reina Del Mar*. There were foreign-flag ships that cruised from British ports, ships such the Spanish *Monte Umbe*, the Greek *Ithaca*, Norway's *Meteor*, Poland's *Batory* and the Soviet *Baltika*.

But there was a slump, a marked disappearance and disinterest almost, by the mid-1970s when, among other reasons, operational costs for British-flag passenger ships were soaring.

The 1990s saw a complete reversal, however. It was as if cruising was re-invented. The travelling public seemed to realize, and all over again, that there is absolutely no better holiday than a cruise. Presently, there is a sparkling, well-served-and-fed, gloriously entertained fleet of fine liners sailing in British cruise service with names such as *Aurora* and *Carousel*, *Braemar* and *Hebridean Princess*, *Saga Rose* and *Minerva II*, and *Ocean Village*.

Whether a holiday-seeking traveller or staff-member with fond, sentimentally laced memories or perhaps an armchair enthusiast intrigued by great ships making grand voyages, the British cruise fleet, past and present, sets sail here in Clive Harvey and Roger Cartwright's superbly researched and illustrated book. Noted for his impeccable research and flawless detail, Clive gives us yet another title to read, absorb, even cherish.

The entire fleet is here for a glorious review. All aboard for *Cruise Britannia*!

Bill Miller
New Jersey USA
August 2004

# Foreword contribution from David Dingle:

The British cruise market has shown spectacular growth over the last decade. Many British passengers prefer a ship dedicated to the UK market, with food, service and entertainment specified to British tastes. There are those who have cruised for many years and whose first experiences date back to classic ships like *Canberra*, *Andes* and *Reina Del Mar*, all of which feature in this book. Indeed, the authors have listed virtually every ship which has provided cruises dedicated to a British clientele since cruising as a true holiday form begin as far back as 1881. P&O were one of the pioneers of the cruise holiday and it is a matter of great pride that as a company we remain the largest provider of cruises dedicated to the British passenger.

This book will be of interest to all those wishing to learn more about British-style cruising or what happened to a favourite ship.

David Dingle
Managing Director, P&O Cruises

# PREFACE

In 1990 the number of Britons taking a cruise holiday was around 200,000. By the year 2003 this number had quadrupled to 800,000. Whilst approximately 6 per cent of the Britons undertaking a cruise did so in ships that operated primarily within the US market (a market that comprised nearly seven million cruise vacationers by 2000) the majority of Britons cruised in ships that were dedicated to the British market.

Cruising is very much a part of the holiday tradition. The first cruise ship to enter service was the *Ceylon,* bought by the Oceanic Yachting Company in 1881 and refitted as a full-time cruise ship.

Britons have comprised the second largest cruise market for many years.

This book is about how the uniquely British cruise market has developed into the thriving industry it is today. As a book it is not just a source of reference about ships but an easy to read explanation of what the cruise market is.

Whether you have bought this book to find out about cruising for the first time, or you are an experienced cruise passenger wanting to know more about the industry, or if you want to find out what happened to your favourite ship, there will be something to interest you.

In their introduction to the book, the authors (who are both well-known names within the industry, not only for writing about it but also for their love of cruising) note that there is a downside to cruise holidays – they are addictive.

The British cruise market has shown spectacular growth over the past decade. Many British cruise passengers prefer a ship that is dedicated to the UK market with food and entertainment to British tastes.

Many of today's cruise passengers had their first cruise experience in *Canberra*, *Andes* or *Reina Del Mar*, ships which feature in this book.

The authors have listed virtually every ship that has provided cruises dedicated to a British clientele since cruising as a holiday style began as early as 1881. P&O were one of the pioneers of the cruise holiday and it is a matter of pride that as a company they are still the largest provider of cruises dedicated to the UK cruise passenger.

*chapter one*

# A BRIEF HISTORY OF CRUISING FROM THE NINETEENTH CENTURY UP TO 1975

The parents of the cruise industry are the passenger shipping and holiday industries. Just like any child, the cruise industry has inherited characteristics of both.

## The passenger shipping industry

Humans have used seas and rivers as trade routes since the dawn of history. However, up to the introduction of steam propulsion even the shortest coastal voyage was hazardous, relying as it did on brute strength, using oars or the vagaries of the wind. People did not go to sea for pleasure, as every voyage was a risk.

After numerous experiments in the UK, the USA and France at the end of the eighteenth century, the first practical steam-driven vessel, a tug named the *Charlotte Dundas* went into service on the Forth & Clyde Canal in Scotland in 1801. Fulton's *Clermont*, built in New York, followed her in 1807. The Royal Navy, with the largest fleet of sailing vessels in the world was loathe to give up sail, as steam was considered unreliable and even too dirty for the spick and span appearance that warship captains insisted upon. Whilst the USA completed a steam warship, the *Demologos,* just too late for the 1812 war with Britain it was not until 1822 that the Royal Navy acquired a steamer in the form of the paddle-driven *Comet*. Early steamships used simple beam engines to drive paddles, the screw propeller not coming into vogue until 1844 with the launch of the *USS Princeton*. These early steamers were wooden vessels, carrying only enough fuel for short coastal voyages. However, a number of far-sighted individuals realised that steam would allow ships to sail to a fixed schedule. Steam-driven ships would be far less dependent on wind direction and strength. The modern cruise sailing ships that were developed in the 1990s can operate to a tight schedule, as they possess powerful engines in addition to their sails.

In May 1819, the fate of the sailing ship was sealed when the *Savannah,* travelling under steam and sail, made the first steam-assisted crossing of the North Atlantic, taking nearly twenty-eight days to make the crossing as the engines were used for only eighty hours.

Atlantic crossings by steam-powered ships, in addition to voyages to South Africa and India, became more frequent and in 1839 the British Admiralty awarded the UK–North

The first Cunarder, RMS *Britannia*, was one of the first ships to usher in transatlantic steam travel.

America mail contract to a Canadian, Samuel Cunard, and on 4 July (in honour of the USA) the *Britannia* sailed from Liverpool arriving at Halifax (Nova Scotia) on 17 July and Boston (MA) on the 20 July. Ships such as the *Britannia* and Brunel's earlier *Great Western* (1838) made the North Atlantic crossing much safer for passengers than the sailing packets, in addition to slashing the journey times.

When Brunel launched the *Great Britain* (3,270grt) in 1843, the world's first iron-hulled, propeller-driven passenger vessel, the pattern for future developments was set. The earliest steam-driven liners carried sails in addition to their engines in case of a mechanical breakdown but sail was dispensed with as the less-efficient beam engines gave way to reciprocating ones and then to turbines. By 1901, the UK White Star Line had placed the *Celtic* (20,904grt) in service, by 1907 Cunard's *Mauretania* and *Lusitania* were over 30,000grt (31,938) and in 1911, White Star introduced the 45,324grt *Olympic*, to be followed in 1912 by the *Titanic*. At that time it was considered that ocean travel was completely safe, a belief that was shattered by the loss of the *Titanic* on her maiden voyage.

Cruising, as distinct from ocean voyages designed to transport an individual from one place to another (the liner or ferry trade), made a fairly early entry into the shipping industry after the advent of steam-powered ships. The key factors that allowed cruising to develop were the ability to sail to a schedule, regardless of the wind, and the increasing safety that came with larger, iron (later steel) steam-driven ships.

It is difficult to define when cruising actually began, and there are several companies that consider themselves to be the pioneers of cruising. It does seem, however, that it is the German Sloman Company that is entitled to claim at least the basic idea. In 1845 they placed an advertisement in a Hamburg newspaper stating:

RMS *Mauretania*, the fastest ship on the North Atlantic for over two decades, was used for cruising and painted white from 1931–1934.

> A full-rigged ship is to go on a voyage of the world, which will not have as its aim any mercantile purposes, but the ship's whole facilities and accommodation, the fixing of the times of sojourn in the towns and countries to be visited, the over-riding aim of the whole voyage will only be consideration for the security, comfort, entertainment and information of the travellers. Only persons of good reputation and education–preferably scientifically educated–shall be taken aboard.

Unfortunately, however, this voyage was not carried out.

Meanwhile, British people used the ships of the Peninsular & Oriental SN Co. for voyages to the Mediterranean, but these ships were on regular routes, carrying cargo to and from scheduled ports, and therefore could not be classified as operating cruises. When Thackeray wrote of his trip to the Levant and the Holy Land that: 'the P&O Company has arranged an excursion in the Mediterranean by which, in the space of a couple of months, as many men and cities were to be seen as Ulysses surveyed and noted in ten years' he had travelled on three of the company's vessels, each of them being on regular service.

The first ocean 'pleasure' cruise was as early as 1881, when the Oceanic Yachting Company bought P&O's *Ceylon* and refitted her as a full-time cruise ship for the European market. The first 'advertised' cruise had been a dummy advertisement for a cruise around the Orkney and Shetland Islands in 1835. A cruise that never took place, although in 1886 the North of Scotland & Orkney & Shetland Steamship Company began to offer cruises to Norway in the *St Rognvald* and the *St Sunniva*. Similar cruises were still offered by P&O (Scotland) up to 2002 (after which the company's the contract

This small trade card is for the company that salvaged the *St Rognvald* of the North of Scotland & Orkney & Shetland Steamship Co., one of the first dedicated cruise ships.

for the North of Scotland services ran out). By the early 1900s, White Star Line, P&O in its own right and the Hamburg Amerika Line were offering regular cruises. Since the late 1890s, the Orient Line had been offering regular Caribbean, Mediterranean and Scandinavian cruises on board three of its vessels. For British passengers the Norwegian fjords and the Mediterranean were the major cruising areas. Both of these areas remain firm favourites with British cruise passengers today.

Two other early ships operating cruises to the Norwegian fjords were *Argonaut* and the appropriately named *Midnight Sun*, which operated from Newcastle. *Argonaut* was built in 1879 at the Blackwall Yard for Wigram's Australian trade, and at 3,274grt, was the last big ship to be built at that yard. In 1882 she was sold to the Royal Mail Steam Packet Co. and until 1893 sailed for them as *La Plata*. She changed hands twice after 1893 before becoming *Argonaut* of the Co-operative Cruising Co. Ltd. On 29 September 1908 she was involved in a collision off Dungeness with a tramp steamer, *Kingswell*. *Argonaut* began to sink immediately. The boats were lowered and all passengers and crew were transferred to the *Kingswell*. However, it was apparent that with her damage the additional people would put *Kingswell* in danger, so the passengers and crew returned to the lifeboats and *Kingswell* took them in tow. They were eventually taken aboard a collier, *South Moor*, and not a single life was lost in the incident.

On 22 August 1903 the 300grt *Balgowan* of the Bucknall Steamship Line made an experimental cruise, a venture to develop weekend excursion traffic, between Cape Town and Saldhana Bay. The trip was advertised to leave Cape Town every Friday morning, giving a seven hour sea passage, arriving in Saldhana Bay in the afternoon. They left there on Tuesday morning, returning to Cape Town in the afternoon (although these were cruises out of South Africa many of the passengers were British). The venture is regarded by the Ellerman Line, which later absorbed the Bucknall Line, as its first venture into cruising. However, it met with limited success and the cruises ran for only six months.

Anticipating the popular fly–cruises of today, in 1903 the Royal Mail Steam Packet Company introduced the 2,000grt *Solent* and, in 1905, the slightly larger *Berbice,* as dedicated vessels cruising the Caribbean for UK and US passengers. Obviously, the cruise passengers could not be flown out but were taken to the Caribbean and returned to Southampton or New York in the regular Royal Mail steamers.

In 1912, Cunard introduced the *Laconia* and the *Franconia* as their first dual-purpose cruise-line vessels. At this stage cruising was still very much an ancillary activity to the main business of regular voyages between fixed points, allowing shipping companies to generate additional revenue during slack periods. Cruising was also an expensive vacation only open to a privileged few. In 1911 the Hamburg Amerika Line converted the liner *Deutschland* into a dedicated cruise ship – the 16,502grt *Victoria Luise*. World War One brought an end to such experiments, as the belligerent powers converted their liners into troop ships or armed merchant cruisers.

Following the end of World War One the shipping companies of the Allied nations and those of Germany experienced a major shortage of tonnage for their core liner business. Even the vessels taken in reparations from Germany were insufficient to meet the increased demands of traffic, especially on the North Atlantic routes that the British and French shipping companies were endeavouring to satisfy. Emigration from Europe to

A small programme for a Fancy Dress Ball at Bergen on board Union-Castle's RMS *Dunottar Castle* in 1909.

The Grand Staircase on board the *Dunottar Castle*, Union-Castle Line's first dedicated cruise vessel.

North America resumed after the war and the geopolitical changes to borders after the peace settlement of Versailles in 1919 caused major population displacements, especially in Eastern Europe, and the United States received many of the displaced refugees. Between 1892 and 1924, when the US Government began to restrict immigration, over 12 million immigrants arrived in the port of New York alone.

Liners designed for scheduled services were often unsuitable for pleasure voyages due to their internal arrangements, with up to four classes of passenger and considerable variation between the facilities for each class.

Even if the issue of the different facilities is discounted, perceived wisdom for the time was that passengers did not wish to interact with their environment, and thus views of the ocean were few and far between. Liners had internal designs that were based on the ones used in hotels and country houses. It was only in the 1930s and the advent of Art Deco that larger windows began to appear in ships. The importance of the changes to the way ship interiors were designed lies in the fact that designs from the late 1920s onwards were based on enjoyment of the voyage in addition to pure functionality. Prior to this time the voyage itself was a 'necessary evil' if one wanted to get from say, Europe to America. Designs began to change so that the voyage became a pleasurable experience in itself.

## Cruising as a mass market

In the 1920s and 1930s the British cruise market was still mainly confined to the more affluent sector. Developments in the USA and Germany showed that cruising could appeal to the masses too.

The first great expansion in cruising was in the United States and was caused by a controversial policy of the US Government.

## Booze cruises

At midnight on 16 January 1920, the 18th Amendment to the Constitution of the United States, prohibiting 'the manufacture, sale or transportation of intoxicating liquors' came into force. This measure had been under discussion for some time in an attempt to combat a belief that alcoholic consumption was affecting the moral and economic wellbeing of the USA. In 1870 there were 100,000 saloons in the USA, one for every 400 citizens. Only wines prepared for personal use in homes were exempted. All of a sudden the people of the United States could not buy alcohol. Gangsters soon developed ways to process and supply alcohol, leading to the formation of the Federal Bureau of Investigation (FBI). There was, however, still one legal way in which an American could buy alcohol – if he or she was in a non-US registered ship outside the territorial limit.

This was the time of the roaring 20s and it soon became apparent to foreign ship owners that there was a market gap they could meet. Whilst US-flagged vessels were unable to serve alcohol, once out of US territorial limits there were no restrictions on non-US flagged vessels. Indeed, Hamburg Amerika, who had been operating the *Resolute* and the *Reliance* under the US flag soon transferred their registry to Panama in order to benefit from what became known as the 'booze cruise market'.

A poster advertising a 'booze cruise' to Halifax on board White Star's *Majestic,* their largest ship.

These booze cruises were in effect 'cruises to nowhere'. The customers undertook the cruises to party and to drink. For the first time there was a considerable market that went on a ship not to go from A to B but purely to sample the facilities that the ship offered.

'Booze cruises' alone would not have led to the first great growth of the cruise industry, but coupled to the flamboyant style of the age, cruising became a more intense experience than the leisurely pre-war operations that had only catered for the rich. In the United States, prohibition registered cruising on the consciousness of the vacationing public (still a small minority) as an acceptable, fun method of the annual get-away.

The impact of the US expansion on British cruising lay in the fact that British shipping companies began to take cruising seriously. Owing to the nature of US legislation, 'booze cruises' could only use foreign flagged ships and the British companies, Cunard and White Star (merged in 1934), were two of the largest operators in the US market. 'Booze cruising' gave the companies experience of mass-market cruising.

In the UK, cruising was still very much a minority experience, although it is reported that 175,000 Britons cruised in 1931 and Moss Brothers (the Gentleman's outfitters) had already produced an 'All at Sea' brochure. The average cost for a cruise was around £30 per head for a fortnight – a figure that seems small by today's standards but was out of reach for the majority of British families.

As the other parent of cruising is the tourist industry it is appropriate at this juncture to consider the development of the British tourism industry.

Tourism in Europe grew out of religious piety. One means of showing faith and piety had been the undertaking of a pilgrimage. In medieval times this really was a sacrifice, involving long journeys with considerable danger. The world's major religions have always had great reverence for the pilgrim, with some making it almost mandatory, for example, the Islamic Hajj to Mecca.

It is not surprising therefore that commercial centres grew up alongside religious ones. If people were travelling to Winchester or York or Santiago de la Compostela (still a popular shore excursion from the north-west Spanish ports of La Coruña and Vigo today), for religious purposes, then they would need to eat and sleep, and where people were gathered together, markets and fairs would develop.

In medieval Britain only the richest could travel on long pilgrimages, but the poor could use their Holy Day (Sunday) to visit the nearest religious centre, and associated with the religious festivities would be a fair. Indeed, towns vied for the charter to hold a fair, as this was a guaranteed source of civic income.

It is interesting to speculate on the difference in origin between the British word 'holiday', from 'Holy Day' and the North American 'vacation' from 'to leave'. Today they are synonymous but their roots are very different. By the time North America entered its period of rapid growth after the Civil War (1861–1865), the emphasis in Europe had shifted from holidays being a 'religious occasion' to a 'time for recuperation from work' and the concept of 'going on holiday' was gaining ground.

The industrial revolution of the early 1800s had a dramatic effect on the social fabric of both Europe and North America. Two aspects especially have impacted upon the development of tourism, the growth of large organisations leading to considerable urban development and the building of an efficient transport infrastructure.

The rich have always been able to take a break; indeed, in the UK, many wealthy families would own at least two homes, one in the city (normally London or Edinburgh) and one in the country. From the sixteenth century onwards many of the wealthier in European society would undertake the 'Grand Tour' of the classical sights of European civilisation, tours that are still offered as coach or cruise holidays today.

It had long been recognised, certainly after both the Black Death (of the fourteenth century) and the Great Plague of London (1665) that country air was healthier than that of the city and the industrial revolution had hugely increased the size of cities;

Manchester (UK) had a population of only 50,000 in 1775 and the combined population of Manchester and Salford (the city on the other side of the River Irwell) had increased eightfold by 1830 when the Liverpool & Manchester Railway commenced commercial operations, and had doubled again by 1850.

Railways allowed much bigger organisations to be developed, as the size of previous ones had been limited by the distance people could walk to work. From the 1830s onwards not only did housing grow up around factories but also as ribbon development alongside firstly the railway lines and then the tramways. By 1914 the majority of British cities had developed an efficient and cheap transport infrastructure.

As early as 1841, Thomas Cook, a printer from Leicester, had organised the first 'package holiday', a day excursion using the recently built local railway. Cook's name lives on not only in the Thomas Cook brand but in the saying 'taking a Cook's tour.' Such tours provided a safe way to travel.

Close-packed housing and pollution led to serious breakdowns in public health in urban areas in both Europe and North America during the latter part of the nineteenth century. The upper and middle classes had long valued the benefits of sea and mountain air, although the journey to such areas could be long and tiresome as roads were only fit for slow-moving carriages. These classes were the first to use the railways for vacations in the true sense, to get away from the city.

The owners of the mills and factories began to realise that there was a limit to the length of day and indeed the number of consecutive days and weeks an employee could work. In the UK various Acts of Parliament were passed protecting the workforce and the idea of time off for rest other than Sunday began to become a right e.g. the Holiday Act (1938). This right has been further protected in the European Union Working Time Directive of 1998. There was also a need to maintain plant and machinery and a concept developed in the northern mill towns of England of a complete cessation of much of the commercial activity for a week, so that such maintenance and improvements could be carried out. Using an old term for a public holiday, these 'Wakes' weeks, where a whole town would effectively shut down except for essential services, became common and the population began to travel to the nearest seaside resort. Each town had a different 'Wakes week' and resorts such as Blackpool in Lancashire developed as working-class holiday destinations. The railways were able to service the travel requirements and whilst the wealthy might go to Scotland, the mill and factory workers from the early 1900s onwards began to take their holiday by the sea, especially where this was a mere hour or so train journey away.

Blackpool, together with other northern English and southern Scottish resorts developed quickly. Even if a full week away was unaffordable, the railway companies ran day excursions to the resorts, a practice that continued until well after the Second World War.

Huge cities could not shut down completely and there, different trades had different holiday periods.

Towns like Blackpool, just as in the current cruise industry, developed a whole range of types of accommodation from extremely large luxury hotels to bed-and-breakfast boarding houses set in the back streets. Stories of the typical boarding house landlady are legion, but as a type of accommodation it developed into the guesthouse and B&B (bed and breakfast) of today.

## Strength through Joy

In Europe the first steps towards opening up cruising to ordinary working people occurred under the German Government of Adolf Hitler. One of Hitler's ministers, Robert Ley, was in charge of the KdF (Kraft durch Freude) 'Strength through Joy'

An unknown Cunarder (probably *Franconia*) is berthed at Monte Carlo while many of her passengers view the cars at the end of the Monte Carlo Rally.

programme that was used to provide, amongst other things, subsidised holidays including cruises to workers. Cruising using two specially built vessels and a number of chartered liners was a political measure used to reward loyal members of the workforce. The propaganda ministry of the Third Reich directly controlled the cruise operation. The organisation ran an all-German cruise operation that offered inexpensive vacations for workers and Nazi Party members. Whilst the organisation commenced using recently-constructed German tonnage from the recognised German shipping companies, by 1938–1939 they had placed in service the 25,000+grt ships *Wilhelm Gustloff* and the *Robert Ley* (both destroyed towards the end of the Second World War, the former with a huge loss of life and the latter being a constructive loss with the remains scrapped in the UK), these being the first specially commissioned cruise vessels of any nationality to enter service.

The *Wilhelm Gustloff* and the *Robert Ley* were the forerunners of today's purpose-built cruise ships. A one-class design they accommodated all of their 1,465 passengers in outside cabins. It was not until the *Royal Princess* of 1984 that there would be another mainstream cruise ship with all its passengers having an outside cabin.

These cruises were also important in the history of the industry in that, for the first time, cruising became available to the middle and working classes as opposed to just the rich. Slower than regular liners and carrying no cargo, they became the prototypes for the purpose-built cruise ships of today.

## Other developments 1918–1939

Prior to the outbreak of the Second World War, a number of companies had experimented with offering cruises to complement their liner trade. The famous Cunard liner, *Mauretania* (holder of the Blue Ribbon), spent her last five years (1930–1935) primarily engaged in cruising, being painted white in 1931. The UK Blue Star line rebuilt the 12,847grt *Arandora* as the *Arandora Star* for cruising in 1928, a function she fulfilled until the outbreak of war in 1939, the ship being sunk in 1940.

As in 1914, the outbreak of war in 1939 brought an end to cruising operations, although the US liner *America* (33,900grt) of 1940 was used for a brief period as a cruise ship in US waters until her conversion to the troopship *West Point* in 1941, after the US entry into the war.

The *Belgenland* (a British-registered ship despite her name) of the Red Star Line made a number of Mediterranean cruises in the early 1930s. In 1935, the Panama Pacific Line purchased the 24,578grt *Belgenland* (ex *Belgic*) of the Belgian Red Star Line, completed in 1917 and rebuilt as a passenger ship in 1923. She was renamed *Columbia* and used solely for cruising but the venture lasted less than a year, the ship being sold for scrap in 1936. At the same time, White Star's *Homeric* operated both short seven-day cruises from the UK to Maderia and longer thirty-five-day UK–Caribbean–UK cruises and the Ellerman Lines used the cargo passenger liner *City of Nagpur* on relatively inexpensive cruises to the Norwegian fjords during the summer months as an alternative to laying the ship up due to a slump in trade.

P&O, Orient Line and Cunard also used cruising as a means of revenue generation and an alternative to laying ships up throughout the 1930s.

Blue Star Line's *Arandora Star*, one of the most delightful of the 1930s cruise ships, here at Hawaii on a world cruise.

*Above:* Cunard's *Laconia* at Funchal, c.1934.

*Right:* A brochure for the Ellerman Line's *City of Nagpur,* for her 1933 cruises to South Africa.

*Opposite:* Panama Pacific's *Columbia* (the ex-Red Star Line SS *Belgenland*) being broken for scrap at Bo'ness, Scotland, at the end of her eventful career, much of which was spent cruising.

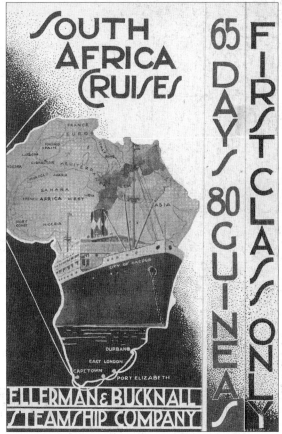

SOUTH AFRICA CRUISES

65 DAYS

80 GUINEAS

FIRST CLASS ONLY

ELLERMAN & BUCKNALL STEAMSHIP COMPANY

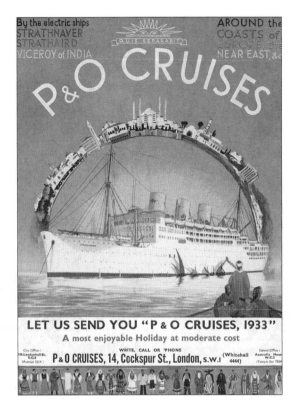

An advert for P&O's three famous cruise ships of the 1930s, the 'White Sisters' *Strathaird* and *Strathnaver,* as well as *Viceroy of India.*

## Post-war developments

In the 1940s and well into the 1950s Britain was under an austerity regime with many goods still being rationed. The British holidayed in their traditional UK resorts. Car ferries were in their infancy, and flying was still only an option for the privileged few.

European shipping companies had suffered huge losses during the war with ships either being sunk or requisitioned by the government for military or troopship service. Cunard, P&O, the Orient Line (the original Orient Line was a separate operation to that of P&O until they merged in 1965, although P&O had long held a majority shareholding in the Orient Line), the current Orient Lines (in no way connected with the Orient Line that merged with P&O and is part of the Norwegian Cruise Line operation that is in turn owned by Star Cruises), Shaw Savill & Albion, Union-Castle and Canadian Pacific (CP ships were registered in the UK) began to rebuild their fleets. P&O had lost nine out of twenty passenger ships during the war whilst Cunard had been reduced to nine passenger ships out of a pre-war total of seventeen.

Until 1958, when the first scheduled Boeing 707 service left New York for Paris, the picture for the passenger shipping companies looked rosy. The Comet airliner had not impacted on the industry as its range and payload were small and it had had a series of confidence-breaking crashes. However, the advent of the Boeing 747 in 1969 was the fatal blow to the liner industry, although it was to prove a boon to the cruise industry offering as it did cheap, mass air transportation.

Between 1945 and 1969 British shipping companies brought out a large number of new passenger liners in addition to refitting older ones. The details of the new builds are shown here:

Canadian Pacific's *Empress of England* at Lisbon in October 1965.

| Date | Name | Size (grt) |
|---|---|---|
| *Bibby Line* | *(UK–Far East troopships)* | |
| 1955 | Oxfordshire | 20,586 |
| | | |
| *British India* | *(UK–India passengers and troops)* | |
| 1951 | Uganda | 14,430 |
| | Kenya | 14,430 |
| 1956 | Nevasa | 20,527 |
| | | |
| *Canadian Pacific* | *(Europe–Canada)* | |
| 1956 | Empress of Britain | 25,516 |
| 1957 | Empress of England | 24,467 |
| 1961 | Empress of Canada | 25,615 |
| | | |
| *Cunard* | *(Europe–USA and Canada)* | |
| 1948 | Caronia | 34,274 |
| 1954 | Saxonia (renamed *Carmania* 1963) | 21,657 |
| 1955 | Ivernia (renamed *Franconia* 1963) | 21,717 |
| 1956 | Carinthia | 2, 947 |
| 1957 | Sylvania | 22,017 |
| 1968 | Queen Elizabeth 2 | 65,863 |

CRUISE BRITANNIA

*Cunard also operated the large passenger/freighters Media and Parthia (250 passengers) on the North Atlantic route.*

| Date | Name | Size (grt) |
|---|---|---|
| Elder Demster | (UK–West Africa) | |
| 1947 | Accra | 11,599 |
| 1947 | Apapa | 11,599 |
| 1951 | Aureol | 14,083 |
| | | |
| Orient Line | (UK–Far East merged with P&O 1965) | |
| 1948 | Orcades | 28,399 |
| 1951 | Oronsay | 28,136 |
| 1954 | Orsova | 29,091 |
| 1960 | Oriana | 41,920 |
| | | |
| Pacific Steam Navigation Company | (UK–South America) | |
| 1956 | Reina Del Mar | 20,234 |
| | | |
| P&O | (UK–Far East) | |
| 1949 | Himalaya | 28,047 |
| 1950 | Chusan | 24,318 |
| 1954 | Arcadia | 29,871 |
| 1954 | Iberia | 29,779 |
| 1961 | Canberra | 45,733 |
| | | |
| Shaw Savill and Albion | (UK–Australia/New Zealand) | |
| 1955 | Southern Cross | 20,204 |
| 1962 | Northern Star | 24,756 |
| | | |
| Union-Castle | (UK–South Africa) | |
| 1948 | Pretoria Castle | 28,705 |
| 1948 | Edinburgh Castle | 28,705 |
| 1950 | Bloemfontein Castle | 18,400 |
| 1951 | Rhodesia Castle | 17,041 |
| 1951 | Kenya Castle | 17,041 |
| 1952 | Braemar Castle | 17,029 |
| 1958 | Pendennis Castle | 28,582 |
| 1960 | Windsor Castle | 37,640 |
| 1961 | Transvaal Castle | 32,697 |

In addition to the above list there were also large cargo/passenger liners built for a number of companies including Royal Mail Lines and the New Zealand Shipping companies. There were also liners built for Germany, Italy, France, Sweden, Norway, the United States and the Netherlands. In the 1950s the shipyards of Europe were busy building passenger liners. What was noticeable about much of the new building was that the ships were being designed not only for liner voyages but also with a cruising capability. Cunard's *Caronia* that entered service in 1948 is credited with being the first liner that was actually designed to undertake more cruises than liner voyages. In 1962 Cunard converted the 1939 liner *Mauretania* (35,738grt) for use as a cruise ship, complete with green hull. She operated mainly on the New York–Mediterranean service and some of these line voyages were sold as cruises. The vessel could not compete with the newer Italian vessels and those of the American Export Line. She had, however, enjoyed success in the late 1940s and early 1950s cruising in the Caribbean out of New York. She was broken up in 1965 at Inverkeithing, Scotland.

## Assisted passages

P&O, the Orient Line and Shaw Savill were able to stave off the challenge of air travel to a degree in the 1950s as they serviced the assisted passages scheme to Australia. Britons could emigrate to Australia for £10 on a voyage subsidised by the Australian government. This provided a market for vessels that might have been disposed of earlier. The market, however, declined rapidly as Australia began to restrict immigration after 1977.

## The growth in air travel

When the Douglas Aircraft Corporation introduced the DC1, 2 and 3 between 1933 and 1935 (the DC3 is better known in the UK as the Dakota, one of the most successful commercial aircraft ever), the world of commercial air travel began to open up, only to be put on hold during 1939–1945. Even after the war commercial aviation was not part of the mass travel market. However, with the introduction of the Sud-Est Caravelle in 1959, the Boeing 727 in 1963 and the BAC One-Eleven in 1965 – inexpensive to operate short-to-medium-haul jet aircraft able to fly holiday makers to more distant destinations on a charter basis, a huge growth in flights linked to holiday packages began. Previous jets, the de Havilland Comet, the Boeing 707 and the Douglas DC8, were essentially long-haul aircraft.

An Iberia Airways McDonnell Douglas DC9 overtakes the *Queen Mary*. It was mainly the jet aircraft that caused the decline in transatlantic passenger numbers.

The introduction of charter operations linked to package holidays from the 1960s onward, together with increasing prosperity in the UK and other European countries, coupled to the opportunities offered by the introduction of jet airliners led to a huge growth in affordable foreign package holidays.

Vladimir Raitz, founder of Horizon Holidays, organised the first package holiday by air in 1950 and by 1970, 2.7 million inclusive holidays were undertaken out of the UK.

One of the results of this expansion was the development of a series of large resorts, especially in Spain, resorts that were often isolated from their original village communities.

According to the UK Civil Aviation Authority (CAA) figures for 1994, the three market leaders in the UK package holiday business at the time, Thomson, Airtours (now branded as MyTravel) and First Choice took over 5.5 million holidaymakers on package holidays in the Summer of 1994. Shortly thereafter all three companies, firstly Airtours, then Thomson and latterly First Choice expanded into the British cruise market.

## Holiday camps

The holiday camp concept provides a useful link between the growth in British tourism in the 1960s and the expansion of the UK cruise market at that time.

In 1936 the British entrepreneur, Billy (later Sir Billy) Butlin established his first holiday camp in Skegness, the camp opening in 1937. This was the forerunner of the modern all inclusive package holiday. Butlin and his competitor (Fred Pontin) established camps throughout the UK, the greatest popularity being in the 1950s and 1960s. All-inclusive with nightly entertainment the camps not only provided a family atmosphere but also launched a number of variety entertainment careers. Many of the later stars of the UK light entertainment and music scenes commenced their careers as Butlin's Redcoats or Pontin's Bluecoats.

In 1971 Thomson introduced weekend short break trips to Majorca for £13 and by 1974 the UK holiday companies of Thomson, Intasun and Horizon had established their own charter airlines. From tiny numbers in 1950, by 1980 there were 6.25 million Britons taking a foreign holiday that involved a charter flight.

Throughout the 1970s the holiday camps began a slow decline. Both Butlin and Pontin experimented with camps in the main foreign resorts but without much success. The holiday camp appears to have been an institution that was successful for a time for UK-based holidaymakers on a UK holiday but which did not appeal when placed in a foreign setting.

Whilst the UK holiday camp industry may have declined (although it is still catering to a specific market), there are echoes of it, albeit much more up market in the all-inclusive resorts operated by some hotel groups, as pioneered by Club Mediterranean, and in some of the cruise products offered by those companies who also operate land-based holidays.

The modern European cruise market can trace its ancestry back to both the liner trade and the original holiday camps. Up to 2002 what had never been seen, however, was the development of self-catering facilities on cruise ships, although such facilities were a part of the holiday camp ethos, which also included restaurants and still remains popular in many European holiday resorts. The introduction of *The World* as a cruise ship on which accommodation can be either booked for short periods or as a permanent apartment, complete with its own kitchen, is the first move in this direction. P&O's rebranding of its *Arcadia* product as *Ocean Village* has seen the restaurant replaced entirely by buffet meals, a type of catering operation often found in the hotels servicing the package holiday market.

## British currency restrictions

Just as a political decision, prohibition, launched the US cruise industry, it was a political decision by the British Government in the 1960s that brought the UK cruise sector to a wider market. No sooner had Britons begun to abandon their traditional British seaside holiday in favour of the shores of the Mediterranean, in particular Spain, than, for economic reasons, the government stepped in to curtail foreign holidays by restricting UK passport holders to taking only £50 in foreign currency or traveller's cheques out of the country. Exceptions were made for business travel but the holidaymaker found that his or her options for a foreign holiday were severely curtailed. Credit cards were virtually unknown in those days and demand for foreign holidays consequently slumped.

However, as British-registered ships used sterling as the currency on board, cruise passengers needed only to use their £50 foreign currency allowance whilst ashore.

Companies such as P&O and Cunard were able to switch tonnage, rapidly outliving its usefulness due to the inroads of air travel, into the UK cruise market, as did Shaw Savill, whose *Southern Cross* and *Northern Star* operated cruises out of Liverpool and Southampton. Originally built for the £10 assisted passage scheme from the UK to Australia, the ships were of a revolutionary design with their funnels situated well aft, thus providing considerable deck space for soaking up the tropical sun. The design has stood the test of time and indeed the *Southern Cross* was still operating cruises (after a number of name changes) in the Caribbean into the twenty-first century. In the 1960s it was the Royal Mail Line's, *Andes*, 24,689grt (420 'first-class' passengers) that was displaced from the UK–South America service by the company's passenger/freighters *Amazon, Aragon* and *Arlanza*, which became one of the first full-time cruise liners dedicated to the UK market. The *Andes* and the ex-Pacific Steam Navigation line *Reina del Mar*, 21,234grt (*Queen of the Seas*), also from the UK–South America (West Coast) run, were the ships that introduced many of today's UK frequent cruise passengers to this form of vacation.

## The Travel Savings Association (TSA)

Originally chartered by the Travel Savings Association, set up by South African born Max Wilson who also chartered the *Empress of Britain* and the *Empress of England*, the *Reina del Mar* was a very popular ship in the 1960s, entering TSA service in 1964. The TSA concept was rather like that of a Christmas club. Customers paid in a weekly or monthly amount and used this to purchase their cruise.

The TSA operation was rather like a seagoing holiday camp and yet it provided a cruise experience for those who would never have been able to afford a traditional cruise.

Union-Castle (as a shareholder in TSA) operated the *Reina Del Mar,* although she had been built for and was still owned by another of the TSA shareholders – the Pacific Steam Navigation Company (PSNC). The ship was painted in Union-Castle colours. Union-Castle became the sole owners of TSA but not the *Reina Del Mar*. The ship retained her PSNC ownership until 1973 but was chartered to Union-Castle until she was bought by the line in 1973. Unfortunately, she went for breaking in 1975.

Operated as a 'sterling zone' the *Reina Del Mar* provided many middle-class Britons with their first cruise and, for many, their first foreign holiday.

The Cunard vessels (the *Saxonia* Sisters) also became early vessels for fledgling cruise operations. The *Carmania* (ex-*Saxonia*) became the *Leonid Sobinov* of the Soviet Union's State Shipping operation in 1973 to be joined by the *Fedor Shalyapin*, formerly *Franconia* (ex-*Ivernia*), both operating through the break up of the Soviet Union and being laid up in 1995. The *Carinthia* and the *Sylvania* were acquired by Sitmar Cruises in 1968 as the

*Above:* Travel Savings Association's *Reina del Mar* in her early service with the company.

*Opposite:* The Cunarder *Carmania* became the *Leonid Sobinov* in 1973. Here she is at Amsterdam, barely a year later on 24 August 1974.

*Fairsea* and the *Fairwind,* respectively. When P&O acquired Sitmar in 1988, they were transferred to the Princess operation to become the *Fair Princess* and *Dawn Princess*.

By the middle of the 1960s there were the beginnings of a thriving European cruise industry, mainly centred on the UK. As a product, it was very unsophisticated compared with today's cruising. Entertainment was mainly dancing and 'crew shows' with fancy-dress competitions and other passenger-derived amusements popular. Many of the ships either operated a two-class system or had difficult passenger flows due to their previous two and three class nature.

The Chandris Company of Greece also entered the UK cruise market at this time, operating a number of its vessels as 'sterling zones'. The Greek Line itself placed in the UK market the ill-fated *Lakonia* (built as the *Johan Van Oldenbarnvelt* in 1930 and acquired by the Greek Line in 1962). The *Lakonia* had a short career as a cruise ship. Carrying a predominantly British complement on a Christmas cruise she caught fire and sank off Maderia with the loss of 128 lives in December 1963.

Chandris acquired the 16,435grt *Queen Frederica* in 1965 for the UK–Australia service but the ship was used almost exclusively on cruising in the Mediterranean, carrying a large number of UK cruise passengers. The *Queen Frederica* had been built as early as 1927, as the *Malolo,* for the Matson Navigation Company of San Francisco and placed on the US West Coast–Honolulu (Hawaii) route. Renamed *Matsonia* in 1937 she served as a troopship in the Second World War, being sold to Home Line for the Italy–New York service in 1948 and renamed *Atlantic.* She was transferred to a subsidiary, National Hellenic America Line in 1954 and renamed *Queen Frederica*, retaining the name when

Shaw Savill's *Ocean Monarch* c.1971, soon after her £1.5 million refit.

bought by Chandris and refitted to carry over 1,000 cruise passengers. This veteran of fifty years was finally withdrawn at the end of 1973 and broken up in 1977, a remarkable record for a ship, which like the *Reina del Mar* gave many UK cruise passengers their first taste of this type of vacation.

The UK company of Shaw Savill were so confident that the growth in the UK market would continue that they bought and converted the *Empress of England* and spent £1.5 million in 1970 converting her to the *Ocean Monarch*. Operating with the *Northern Star,* the market declined rapidly and the *Ocean Monarch*, together with the *Northern Star*, was broken up in 1975, *Southern Cross* being sold in 1973 to have a long career in the Caribbean.

## Sovereign Cruises

The UK entrepreneur Ted Langton chartered the *Queen Frederica* from the Chandris Company from 1970 until 1973 as a UK market ship. Naming the operation Sovereign Cruises, he had large Maltese Crosses placed on each of her two funnels. A seven-day Mediterranean cruise cost around £50 including a charter flight out of London's Gatwick airport. Gatwick was then a relatively small airport but is now one of the major airports of the world, handling a large number of scheduled and charter flights.

The Sovereign Cruise operation was an example of one of the earliest UK market 'fly cruises'.

## Thomson

Thomson, one of the major names in the UK package holiday market made a dramatic re-entry into the UK cruise market in the late 1990s, as will be recounted in the next chapter. However, the company had chartered the *Ithaca* (converted from the former cargo/passenger liner *Amelia de Mello* ex-*Zion,* and the *Calypso* ex-*Southern Cross*) from the London–Greek company of N&J Vlassopoulos for Mediterranean fly cruises in the 1970s. These cruises were costed at a mere £49 for the cheapest accommodation on a seven-day fly cruise in the Mediterranean.

## Fly cruises

The attraction of fly cruising for the British market lay in the fact that the cruise customer did not have to spend two days out and two days back on his or her search for the sun. Fly cruising to the Mediterranean also avoided crossing the Bay of Biscay – notorious in anecdotes, if not in reality, for causing seasickness.

Such was the demand for ships in the Mediterranean that even small passenger ferries displaced by more modern car-carrying vessels were converted to cruise vessels. In addition to their larger ships, Chandris had a number of such vessels. The 4,325grt *Fantasia* of 1964 had commenced operations in 1935 as the *Duke of York* for the London, Midland & Scottish Railway service from Heysham to Belfast. Rebuilt in 1950, Chandris fitted her out for 381 cruise passengers paying from £49 to £119 for two-week cruises in the Eastern Mediterranean and Aegean operating out of Venice. She was joined by two

The Chandris liner *Britanis* sailing from Tilbury on 21 June 1975, on a cruise to Scandinavia.

other ex-UK passenger ferries, *Fiesta* (ex-*Mona's Queen*) and *Fiorita* (ex-*Amsterdam*), finally being broken up in 1974 after thirty-nine years of service, including war service as HMS *Duke of Wellington* (the name *Duke of York* being in use on a King George V class battleship). Epirotiki Lines also used ex-UK passenger ferries for their Mediterranean cruise operations.

Chandris were a major player in the European market through their various subsidiaries, with four large vessels, *Queen Frederica* (see earlier), *Britanis* (18,655grt), *Elenis* (24,351grt) and *Australis* (26,485grt) – originally acquired for the Europe–Australia service but later switched to cruising – plus a fleet of smaller, converted vessels as mentioned above. For the UK market, Chandris was at the lower end of the price range.

## Foreign shipping companies operating cruises from the UK for the UK market

In recent years a number of companies operating cruises for the US market have used British ports as the starting and finishing points for their cruises. However, in the 1960s Spanish, Norwegian and even Russian shipping companies provided British market cruises out of UK ports.

The Spanish shipping company, Naviera Aznar SA of Bilbao operated a cruise operation from Liverpool down to the Canary Islands and back, initially using the cargo/passenger *Monte Umbe* (9,961grt) and later two 13,500grt car ferries in the 1960s

The cover of an Aznar Line brochure advertising their cruises to the 'Sunny Canaries', a perennial British cruising favourite.`

and 1970s. The Canary Island–Liverpool trade was an important one due to the fact that the Canary Islands provided tomatoes for the UK market. The ships were unsophisticated as cruise ships as they also carried cargo and, later, vehicles. By 1977 the availability of package holidays using flights to the Canaries and, more importantly, the death of Franco and Spain's changed political climate made it unviable.

The Norwegian shipping company owned by Fred Olsen operated (as the company still does) cruises using the dual-named car ferry *Black Prince/Venus*. When used on a similar UK–Canary Islands cruise schedule to that of the Aznar Line (see above) in winter the ship was in Fred Olsen colours and named *Black Prince*. During summer months the ship sailed on the Norway–UK service as the *Venus* of the Bergen Line. Bergen Line had operated in Norwegian waters for some years and these had been popular with British passengers.

The ship became the outright property of Fred Olsen in 1986 and was converted to a full-time cruise ship using solely the *Black Prince* name.

Acquiring hard currency was a priority of the Russian government and a number of Russian ships operated cruises for the UK market mainly out of Tilbury. The cruises were known for their exceptionally low prices, although the food and the entertainment often reflected this. The best known of the Russian ships operating in the UK market in the 1960s and 70s were the *Baltika*, the *Mikhail Kalinin* and the ex-Cunard vessel *Leonid Sobinov* (ex-*Carmania*) and *Leonid Bvezhnev*.

In 1973 the small Portuguese liner *Funchal* (9,824grt) was converted into a full-time cruise ship and continues to operate for the UK market for part of the year and the Brazilian market for the rest of the time.

## School cruises

British India's liner operations had been in decline since Indian independence in 1948. The company (part of the P&O Group) had, together with the Bibby Line, been a supplier of troopships to the Ministry of Defence. As Britain scaled down its military presence east of Suez during the 1960s the company's newest ships the *Uganda* and *Nevasa* joined the pioneering *Dunera* as educational cruise ships carrying a mixture of school children, teachers and ordinary cruise passengers, the latter being kept separate from the school children. The educational cruise market declined during the 1970s. *Nevasa*, the younger of the two ships was broken up in 1975, *Uganda* going for scrap in 1986 following a brief return to cruising after her troop and hospital ship duties during the Falkland's conflict of 1982. School cruises have been continued by the UK Voyages of Discovery company.

## Cultural cruises

Swan Hellenic was a company founded in 1954 as an offshoot of the Swan Travel Bureau. Swan Hellenic provided cruises in the Aegean and surrounding areas for those who were interested in the culture rather than the sun. The company chartered suitable vessels, including the *Orpheus* (ex-*Munster* of the British & Irish Steam Packet Company) of Epirotiki Lines and the Turkish-owned *Ankara*. Swan Hellenic is now part of the P&O Group and used the 12,500grt *Minerva* until 2002 when the ship became the *Saga Pearl*, the replacement being *Minerva II* one of the R ships made available following the failure of Renaissance Cruises.

# The apparent decline of the UK market

Between 1960 and 1970 the British cruise customer had a good choice of cruise products tailored to the UK market as shown below:

| Operator | Ship | Fate |
|---|---|---|
| Aznar | Monte Umbe | Sold 1975 |
| British India | Uganda | Scrapped 1986 |
| | Nevasa | Scrapped 1975 |
| Chandris | Queen Frederica (Sovereign Cruises) | Scrapped 1977 |
| | Australis | Transferred out of UK market 1978 |
| Cunard | Mauretania | Scrapped 1965 |
| | Caronia | Sold 1968 |
| | Franconia ex-Ivernia | Sold 1973 to Russia (see under Russian vessels) |
| | Carmania ex-Saxonia | Sold 1973 to Russia (see under Russian vessels) |
| | Carinthia | Sold 1968 |
| | Sylvania | Sold 1968 |
| | QE2 | Still in service |
| Empresa Insulana de Navegação | Funchal | Still in service with new owners |
| Fred Olsen | Black Prince | Still in service |
| P&O/Orient Lines | Canberra | Scrapped 1997 |
| | Oriana | Sold 1986 |
| | Arcadia | Scrapped 1979 |
| | Iberia | Scrapped 1972 |
| | Chusan | Scrapped 1973 |
| | Himalaya | Scrapped 1974 |
| | Orsova | Scrapped 1974 |
| | Orcades | Scrapped 1973 |
| | Oronsay | Scrapped 1976 |
| Royal Mail | Andes | Scrapped 1971 |
| Russian Vessels | Baltika | Scrapped 1987 |
| | Mikhail Kalinin | Scrapped 1984 |
| | Leonid Sobiov (ex-Carmania) | Scrapped 1999 |
| Shaw Savill & Albion | Southern Cross | Sold 1973 |
| | Northern Star | Scrapped 1975 |
| | Ocean Monarch ex-Empress of England | Scrapped 1975 |
| Swan Hellenic | Ankara | Scrapped 1982 |
| Thomson (charter) | Ithaca | Charter ended 1976 |
| Union-Castle | Reina Del Mar | Scrapped 1975 |

The seamen's strike of 1966 and the massive oil rises of the early 1970s brought this expansion to an end and the UK sector began to go into decline.

Up to the 1970s British market cruises were still very much traditional liner voyages, except that they began and ended at the same port. The cruise passengers, especially those

P&O Short Sea Tours descriptive handbook from the mid-1920s.

The 12,620grt SS *Dunera*, in her role as the British India Steam Navigation Co.'s educational cruise ship.

who embarked and disembarked the cruise at a UK port, tended to be from the more affluent middle and upper classes and maintained many of the traditions of the liner trade.

Many of the ships remained two-class or had been converted from two-class ships. The *Reina Del Mar* was built as a three-class ship (207 First Class, 216 Cabin Class and 343 Tourist Class). During her conversion to a cruise ship she was equipped with a cinema and extra cabins in what had been her forward holds. The difference between these newer (cheaper) cabins constructed using laminates and formica and the beautiful wooden fittings in her top of the price range cabins was marked. The *Queen Elizabeth 2* was single class when cruising but had segregated sailing when on the scheduled transatlantic service.

Typically, in a two-class cruise ship the first-class passengers would be about a third of the complement but would have two thirds of the available space. However, class distinctions in British society were becoming less well marked by the 1960s and two-class ships were rapidly losing acceptability with the holidaying public. The current cruise concept where all facilities are shared but there is a considerable difference in the cost of accommodation was gaining ground, as indicated by the one-class nature of the *Andes* and the *Reina Del Mar*. As a liner, the *Canberra* operated as a two-class ship until she was converted to a single-class cruise ship in 1974.

# chapter two

# DECLINE AND REBIRTH

The seamen's strike of 1966, the spiralling costs of fuel, old ships plus the removal of currency restrictions and the cheapness of package holidays dealt the British passenger shipping industry and its cruise operations a crippling blow in the early 1970s.

Of the thirty-three ships listed in the previous chapter as operating in the UK cruise market in the 1960s and early 1970s, eleven were sold out of the UK market and no fewer than thirteen scrapped by 1980. Of the remaining vessels only the *Queen Elizabeth 2* and the *Black Prince* still operate cruises within the UK market and even the *Queen Elizabeth 2*, now part of the Carnival Corporation of the USA (the owners of Cunard since 1998) is operated much of the time as a US market vessel. The *Queen Elizabeth 2* has been one of the few vessels to carry on a scheduled service to some degree with her UK–US transatlantic voyages.

Figures produced by P&O state that the number of UK cruise passengers dropped from 150,000 in 1974 to 100,000 in 1981 and as low as 55,000 by 1982. 1982 was an unusual year as a number of ships were engaged on support duties for the Falkland's conflict. Both the *Queen Elizabeth 2* and *Canberra* served as troopships, the latter vessel going to the landing site itself.

The 1970s and 1980s not only saw the sale or scrapping of well-known UK ships but also the demise of some of the respected names in the UK passenger shipping industry. By the end of the 1970s Union-Castle, Shaw Savill and Royal Mail had ceased passenger shipping operations leaving P&O, Cunard and Fred Olsen to service the UK dedicated cruise market.

Between 1970 and 1990 there was little new building or acquisitions for the purely UK market. Cunard took delivery of the *Cunard Adventurer* (14,151grt) in 1971 but sold her to Norwegian Cruise Line in 1977. In 1972 the line took delivery of the *Cunard Ambassador*, sister to the *Cunard Adventurer*. She was sold to a Danish company for conversion to a livestock carrier in 1974 after a fire had severely damaged the ship. Both the *Cunard Adventurer* and the *Ambassador* cruised mainly in the Caribbean and, although British, were very US market in orientation.

P&O purchased the hull of a sister ship to Norwegian Cruise Line's *Southward* (the ship was to have been named *Seaward* by NCL) in 1972. NCL had withdrawn from the contract with her Italian builders due to a price rise following the nationalisation of the yard. P&O named the ship *Spirit of London*. In 1974 P&O transferred her to Princess Cruises after P&O had acquired the Princess operation (see later). The ship was renamed *Sun Princess* and was used for cruising in the US market. She was later to return to the UK/European market as the *Southern Cross* of CTC and then as the *Flamenco* of Festival Cruises.

Fred Olsen's *Black Prince*, one of the few survivors of the 1960s cruise ships, still trading in the British cruise market.

*Sea Princess* at Santa Cruz, Tenerife in December 1992.

Cunard then took delivery of the new-build 17,500grt *Cunard Countess* and *Cunard Conquest* (renamed *Cunard Princess*) in 1976. These ships, although marketed in the UK, were based in San Juan, Puerto Rico, and aimed squarely at a US market.

In 1978 P&O bought the ex-Swedish America liner *Kungsholm* from Flagship Cruises, who had acquired the vessel in 1975. The ship underwent a major reconstruction to emerge as the *Sea Princess* in 1979. Originally used in the Australia market from 1979 until 1982, she replaced *Oriana* in the UK when *Oriana* was transferred to the Australian operation. In 1986 she was transferred to the Princess operation in the US. She returned to the UK market in 1991 to partner *Canberra* and was renamed *Victoria* in 1995 to free up the *Sea Princess* name for a new vessel destined for the Princess Cruise's fleet.

In 1983, Cunard acquired the *Sagafjord* of 1965 and the *Vistafjord* of 1973 from Norwegian America Cruises. The ships operated for British, European and North American customers.

Whilst 1982 was the nadir of UK market cruising, developments in the US market were to change the face of cruising and impact not just on the US market but also on the British one.

## The purpose-built cruise ship

The new generation of ships were purpose built for cruising rather than for the rapidly declining liner trade. The trend had been set by Cunard's *Caronia* of 1949, a ship that, although carrying two classes, was intended for a joint cruising and liner service career. She was a huge success, particularly catering for the American market.

Following on from *Caronia* was the Home Lines *Oceanic*. On her maiden entry to New York in 1965 the 39,000grt *Oceanic* was referred to as 'the ship of tomorrow'. Although she had been designed originally as a two-class transatlantic liner for the Northern Europe to North America (St Lawrence) service she was completed as a cruise ship for the US market and carried 1,601 cruise passengers. Every cabin on the ship was equipped with en-suite facilities and her two swimming pools could be covered by a 'Magrodome' a feature that did not appear on a UK market ship until the debut of P&O Cruises' *Aurora* in May 2000. North Americans clambered for cruises on *Oceanic*, the ship being fully booked for her weekly New York–Nassau cruises for years ahead.

In 1966, Ted Arison (later to found Carnival Cruises and the Carnival Group) and the Norwegian shipping company of Kloster Reederei formed a partnership to offer Caribbean cruises from the then little-known port of Miami in Florida.

Kloster provided the *Sunward* which had been built as a passenger ferry designed for the UK–Spain service while Arison marketed the cruise package to the US market. The *Sunward* had suffered from the UK currency restrictions that had caused a drop in demand for foreign holidays as described in the previous chapter. The new company was given the name of Norwegian Caribbean Line (renamed Norwegian Cruise Line in 1987). Disagreements between Knut Kloster and Arison led to a parting of the ways in 1972 and Arison set up Carnival Cruises.

Following the success of NCL, two other Scandinavian companies entered the Caribbean market, Royal Caribbean Cruise Line (still operating today as Royal Caribbean International) and Royal Viking Line (acquired by Kloster in 1984, then Cunard in 1994 and thus eventually in 1998 by Carnival as part of the takeover of Cunard). The Scandinavian influence has remained strong within the US-based marketplace.

*Sunward* was followed by a distinctive design of vessels (*Starward* (1968), *Skyward* (1969), and the 1971 *Southward*) of between 12 and 17,000grt designed for seven-day Caribbean cruises out of Miami.

From 1969 to 1971 Royal Caribbean Cruise Line (RCCL), now Royal Caribbean International (RCI), introduced three 18,500grt, 700–880 passenger vessels with distinctive lounges placed halfway up their funnels (*Song of Norway, Nordic Prince* and *Sun Viking*) the first two being later lengthened to accommodate over 1,190 passengers. Royal Viking Line followed suit with their trio of ships, albeit to a slightly different philosophy. *Royal Viking Star* (1971), *Royal Viking Sky* (1972) and *Royal Viking Sea* (1973) were bigger at 21,800grt but carried only 550–560 passengers. They too were lengthened later to become over 28,000grt and carry 812 passengers. In their later lives many of these US market ships were sold to new entrants into the cruise industry and a number of them operated in the UK market for new owners.

The US led the growth in the cruise industry in the 1970s and 1980s with new companies being formed each year (as well as ones leaving the market or being bought up). The US market product was also more destination intensive than that of the UK. There were as few days at sea as possible and the cruise called at the maximum number of ports.

Entertainment on the US market ships became more lavish, with professional performers being booked for solo performances and professional dancers and singers being contracted to provide production shows that were less elaborate versions of those provided in resorts such as Las Vegas and Atlantic City. A common feature of Las Vegas and Atlantic City were the gambling facilities that were a hallmark of the two cities. In the US it is state law rather than federal law that gives permission or not for gambling and casinos. Cruise companies operating for the US market soon saw that the provision of on-board casino facilities would be a major generator of revenue and more and more space began to be allocated for this particular form of entertainment. Whilst the British do gamble, the facilities the UK cruise market demands for on-board gambling are not to the same scale as the US market, and thus even today the casino on a UK market cruise ship is likely to be a much smaller affair than on a comparable US market vessel.

## One-class ships

There are considerable advantages gained in operating a one-class ship. Firstly, there is no need to reserve parts of the ship for one particular class and thus there is no resentment caused by seeing others enjoying better facilities.

Secondly, there is no need to provide parallel facilities. The lounges, pool areas, restaurants, etc., are open to all. The single-class design allows for freer passenger flow around the ship and avoids the need for non-structural partitions designed to prevent access by a particular class of passengers.

The only vestiges of the old two (or more) class ships are in the dining arrangements on board ships such as the *Queen Elizabeth 2,* where restaurants with different menus are allocated according to the price grade of accommodation, and Festival Cruises' *Mistral,* where dinner in the grill room was included for those in mini-suites (the highest grade of accommodation) but has to be paid for as a dining alternative by others.

Ships designed for regular liner services tended to be built for as speedy a voyage as possible. The competition to win the Blue Riband of the Atlantic led to governments commissioning large and fast 'ships of state' such as the *Mauretania, Queen Mary, Normandie, Rex, Bremen* and the *United States.* Cruise ships had less need for speed, especially in the US market where the distances between Caribbean islands were relatively small. Ships designed for speed have deep V-shaped hulls. By designing ships that have less draft (the measurement of the distance from the water line to the keel) it was possible to build cruise ships that could go alongside at destinations where the waters were shallower than at major ports. Deeper draft vessels needed to use their lifeboats or specially-built tenders to get their cruise passengers ashore at may ports of call. Using tenders is time consuming and it is much safer to put passengers (especially the frail and elderly) directly ashore from the ship to the quayside.

The *Queen Elizabeth 2* (1969), the *Norway* (ex-*France*) of 1961 and the smaller (46,000grt) Italian liners *Michelangelo* and *Raffaello* of 1965 (both sold to the Iranian Navy in 1977) were the last conventional transatlantic liners to be built, although the *Queen Elizabeth 2* was intended for a dual line–cruising role. The drafts of the *Queen Elizabeth 2* and the *Norway* are 32.4 and 35.4ft, respectively. When cruising in the Caribbean the *Norway* used military-style landing craft at nearly every port of call as she drew far too much to go alongside. As the chart below shows, modern cruise ships, whilst having a much greater gross registered tonnage (i.e. more enclosed space), draw far less due to their flatter bottom design.

| Ship | Market | grt | Date | Draft (feet) |
| --- | --- | --- | --- | --- |
| Queen Elizabeth 2 | UK/US | 70,327 | 1969 | 32.4 |
| Norway (ex-France) | US | 76,049 | 1962 | 35.4 |
| Carnival Destiny | US | 101,353 | 1996 | 27.0 |
| Grand Princess | US | 108,806 | 1998 | 26.2 |
| Voyager of the Seas | US | 137,280 | 1999 | 28.8 |
| Oriana | UK | 69,153 | 1995 | 25.9 |
| Aurora | UK | 76,152 | 2000 | 25.9 |

In recent years cruise ships built for the US market have had flatter sterns that can accommodate cabins at the very back of the ship. The *Aurora*, as a UK market ship, has sun terraces at the stern, whilst the *Golden Princess* has a much flatter stern with accommodation. It appears that Britons prefer sunbathing more than North Americans.

## The Love Boat®

Stanley B. McDonald had founded Princess Cruises on the western seaboard of the USA in 1965. Princess Cruises was purchased by P&O in 1974, although the US operation continued to operate under the Princess brand. This provided P&O with an easy entry into the US market where the P&O brand was less well known. The P&O acquisition of Princess and later Sitmar Cruises is often quoted as a textbook example of how an organisation can expand into a new market by acquisition, thus retaining the customer base of the acquired company.

During 1974 P&O purchased the *Pacific Princess* and *Island Princess* (the latter ship coming into the UK market in 2002 as the *Discovery* of the Voyages of Discovery company) from Flagship Cruises who had ordered the vessels in 1970. In 1977 both ships were made available to Aaron Spelling Productions and became the stars of 'The Love Boat®', a highly successful TV series starring Gavin Macleod as Captain Stubbing. So successful was the Love Boat that even in the 1990s Princess were still saying, 'It's more than a cruise, it's the Love Boat®'. A revamped 'Love Boat®' series was made for televison in the early years of the twenty-first century using one of the newer Princess ships.

Americans became entranced with the fun, sun and romance depicted in the series and it was just as successful when shown to UK audiences. German audiences had their own long-running show 'Traumshiffe' (Dreamship), which started in the 1980s and featured the 9,570grt MV *Berlin* of Deilmann Reederie.

In the 1990s, a UK documentary featured one of the Celebrity Cruises' ships operating for the US market, the 'star' of the show emerging as the UK singer Jayne McDonald whilst a 2002/2003 documentary was based around the *Island Escape* (ex-*Viking Serenade*) operated as a joint venture between First Choice Holidays and Royal Caribbean Cruises. The First Choice cruise operation is considered later in this chapter.

The appearance of a regular cruise-related soap opera on both US and UK television screens did a great deal to raise awareness of cruising as a fun experience and one for all people and not just a wealthy minority. The role of *Canberra* in the Falkland's conflict also helped raise UK awareness of cruising.

## Cruise ship design in the 1970s

The earliest purpose-built cruise ships discussed above followed a design philosophy inherited from their liner ancestors.

The majority of non-premium accommodation was in the hull, followed by one or two public decks of lounges, bars, shops, etc. higher up in the ship, normally at the promenade deck level where the hull and superstructure meet. The highest priced premium accommodation was then placed above the public rooms. Many companies included an observation lounge either at the extreme front of the superstructure or, in the case of the Royal Caribbean ships, part way up the funnel.

These design changes can be seen by comparing Fred Olsen's *Black Watch* (28,492grt after lengthening in 1981) built as *Royal Viking Star* in 1972 (acquired by Fred Olsen in 1996) with the *Oceana* of P&O. Most of the standard accommodation is below the main public deck. Compare this with another vessel built for the US market and transferred to the UK market in 2003, P&O/Princess Cruises' *Ocean Princess* (77,499grt) of 2000, transferred to the UK operation of the company as the *Oceana*.

*Black Watch* has sun terraces at the stern whilst the sternmost areas of B, C and D decks on the *Oceana* are used for suites and mini-suites (premium accommodation). On the lowest passenger decks of *Oceana* there are only sixty-eight outside and fifty-two inside cabins out of a total of 603 outside and 372 inside cabins. Whilst *Black Watch* has nine balcony cabins (all suites) out of a total of 422 cabins, *Oceana* has no fewer than 410. The trend throughout the 1990s was for a greater proportion of balcony cabins, even when this reduced the living area of the cabin. Whilst balconies were once only provided in premium accommodation, newer ships have a far greater percentage of balcony cabins.

In general cruise ships have become shorter, wider as a function of length, squarer in the stern, more slab sided and draw less water than their line ancestors. The *Carnival Destiny* of 1996 was the first passenger ship that had a beam that made her too wide to use the Panama Canal. All of the UK market ships operating in 2002 could use the Panama Canal but an increasing number of US market ships are too wide for the canal, thus making repositioning from the Atlantic to the Pacific difficult.

The *Norway* (ex-*France*) was built as a traditional liner, whilst *Aurora* is a purpose-built cruise ship. The differences in their dimensions are shown below:

|                | *Norway*        | *Aurora*     |
| -------------- | --------------- | ------------ |
| Built          | 1962            | 2000         |
| grt            | 76,049          | 76,152       |
| Length (ft/m)  | 1035.1/315.5    | 885.8/270    |
| Beam (ft/m)    | 109.9/33.5      | 105.6 /32.2  |
| Draft (ft/m)   | 35.4/10.8       | 25.9/7.9     |

A squarer ship can have more cabins because cubes (cabins) are easier to fit into a more box-like superstructure. The use of lightweight materials has led to an increase in accommodation higher up the ship. This aids the economics of cruising as a 2 per cent increase in accommodation can lead to upwards of £1 million in annual income.

# British cruising in the 1980s

The choices for British cruise customers in the 1980s were nowhere as great as they had been in the 1960s–early 70s and were to be again by the middle of the 1990s.

P&O's *Canberra* gained a very loyal following in the 1980s. *Canberra's* future had seemed bleak in the 1970s as her deeper draft than *Oriana* (32ft as against 31ft) was believed to limit her usefulness as a cruise ship. As it was she underwent conversion to a full-time cruise ship and replaced the *Orsova* in the UK cruise market.

Through their ownership of British India, P&O also offered places on their educational cruise ships, with *Uganda* operating as a school ship until the Falkland's conflict of 1982. Taken up for Ministry of Defence service, *Uganda* had only a brief return to educational cruising between September 1982 and January 1983 when she was chartered again for MoD duties.

In 1988 *Canberra* was joined by the *Sea Princess* (ex-*Kungsholm*), which was renamed *Victoria* in 1995. In 1983 P&O acquired Swan Hellenic and were able to offer cruises with a cultural theme on the chartered *Orpheus*.

*Canberra*, the quintessential British cruise ship at Bonaire, March 1997, shortly before she was sold to shipbreakers.

Cunard's *Queen Elizabeth 2*, arguably the most famous cruise ship in British history, at South Queensferry, July 2001.

Cunard had the *Queen Elizabeth 2* and the 17,500grt *Cunard Countess* and *Cunard Princess*. *Sagafjord* and *Vistafjord* joined the Cunard fleet in 1983.

The Russians operated a number of cruises out of Tilbury, these cruises being very much at the lower end of the market. The small Portuguese line *Funchal* had (as it still does) a loyal British following despite the ship's lack of modern facilities at the time.

A survivor of the period is Fred Olsen's *Black Prince* (11,209grt), another small ship; she was still in service in 2004 and has a very loyal following of people who appreciated her intimate nature.

Apart from the above it was necessary to fly out and take a cruise on one of the US market ships. Even by 2002, when there had been considerable growth in the number of ships operating for the British market, research for the Competition Commission revealed that approximately 6 per cent of those cruising on one of the major US market ships would be from the UK.

# A British boom

In the 1990s the British rediscovered cruising. In 1992, 225,000 Britons cruised. This number increased to 640,000 by 1996 and by 2000 it was 800,000. Any market that increases over threefold in eight years is worthy of study. An interesting experiment in the 1980s was the introduction of the *Vacationer*. Converted from a container ship the new owners Vacation Liners offered a totally 'no-frills' cruise operation; no cabin service (passengers made their own beds), buffet meals and minimal entertainment., the ship operating with a crew of just twenty-nine. Although Vacation Liners was a Dutch company, the *Vacationer* was initially aimed at the British market, being sold through Cadogan Travel, and began cruising in Spanish waters from her base in Gibraltar in March 1982. During the winter of 1983/84 she was positioned in the Caribbean, and in 1986 was renamed *Carib Vacationer*. During the summer months she still operated cruises in the Mediterranean. However, this was a flawed concept, and in 1987 she was placed in lay-up in Curaçao. Whilst there have been several attempts to return her to service the ship remains idle. In 2003 P&O introduced a new brand – Ocean Village – using the *Arcadia* which was renamed *Ocean Village*. Designed for a younger age group this operation also offered buffet-style meals only, although there was a full service and entertainment package provided.

The global cruise industry throughout the 1990s saw mergers, acquisitions and new companies, some of which survived and some that did not. The global market increased from just under 5.5 million in 1992 to nearly 10.3 million in 2000. The largest market was, and remains, the US but it is worth noting that it is a market that is slowing down whereas the UK market is still expanding.

By the start of the twenty-first century, four companies dominated the global cruise market. The largest by far was that of the Carnival Group that includes Carnival itself, Holland America, Costa and Cunard amongst others. Carnival was started by Ted Arison and is now controlled by Mickey Arison. It only commenced operations in 1972 and now has brands in nearly every segment of the cruise industry. The Carnival Group held a 29 per cent share of the UK package/cruise holiday company Airtours (now My Travel) but has now relinquished this holding. Royal Caribbean operates US market cruise ships in its own name and commenced UK operations in 2003. Royal Caribbean also acquired Celebrity Cruises, the successors to Chandris. P&O Princess Cruises was demerged from the main P&O Group in 2000 and floated on the New York and London Stock Exchanges as a separate company, although still using the P&O logo and name. The companies have separate boards. The demerger reflected the growing strength of the cruise sector. P&O Princess Cruises includes as its functional components Princess Cruises, the North American premium brand; P&O Cruises, the UK's largest and oldest premium cruise brand; Aida Cruises, one of Germany's fastest growing cruise companies; and P&O Cruises (Australia), Swan Hellenic, and Seetours in Germany.

Norwegian Cruise Lines, together with Orient Lines, is owned by Star Cruises of Asia.

During the 1990s the uniquely British cruise market saw a number of very successful new entrants. A number of these companies have come from the package holiday sector. In addition to the new entrants, P&O Cruises and Fred Olsen both increased their capacity to a considerable degree. Cunard did not increase its UK operation during the 1990s but that all changed in 2004 when *Queen Mary 2* was added to the fleet, with an announcement for another liner to be in service in 2007.

# P&O Cruises

In 1994 P&O Cruises operated two ships for the UK market in their own name plus one ship chartered under the Swan Hellenic brand. The two P&O ships were *Canberra*

(44,807grt), carrying a maximum of 1,641 passengers, and *Sea Princess*, ex-*Kungsholm* and later *Victoria* (27,670grt) with a maximum of 743 passengers. The Swan Hellenic operation used the chartered *Orpheus*, ex-*Theus*, ex-*Munster 1*, ex-*Munster* (5,092grt), with a maximum capacity of 318.

In 1995 the company introduced what was the first purpose-built vessel for the UK cruise market – the 69,153grt *Oriana*, with a maximum capacity of 1,975. *Canberra* was withdrawn in 1997, by which time the *Star Princess* (ex-*Sitmar Fair Majesty*), from the company's US Princess Cruises operation, was transformed into the 63,524grt *Arcadia* with a maximum capacity of 1,549. In 2000 a semi-sister to *Oriana* was introduced – the 76,152grt *Aurora* with a maximum capacity of 1,975 and also purpose built for the UK market. In 2002 it was announced that *Arcadia* was to be-named *Ocean Village* as the flagship for a new P&O/Princess operation in the Mediterranean for the 'dress down Friday' generation of younger holidaymakers from the UK. *Ocean Village* is designed as a more flexible product than traditional cruises. There are no set meal times and all meals are buffet style. The aim is to visit a different Mediterranean resort each day with all sea time being at night. *Victoria* left the fleet in late 2002 to become the *Mona Lisa* of the German company Holiday–Kreuzfahrten. The UK market is still growing and to replace *Arcadia* and *Victoria* for the 2003 season, the *Ocean Princess* and *Sea Princess* from the US operation were refitted for the UK market and renamed *Oceana* and *Adonia*. These sister ships of 77,000grt have a maximum capacity of 2,272. *Oceana* and *Adonia* and were branded as the 'White Sisters', echoing the branding of the *Strathaird* and the *Strathanver* in the 1930s. In 2005 *Adonia* will return to Princess and a new *Arcadia* will come into service with *Royal Princess* operating in the UK market as *Artemis*.

## Adult-only cruising

Cruising has become a much more family-orientated holiday in recent years. Whereas the traditional image of cruising was of a holiday package for the middle-aged and elderly, the majority of the companies and ships in the global cruising market have considerable facilities for children. The Disney Cruise Line uses ships that have been designed to reflect a child's drawing of 'an ocean liner'. There is, however, still a market for those who want to cruise in a ship where there are no children. Saga Cruises (covered later in this chapter) operate for the over-50s (although a partner or companion over 40 can accompany the over-50s). P&O dedicated the *Arcadia* as an adult-only ship from May 2002. With the transfer of *Arcadia* to the *Ocean Village* operation in 2003, the role of adult-only ship was given to *Adonia*.

In 1996 Swan Hellenic chartered the 12,500grt *Minerva* with a maximum capacity of 474, replacing her with the *Minerva II*, one of the eight Renaissance Cruises 'R' ships made available by the failure of that line in 2002. Of 30,277grt, *Minerva II* (ex-*R Eight*) has a maximum capacity of 824. As befits the cultural nature of the Swan Hellenic operation there are no facilities for children. The *Minerva* herself (built on the uncompleted hull of a Soviet spy ship – the *Okean*) was chartered by Saga Cruises (see below) and entered service as the *Saga Pearl* in 2003.

The huge expansion of the UK cruise market between 1994 and 2003 can be shown by the comparative figures for tonnage and available berths offered by the UK P&O/Princess Cruises operation.

| Year | Tonnage (grt) | Berths (maximum) |
|------|---------------|------------------|
| 1994 | 77,500        | 2,702            |
| 2003 | 393,106       | 10,867           |

*Arcadia*, P&O's adults-only ship, now sailing as *Ocean Village*.

These figures represent a five-fold increase in both tonnage and capacity in less than ten years.

In 2001 P&O announced plans to purchase Festival Cruises (known as First European Cruises in the US). Festival operated a number of older ships at the time plus a brand new vessel – *Mistral*. Festival's operation was neither UK nor US market orientated but aimed at the general European market. The company used the Euro for on-board purchases before those countries that entered the Eurozone relinquished their national currencies. At the last minute the purchase plans were withdrawn and Festival did not become part of the P&O operation, although the company subsequently expanded into the German market.

In 2002 plans were put forward for a merger between P&O/Princess and Royal Caribbean. A counter bid for P&O was made by the Carnival Group. The competition authorities in the UK, the EU and the USA cleared the proposed merger and in the spring of 2003 it was announced that P&O and Carnival would merge as a dual-listed company and that the respective brands would be retained. In the 1980s Cunard had made an unsuccessful bid for P&O and it is interesting to speculate how British cruising would have developed if P&O and Cunard had merged then.

## Fred Olsen

The Norwegian company of Fred Olsen has been a continual feature of the UK cruise market for many years. Fred Olsen has interests in the Canary Islands and it was to there that the company's first cruises were offered. Initially the Olsen operation used the *Black Prince* for winter cruises from the UK to the Canaries, whilst the ship was used by the

Bergen Line as the *Venus* for the UK–Norway ferry service in the summer. The first *Black Prince* cruise was in October 1966. In 1986 the ship was converted to a full-time cruise ship of 11,500grt with a maximum capacity of 517.

The Olsen ferry *Bolero* (1972, 11,344grt) also undertook some winter cruising between 1972 and 1976, as did the *Blenheim* (10,420grt) from her launch in 1970 until her sale in 1981 when she entered the US cruise market as the *Scandinavian Sea*.

Throughout the 1980s and early 1990s the *Black Prince*, small as she is, gained a loyal UK following. Having only 517 berths to offer made Fred Olsen a very small player in the UK market. However in 1996 the company acquired the 28,492grt *Star Odyssey* (ex-*Westward*, ex-*Royal Viking Star*) with a capacity of 892 and renamed her *Black Watch*. When the ship was launched in 1972 she was of 21,847grt with a capacity of 539 and was lengthened in 1981. A planned refit in 2005 will add extra balcony cabins.

Further expansion occurred in 2001 when Fred Olsen acquired the 19,069grt *Braemar* (ex-*Norwegian Dynasty*, ex-*Crown Majesty*, ex-*Cunard Dynasty* ex-*Crown Dynasty*). This smallish vessel fitted into the Olsen 'small is beautiful' philosophy and with a maximum capacity of 821 enabled the company to offer 2,325 berths from 2002. In recent years the *Black Prince* has been used to pioneer new itineraries, such as South America and Cuba, as well as being available for charter to other travel companies including Page & Moy (see later) and even the National Trust for Scotland. *Black Prince* is one of the smallest vessels to cruise across the Atlantic.

## Cunard

P&O itself was the subject of a takeover attempt by Cunard in 1983 – a turbulent decade for one of the oldest names in the shipping industry. Cunard had been sold to Trafalgar House Investments in 1971. In 1983 Trafalgar House purchased Norwegian American Cruises, a deal that added the *Vistafjord* and the *Sagafjord* to the *Queen Elizabeth 2, Cunard Countess* and *Cunard Princess*. The *Queen Elizabeth 2* was regarded by much of the UK public as the flagship of the British Merchant Navy. In 1986 Cunard acquired Sea Goddess Cruises and added the luxury 4,260grt, 116 passenger 'mega-yachts' *Sea Goddess 1* and *Sea Goddess 2* to the fleet. These vessels were mainly intended for the international luxury cruise market.

*Cunard Princess* was chartered by the United States military in 1990 for a period of six months to act as a floating R&R (rest and relaxation) centre for US personnel involved in the Gulf War that followed Iraq's invasion of Kuwait.

In order to expand its US market operation, Cunard joined with the Effjohn Company to form Cunard Crown Cruises in 1993, and in the following year there was further expansion of the US market when Trafalgar House acquired the Royal Viking Line name together with the 37,845grt *Royal Viking Sun*, one of the highest rated cruise ships at the time.

*Cunard Princess* was sold to the Mediterranean Shipping Company (MSC) in 1995 to become the *Rhapsody*. *Cunard Countess* was sold in 1995 to the Epirotiki Line who sold her on in 1996 to the ill-fated Awani Cruises of Indonesia with the intention that she should become *Awani Dream 11*. Unfortunately, this was a period of political and economic turmoil in Indonesia and the company rapidly became defunct. The ship was sold to Royal Olympic (nee Epirotiki )Cruises in 1998 to become the *Olympic Countess* and was later renamed *Olympia Countess*.

Kvaerner, a Norwegian group that includes paper, oil and shipbuilding amongst its activities, acquired Trafalgar House and thus Cunard in 1996. Two years later Kvaerner sold Cunard to the Carnival group for $500 million. Carnival kept the brand name of Cunard in line with the group's practice of retaining well-known brand names that it has acquired.

As described in the section on Saga Cruises (below) *Sagafjord* was sold to Saga Cruises to become *Saga Rose* in 1997 (she was briefly named *Gripsholm* before the sale) whilst *Vistafjord* was renamed *Caronia* in 1999 after a major refit.

At the start of the twenty-first century the Cunard brand only offered the *Queen Elizabeth 2* and *Caronia* with a total of 2,638 berths for the UK/US market. However, the *Queen Mary 2* of 150,000grt made her debut in 2004. *QM2* is primarily designed to reintroduce the transatlantic service but will also undertake some cruises from the UK and the Caribbean. There will be a new build named *Queen Victoria* for the UK market, the ship being of 90,000grt. This ship is due to enter service in 2007. Meanwhile, *Caronia* has been sold to Saga as *Saga Ruby* to join her sister, *Saga Rose* in 2005.

## Saga

In 1951, in Folkestone (UK) Sidney De Haan realized that retired people would appreciate the opportunity to take lower-cost seaside vacations outside of the main vacation periods. The main vacation periods coincide with school vacations and hoteliers offer discounts for those who vacation outside of the busiest periods. The first vacation De Haan offered cost £6.50 and included full board, travel to the resort and three excursions. Initially for the over-60s, Saga now provides holidays for those over fifty who may take a partner or companion with them provided that the partner or companion is over forty.

Research carried out by Roger Cartwright and Carolyn Baird in 1999 showed that the older a holidaymaker was the more safety and security were likely to feature as choice factors in booking a holiday.

Saga provides their customers with an escort for every vacation that the company offers. Many of the vacations are organized through established travel and vacation operators. Saga, however, also provide their own representative for the vacation, thus giving the customer a Saga point of contact all the time they are away from home. Saga also charter river cruise boats to provide a 'Saga customers only' holiday.

In 1996 Saga, in addition to booking customers onto the ships of the major cruise lines, commenced their own dedicated cruise operation. Believing that there was a large enough UK market for a cruise ship for the over-50s, Saga acquired the 24,500grt *Sagafjord* from Cunard and renamed her *Saga Rose*.

Saga's requirements were for a ship with sufficient range to undertake an annual world cruise (retired people can afford to take the 100 days required to circumnavigate the globe), larger cabins than the industry norm and a good proportion of single cabins. The latter requirement is very important as many older people travel on their own and cannot afford the huge single supplements charged by many holiday operators. *Saga Rose* carries a maximum of 587 passengers and 350 crew. There are sixty-three dedicated single cabins.

It is a fact that women tend to live longer than men do and thus there are likely to be more single females than males on the *Saga Rose*. Recognizing this, Saga is one of the few remaining cruise companies (Fred Olsen Lines is another) to provide two male dance hosts for the female passengers.

Saga's cruise business was such that in 2002 it was announced that they were to increase capacity by chartering the *Minerva* (see earlier) with accommodation for 352 passengers. The ship was renamed *Saga Pearl* and is operated to the same high standard as *Saga Rose*. She leaves the fleet in 2005 when the *Caronia* of Cunard joins and becomes *Saga Ruby*.

## New entrants to the cruise market

The three main providers of package holidays in the UK are My Travel (formerly Airtours), Thomson and First Choice. In the 1990s all three companies entered the UK cruise market in their own right. The companies had offered cruises and cruise and stay holidays with traditional cruise operators but this new development involved them offering cruises in ships that were owned by them or chartered for their sole use. The advantage that these companies have in the fly cruise market is that they have their own airlines that are already flying to the embarkation regions carrying land-based holidaymakers in addition to cruise customers. These companies offer cruises of seven or fourteen days (with occasional longer voyages when re-positioning ships). There are usually two seven-day itineraries that can be combined for a fourteen-day cruise. An alternative option is for a seven-day cruise and a seven-day hotel stay. Not surprisingly the base ports for these operations have tended to be in the areas that the maximum land-based UK holidaymakers use, e.g. Majorca or the Canary Islands.

## Airtours (My Travel)

My Travel is the recent name for Airtours. Airtours entered the cruise market in 1995 using the 16,607grt *Seawing* (ex-*Southward* of 1971) and the 23,000grt *Carousel* (ex-*Nordic Prince*, also built in 1971). The distinctive funnel-mounted lounge of the *Nordic Prince* was removed, altering the profile of the vessel.

Photographed at Lisbon in May 1996 is *Seawing* of Airtours/My Travel. Her last cruise for the company is in September 2004.

For the 1996 season Airtours were able to offer 2,062 berths. Also in 1996 the Carnival Corporation acquired a 29.6 per cent share of Airtours and in 1997 Carnival and Airtours each acquired 50 per cent of the Italian cruise operator Costa. Costa operated primarily in the Italian and US markets.

In 1997 a sister ship to the *Nordic Prince*, the *Song of Norway* was acquired and renamed *Sundream*. This brought the number of available berths up to 3,319. In 1999 Airtours bought the 37,584grt *Song of America* of 1982 from Royal Caribbean and renamed her *Sunbird*. The funnel-mounted lounge was retained as, unlike that on the earlier ships, it went all the way around the funnel and could not be removed. Had RCL demanded its removal, as had been the case with the previous purchases, it would have meant a completely new funnel. This new acquisition meant that Airtours were able to enter the twenty-first century with four ships and an availability of 4,914 berths.

In 2001 Carnival sold their shares in Airtours and took complete control of Costa. Airtours, as the owners of the largest fleet of the newcomers, have offered cruises to Scandinavia and Northern Europe from Southampton and Harwich. For the winter 2002/03 season the *Seawing* went out to the Far East, thus opening up another cruising area for the UK market. Thailand has become a major UK long-haul holiday destination and thus it makes sense for a package holiday company to be able to offer cruise and stay holidays using its own ships rather than having to rely on those of other cruise companies. My Travel also operates cruises in the Caribbean.

Whilst Airtours sub-contracted their cruise management and day-to-day operations in the first instance they now operate the ships in-house as an integral part of their business. All this is to change as, in 2004, My Travel announced that it was to leave the cruise market. Its leased ships are to return to their owners, with *Sundream* leaving the fleet in September 2004 and the other ships going to Louis Cruises.

## Thomson

The package holiday company Thomson have offered cruises and cruise and stay holidays using the vessels of other cruise companies for some time. The company had also chartered the *Ithaca* and *Calypso* as described earlier.

Thomson re-entered the cruise business in its own name in 1995 using ships that were (and still are) owned by Louis Cruise Lines of Cyprus plus a partial charter of the 38,175 *Island Breeze* (ex-*Festivale*, ex-*Vaal*, ex-*Transvaal Castle*) of 1962. *Island Breeze* sailed for Thomson during the summer from 1996 until 2000.

A Louis Cruise Line ship that sailed in Thomson colours was the *Sapphire* (ex-*Princesa Oceanica*, ex-*Sea Prince*, ex-*Ocean Princess*, ex-*Italia*), 12,163grt and with a maximum capacity of 650. *Sapphire* operated for Thomson between 1996 and 2000. She is an interesting ship as she actually sank in the Amazon in 1993 and was raised and refitted.

The mainstays of the Thomson operation from 1998 until April 2003 were the *Topaz* (ex-*Olympic*, ex-*Fiesta Marina*, ex-*Carnivale*, ex-*Queen Anna Maria*, ex-*Empress of Britain*) on a five year charter and the *Emerald* (ex-*Regent Rainbow*, ex-*Diamond Island*, ex-*Santa Rosa*). Built in 1956, the 31,500grt *Topaz* is one of the great classic ocean liners and had a capacity of 1,386 in Thomson service. The 26,431grt *Emerald* has a maximum capacity of 1,198. *Topaz* operated all-inclusive cruises where all drinks (with the exception of premium brands) were included in the price of the cruise. The replacement for *Topaz* in Thomson service was announced in 2002 and is the ex-Holland America liner *Nieuw Amsterdam*, built in 1983. Renamed *Thomson Spirit*, the 33,930grt vessel has a capacity of 1,350. Thomson has also expanded its cruise operations to include the Caribbean. By 2005, Thomson will be operating

*Island Escape* leaving Setubal after her refit in March 2002.


## First Choice

The cruise operations of the third of the major UK package holiday companies, First Choice, have been smaller than its rivals. First Choice entered the market in 1999 with the charter of the *Bolero* (ex-*Starward* of 1968) from Festival Cruises. The 16,107grt vessel had a capacity of 984 passengers. The vessel was chartered to First Choice for seven months in 1999. First Choice had originally intended to charter the 12,609grt *Ausonia*. Built in 1957, the classically designed *Ausonia* with a capacity of 701 was bought by Louis Cruise Lines in 1998. For various reasons the ship did not begin the charter until 2000. Whilst most of her cruises were in the Mediterranean she also offered a number of Southampton–Cyprus (and vice versa) cruises. In 2002 First Choice formed a joint venture with Royal Caribbean to offer 'aspirational' cruises for the UK market. This operation formed the subject of the television documentary mentioned earlier in this chapter. The *Viking Serenade* (ex-*Stardancer*, ex-*Scandinavia*) originally built as a luxury car ferry but refitted in 1985 as a 40,132grt cruise ship with a capacity of 1,863 was renamed *Island Escape*. On-board services are not only provided by Island Cruises (the brand for the joint venture) but also by high street names such as Oddbins (for wine) and Costa Coffee. The ship serves the UK market in both the Caribbean and the Mediterranean.

The Island Cruise operation appears very similar to that of P&O's Ocean Village in that it is designed for the younger holidaymaker.


## Voyages of Discovery

In 1932 a government-sponsored scheme saw a party of Scottish schoolboys undertaking a two-week cruise to Scandinavia in a troopship. English schoolboys (but not girls) had their turn in 1933.

In 1962, British India (part of the P&O Group), a company that had played a major role in troop transporting, converted two of its ships, *Dunera* and *Devonia* to school cruising. The traditional British India market had contracted due to the withdrawal of British forces from east of Suez and the independence of India and Pakistan in the late 1940s. The school cruise concept proved successful and the troopship *Nevasa* (20,527grt), built in 1956, was converted to school cruising in 1964. *Dunera* and *Devonia* were replaced in 1968 by the 14,430grt *Uganda,* built in 1952. Although *Nevasa* was withdrawn and scrapped in 1975, *Uganda* carried on with educational cruising until she was requisitioned for military duties during the 1982 Falklands conflict.

In addition to their school passengers, *Nevasa* and *Uganda* also carried a small number of regular cruise passengers in separate accommodation.

It might be thought that educational cruising had ceased with the re-chartering of *Uganda* by the MOD in early 1983 but, in fact, the market for such cruises has continued. In 1984 a Sussex-based company known as 'Schools Abroad' chartered or arranged educational cruises on a large number of vessels. Latterly, the *Ocean Majesty, Funchal, Aegean 1* and *Arion* have been used by the company – now known as 'Voyages of Discovery'.

The company is also offering cruises in the newly named 19,907grt *Discovery*, ex-*Island Princess*, ex-*Island Venture* of 1971 – one of the two original 'Love Boats®' from the television series. The vessel, owned by the shipping entrepreneur Gerry Herrod, was refurbished to a high standard for the 2003 season. Since moving into the adult cruise market in the late 1980s the company has found that there is a ready market for cruises that are informative and which have an intellectual content.

Since 1984 the company has provided nearly 200 cruises accommodating some 90,000 students, teachers and adult passengers on destination-intensive cruises designed to bring geography and history to life.

## Page & Moy

The UK travel company Page & Moy regularly charters cruise ships for the exclusive use of their customers, placing their own staff on board to work alongside the ship's company. Page & Moy often include the *Black Prince* (see Fred Olsen earlier in this chapter) and the *Ocean Majesty.* At 10,414grt and with a capacity of 621 the *Ocean Majesty* (ex-*Kypros Star*, ex-*Juan March)*, built in 1966, was converted from a ferry in 1994. Under the Page & Moy brand she is another of those small ships that has a loyal following. In this respect she is very similar to the *Black Prince. Ocean Majesty* has been a regular summer season vessel for Page & Moy since the late 1990s.

## Direct Cruises

In 1997, Direct Cruises was set up by the UK-based Direct Holidays to operate the 32,753grt *Eugenio Costa* as the *Edinburgh Castle.* The operation commenced at the time P&O were withdrawing the *Canberra*. Although slightly smaller than *Canberra, Edinburgh Castle* had something of the looks of the much loved favourite and the company's initial brochures actually made direct comparisons to the *Canberra* and their quoted savings were directly linked to *Canberra* fares.

It seems that Direct Cruises had their eye on the *Canberra*'s customer base, hence two mentions of a competitor's vessel in their brochure.

Unfortunately for Direct Cruises, whilst their initial uptake was enough to need a second ship for the first season, the *Apollo* (actually the 28,574grt *Apollon* – the name carried on her bow – ex-*Star of Texas*, ex-*Mardi Gras*, ex-*Empress of Canada)*, the company did not have the most auspicious of starts. Press reports indicated that the *Edinburgh Castle* was not fully complete in time for the first cruise, although this was related to only a few cabins; the *Apollo* was late out of refit and cruises had to be cancelled and in the summer of 1998 the *Edinburgh Castle* was the subject of a Legionnaires Disease scare. Later in the summer of 1998 the Direct Cruise operation was purchased by Airtours, although the cruises continued to be operated and branded separately for a short time before disappearing completely. On 24 February 1999, the company actually owning the *Edinburgh Castle* (Direct Cruises being the operators) went into liquidation.

# chapter three

# BRITONS CRUISE THE WAVES – THE BRITISH CRUISE MARKET IN THE TWENTY-FIRST CENTURY

The previous chapters have been concerned with the history of both the companies involved in the British cruise industry and the ships that have operated cruises aimed directly at the British cruise passenger. This chapter is concerned with the three other components of what makes a cruise – the nature of the cruise experience, the cruise passengers themselves and the destinations visited.

## The cruise experience

People take a cruise for a number of reasons; it may be to relax, to celebrate a special event or anniversary, it may be to see new places or just to seek the sun. Different cruise products suit different reasons for cruising.

The overall cruise market can be divided into four main sectors that can and do overlap each other:

traditional cruises
resort cruises
niche cruises
world cruises

All of these sectors are represented within the UK cruise market.

## Traditional cruises

The traditional cruise experience can be identified by:

a degree of formality
a number of sea days per cruise
cruises of from ten to twenty-one days' duration
the ability to choose one's cabin when booking at no extra cost
a variety of itineraries with each cruise in a season being different from the others

The companies offering traditional cruises dedicated to the UK market were:

P&O Cruises: four ships in 2003; *Adonia, Aurora, Oceana, Oriana*
Cunard: two ships in 2003; *Caronia, Queen Elizabeth 2*
Fred Olsen: three ships in 2003; *Black Prince, Black Watch, Braemar*
Voyages of Discovery: one ship in 2003; *Discovery*
Page & Moy: one ship in 2003; *Ocean Majesty*
Saga: two ships in 2003; *Saga Pearl* (see also under niche cruising), *Saga Rose*

Page & Moy charter the 10,417grt *Ocean Majesty* for a number of months of the year and also book customers onto the ships of other companies. The company has also chartered the *Black Prince* from Fred Olsen.

Saga operate the *Saga Rose* but also book Saga customers onto Cunard, Holland America, Costa, Fred Olsen, Orient Lines and Star Cruises vessels. Saga began a charter of the *Saga Pearl* (ex-*Minerva*) in 2003 – an operation also covered under niche cruising.

A large number of traditional cruises for the UK market operate out of UK ports, thus avoiding the need to fly. A number of fly cruises are also offered together with world cruises from Cunard, P&O Cruises, Saga and, from 2004, Fred Olsen. The traditional cruise companies are beginning to offer regional airport departures for fly cruises instead of just Gatwick and Manchester. Fred Olsen also operates a small number of cruises from Scotland.

There is no doubt that the traditional cruise is still important to a large number of cruise passengers, especially those who have been cruising for some time. There is also another type of cruise – the resort cruise – that has gained a considerable share of newcomers to cruising.

## Resort cruises

The UK market for resort cruising has been pioneered by the three main UK package holiday companies of Thomson, First Choice and My Travel (formerly Airtours).

These companies have become known for their package holidays and have expanded their operations to include cruising, albeit in a less-traditional manner. The three companies operate their own charter airlines out of regional UK airports and are thus able to offer a highly effective fly-cruise programme.

Many British holidaymakers switched from UK seaside destinations to the resorts of Spain in the 1970s and 1980s, so their successors are now beginning to move into resort cruising – a product that has its roots in the package holiday sector rather than the traditional cruise sector.

Resort cruises tend to be characterised by:

seven-day alternating itineraries
seven-day hotel stays
extra charge for pre-booking a particular cabin
a more informal dress code
fly cruises rather than UK ship departures (with the exception of *Sundream*)
regional airport departures for fly cruises
only one sea day per seven-day cruise – resort cruises tend to be more destination intensive than traditional cruises.

A resort cruise uses the ship as a floating hotel in a different port nearly every day whereas on a traditional cruise there are lazy days at sea in between ports of call.

Whist traditional cruises have offered extended stays at the beginning and or end of fly cruises, the resort cruise operations nearly always offer a cruise and stay option. The cruises tend to be based around a pattern of a seven-day itinerary (A) followed by a seven-day itinerary (B). Customers can choose between a seven-day hotel stay followed by either itinerary A or B, or an A or B itinerary cruise followed by a seven-day hotel stay or the combination of itineraries A and B. The latter option provides a cruise of a more traditional length but menus and shows will in all probability be repeated on the second part of the cruise.

The relationships that the package holiday companies have built up with resort hotels mean that they can offer very competitive packages. The majority of resort-style cruises involve flying to popular package holiday destinations such as Majorca (where My Travel, Thomson and First Choice base vessels) or Cyprus in order to join the ship.

In 2003 My Travel began to offer more traditional cruises basing *Sundream* in the UK and offering thirteen- or fourteen-night cruises out of Southampton or Harwich. Following the charter of the *Ausonia*, First Choice began a partnership with Royal Caribbean Cruises (a major player in the US cruise market) to offer a resort-style cruise operation using the 40,132grt *Island Escape* (ex-*Viking Serenade,* ex-*Stardancer,* ex-*Scandinavia*) on two western Mediterranean seven-day itineraries out of Palma, Majorca. The Island Cruises operation also involved the Costa Coffee and Oddbins (wines) companies who operate on-board concessions.

P&O Cruises also entered the resort cruise market in 2003 with the re-branding of the 63,524grt *Arcadia* as *Ocean Village*, operating two seven-day itineraries out of Palma, Majorca. The cruises are designed for the 'thirty-something/dress-down Friday generation'. Dress is casual; the ship stays late in some ports so that local nightlife can be sampled, meals are buffet style, there are mountain bikes available for use on shore and a range of sporting activities can be purchased. *Island Escape* is not only the most recently built of the UK market resort ships (1987 as opposed to 1982 for the next youngest – *Sunbird*) but is also the largest by a considerable margin, 63,364grt compared with *Sunbird* at 37,584grt and the Thomson Spirit (ex-*Nieuw Amsterdam*) at 33,930grt. Cruise passengers on board *Ocean Village* have more space than on board other ships as many of her cabins are closer to 180sq.ft rather than the 150 sq.ft that is now common for many traditional and resort cruise ships. She also has sixty-four premium cabins with balconies. The only resort ships with balcony accommodation in 2003 were *Sunbird* (nine) and *Island Escape* (five). My Travel, Thomson, Island Cruises and Ocean Village all include tips as an integral part of the holiday price. Thomson, My Travel and Island Escape all charge extra to reserve a particular cabin rather than just a particular grade. The resort cruise companies also offer enhanced flight service at an additional cost.

In contrast, My Travel seems to be moving away from the resort cruise to some extent to the more traditional cruise product with longer itineraries and even butlers servicing the premium accommodation on *Sunbird*. Initially, My Travel, as Airtours, used an outside management company to operate cruises but the company now operate the cruises as an integral part of the business.

All-inclusive packages where many beverages are provided as part of the total cost or with an extra payment are also a feature of many resort cruises.

The companies offering resort cruises dedicated to the UK market are:

My Travel (Airtours): four ships in 2003; *Carousel, Seawing, Sunbird, Sundream*
Island Cruises (First Choice): one ship in 2003; *Island Escape*
Thomson: three ships in 2003; *Topaz* (until April 2003), *Thomson Spirit* (from May 2003),
  *Emerald, Thomson Celebration* and *Thomson Destiny* (from May 2005)

## Niche cruises

Many of the traditional cruise companies engage guest speakers, including 'stars' of TV programmes such as Antiques Roadshow, to provide extra activities on sea days. These themed cruises can, however, be enjoyed fully without having an interest in the theme.

The Swan Hellenic Cruises, operated by *Minerva II* are designed for those who wish to gain a more in-depth knowledge of the areas visited and attract cruise passengers with specific interests. The 2003 itinerary for *Saga Pearl* (ex-*Minerva*) kept to the Swan Hellenic style of cruise with renowned expert speakers accompanying each cruise.

Organisations such as the National Trust for Scotland also charter cruise vessels for themed cruises linked to the work of the organisation. The *Black Prince* of Fred Olsen Cruises has often been engaged in such charters.

Other types of niche cruising include expeditions to more remote parts of the world and cruising on the new generation of luxury sailing vessels. These cruises tend to be international in flavour.

## World cruises

For many people one of the first things on their 'what to do if I win the lottery' list is a world cruise. World cruises have long been a feature of the UK cruise market. The 42,350grt Canadian Pacific liner *Empress of Britain* of 1931 made an annual 125-day world cruise during the winter. Departing New York just after Christmas, she would sail eastward across the Atlantic before transiting the Suez Canal and cruising the Indian Ocean and the Pacific, returning to the Atlantic via the Panama Canal.

By the start of the twenty-first century three UK market cruise liners plus the *Queen Elizabeth 2* were making 80–100-day world cruises while one of the Fred Olsen ships undertook an extended voyage to the Far East and back. Fred Olsen announced that they would begin to operate a full world cruise from 2004. One after the other the ships leave the UK in early January and head for the sun. P&O Cruises send one of their ships eastward and another westward. In 2004 *Aurora* headed west across the Atlantic to the Caribbean and then the Panama Canal into the Pacific whilst *Adonia* headed eastward towards Suez. The ships are both in Australian waters towards the end of February making for the option of a 'boomerang' cruise – out on one ship and back on the other, with a few days in Australia.

*Saga Rose* took a westward track for her 103-night, 33,775 nautical mile world cruise in 2003 whilst Fred Olsen's *Black Watch* left Southampton in January 2003 for a seventy-two-night cruise around South America.

A world cruise remains the ultimate 'long vacation' and with people retiring earlier with increased disposable income such a cruise is within the reach of many more potential cruise passengers. The ready availability of air travel means that those who cannot spare the time for the full world cruise can still undertake sectors on a fly-cruise basis.

## Children

As the cost of cruising has declined in relative terms, so the market for family cruise holidays has increased. Many of the cruise companies, especially in the resort cruise market, have invested in facilities for children. In the US market there are two purpose-built 'family-friendly' cruise ships – the *Disney Magic* and *Disney Wonder*, both of 85,000grt with two funnels. In fact, the ships look very similar to those drawn by young children – a clever piece of design and marketing.

## Accommodation

As late as the mid-1990s, *Canberra*, the quintessentially British cruise ship, had 236 out of a total of 780 cabins that were without private facilities. In the 1970s, the *Orsova* had a number of first-class inside cabins that comprised bunk berths and had no private facilities.

The British cruise passenger is now far more sophisticated and such a lack of facilities would not be tolerated. Many houses now have two or three WCs and only the most frugal of hotel/guesthouse accommodation does not offer en-suite facilities.

By 2003 practically every cruise ship in the world had private facilities attached to all cabins. The exceptions being the five-star *Hebridean Princess* (a small ship offering luxury cruises around Scotland and Scandinavia) that, despite its high rating in the *Berlitz Guide to Cruising* and *Cruise Ships 2003* had two cabins that were not provided with private facilities; the expedition cruise ship *Akademik Sergey Vavilov*, where the occupants of some cabins share facilities; and the *Princesa Cypria* (a combination car ferry and cruise ship operating out of Cyprus) which has 171 out of 274 cabins without private facilities. As a matter of interest, the first ship to offer en-suite facilities was the Cunard Line *Campania* of 1893, the ship also being the first to offer dedicated single cabins.

Ships designed for the US cruise market tend to have showers rather than baths in the lower priced accommodation as US cruise passengers tend to shower rather than take a full bath. On such ships baths are only found in premium accommodation. P&O's *Aurora*, built specifically for the British cruise market, has 542 cabins with baths and showers and only 392 with only showers. The shower-only cabins include twenty-two that are wheelchair accessible. The company's *Ocean Village* (ex-*Arcadia*) was built for the US market as the *Star Princess* (she was laid down as the *Sitmar Fair Majesty* but renamed during building) and has only her fourteen suites and thirty-six mini-suites equipped with both a bath and shower whilst the remaining 572 cabins have only a shower. In everyday life Americans adopted the shower and en-suite facilities long before the British.

## Verandas

Private balconies at sea were once the preserve of the rich. The provision of balconies in land-based resort hotels has become very much the norm and it is no surprise that this development has been mirrored in the cruise industry.

In 1992 none of the ships operating in the UK cruise market offered cabins with balconies and even in the US market balcony cabins only accounted for 6 per cent of the total. By 2003, 34 per cent of accommodation in the US cruise market was in balcony cabins with the figure for the UK market being somewhat lower at 15 per cent. Both those figures, however, include a number of older vessels that were still in operation. If ships entering the US or the UK market for the first time (either newly built or transferred) are considered, the figures increase to show that 34 per cent of the latest UK market accommodation is in balcony cabins compared with 56 per cent for the US market.

Just as power steering and CD players in cars were once only found at the top of the market but are now available as standard on the majority of cars so balconies, which were once reserved for the occupants of suites if they were present at all, are now to be found as an extra on normal cabins.

## Cuisine

Cruise company brochures stress the quality of the food served on board. In recent years there has been a move away from set sittings for dinner towards a more 'freestyle' approach more akin to that found in hotels where one books a table for a particular time, perhaps with friends. The traditional cruise approach to evening dining is to allocate people to a sitting and to place them on a table for between two and ten people. Many cruise passengers enjoy the social aspect that this arrangement provides. There is also the opportunity for waiters to get to know the preferences of those they serve on a regular basis.

Many ships, including those operating for the UK market offer alternative dining options with an à-la-carte restaurant in addition to the regular restaurants. For a small cover charge friends not seated together in the main restaurant can enjoy a meal and those who are normally on a large table can have a more intimate dining experience.

Food is one of the areas where we like our national preferences in addition to trying something new. Cruise companies operating in the UK market stress the availability of a 'good British breakfast'. As Britons we do not order our eggs 'over easy' and have fruit on the same plate as our bacon. An important part of the environmental bubble is providing people with a choice between food that is new and traditional national dishes. The British are more adventurous with cuisine than in the past but as the cafés, bars and restaurants of the Spanish Costas show – we still like the option of our national dishes whilst on holiday.

Cruise ship food is usually good, given that for the vast majority of ships it is banquet-style catering. Fewer and fewer companies are providing silver and partial silver service where the waiter brings the vegetables, etc. as a separate item. Plated service, where the complete meal comes on the plate, is now very much the norm. To those seated at a table for six, eight or ten this may be an advantage, as they will not have to wait, with their food going cold whilst their companions are served. It does, however, take some of the mystique out of the meal.

In the 1960s and 1970s the quality and range of food on UK market cruise ships was well in advance of that the cruise passenger would normally enjoy. That was a time, for many, when wine was something one had on holiday or only at Christmas. More and more people eat out today and UK wine sales are amongst the highest in Europe. Cruise ship cuisine and what we eat at home are converging quite rapidly. The advantage on a cruise, as on all-inclusive holidays, is that the cruise passenger does not have to cook the meal nor wash up afterwards! Nobody has suggested a self-catering cruise yet although the 43,525grt floating apartments/cruise ship *The World* has kitchens attached to the apartments but not in the guest accommodation.

## Entertainment

A cruising guide once described the entertainment on a UK market ship as 'end of the pier style'. Judging by the tone of the review the comment was meant to be negative. However, the variety shows that were, and still are, staged in the pier theatres at British holiday resorts represent good variety entertainment of a type that is much appreciated by UK audiences. The success each year of the Royal Variety Show demonstrates that there is room for this type of entertainment alongside the West End/Broadway musicals.

Cruise ship entertainment is usually a blend of musical (often a shortened version of a stage or film musical), variety acts and cabaret. Whilst music travels well, comedy often does not. The comedians who work the UK cruise ships use material suitable for a UK audience whereas those on US market ships target their act on US humour (humor)!

In many ways the growth in UK cruising has aided a revitalisation of UK variety entertainment. No longer are variety artistes reliant on clubs and summer seasons at holiday resorts – cruising can provide year-round employment.

In addition to headline acts, the cruise ships have their own entertainment staff and dancers. Where holiday camps once provided a start in the entertainment business today the modern 'red or bluecoat' may be found on a UK market cruise ship.

Guest speakers who can provide seminars and lectures on topics of interest to UK cruise passengers are found on many of the cruise ships, especially those ships that provide a traditional cruise experience. Life enhancement, crafts and topics related to the particular cruise itinerary are provided on sea days as additional activities and are often very well attended.

The standard of entertainment on the UK market cruise ships is generally high, although this is an area where cost cutting becomes readily apparent. The increasing sophistication of home entertainment systems and live events in land-based theatres has exposed people to high-quality entertainment and they expect similar sophistication on their cruise ship. A group of dancers with feathers and glitter does not impress today's cruise generation as it might have done in the past. Whilst the shows may not be as 'glitzy' as those on some of the US market vessels, they cater for and reflect the entertainment preferences of a British audience.

Entertainers on a cruise ship face different challenges from their colleagues on land. They cannot pack up and go home after a show – they live with their audience and become, to a certain extent, public property during the cruise. They need enhanced social skills and emotional resilience, as they have to interact with their public both on and off stage.

## Tipping

The origin of the word 'TIPS' lies in the phrase 'To Insure Personal Service'. Logically that suggests that tips should be given at the beginning of a cruise and not at the end. However, it would be unacceptable in this day and age to expect cruise passengers to have to pay up-front for good service. Indeed, it is not necessary to tip at all – service on the vast majority of UK cruise ships is exemplary. Tips are traditionally given on the final night/morning of a cruise. The recipients are normally the cabin steward or stewardess and the dining room servers. These are the people who have the most contact with the individual cruise passenger. However, to provide good cabin and table service requires the contribution of people who the passenger may never meet – laundry staff, washing-up staff, cooks, etc. They may receive nothing in tips unless company policy is that all tips are pooled. The resort cruises tend to avoid tipping altogether, as do Saga cruises. These companies 'include' gratuities in the price. Other companies do not, as they believe it is for the individual cruise passenger to decide how much and to whom a gratuity should be given. The advent of alternative dining options means that one may be served by many different people when eating – which do you tip? Cunard is the first company in the UK market to adopt the US idea of adding gratuities to a cruise passenger's account for settling at the end of a cruise or even in advance – the tips then being pooled. Whilst this might sound 'cheeky' it is perfectly possible for an individual to alter the amount of gratuity or indeed to pay none at all. This approach, and the inclusion of tips within the overall fare, does ensure that no individual crew members are disadvantaged by not working at the customer interface.

## Who goes cruising?

Who are the 800,000 Britons who cruised in 2002?

At one time, not in the too distant past, many of the passengers on a UK market cruise would have been retired and in possession of a reasonable pension. The trend towards younger couples, singles and families cruising began in the US and is now a trend in the UK market.

The resort-style cruise ships offer a holiday that resembles that of land-based packages. *Ocean Village* is designed for the 'thirty somethings' and traditional companies like P&O offer both family facilities on board with an adult-only option on *Adonia,* whilst Cunard market *Caronia* as an adult product.

Cruising is no longer a 'once in a lifetime' or even a 'once every few years' holiday choice for many people. The high levels of repeat business and customer loyalty in the UK cruise market indicate a growing trend towards cruise passengers who undertake at least one cruise every year.

As people gain more leisure time they have a greater opportunity to take either more cruises and/or longer cruises. Cruising is still at the top end of any particular holiday segment in terms of cost, but in real terms the cost of cruising in relation to average incomes is coming down.

There has been heavy discounting of prices in recent years but even without discounts a seven-day cruise in an outside cabin in the Mediterranean in 2003 could be had for £599. A land-based holiday in the same area in equivalent accommodation, full board and with entertainment would not be that much cheaper.

Single people have the same problem cruising as they do with land-based holidays – single supplements. Most cruise ship cabins are for two people, although Cunard – *Caronia* (73 single cabins out of a total of 324), *Queen Elizabeth 2* (151/950); Fred Olsen – *Black Prince* (29/167), *Black Watch* (38/352), *Braemar* (16/251); Page & Moy – *Ocean Majesty* (11/186); Saga – *Saga Pearl* (4/126), *Saga Rose* (60/290); Thomson – *Emerald* (2/338), *Thomson Spirit* (6/528); and Voyages of Discovery – *Discovery* (2/305) all have single cabins.

There are no dedicated single cabins in the ships of P&O Cruises but standard double cabins can be booked for single occupancy at a premium of between 15 per cent and 70 per cent depending on the ship and cruise chosen. Suites and mini-suites on nearly every cruise line carry a premium of 100 per cent for single occupancy. Single occupancy cabins, even when there is dedicated provision, carry a premium over those for twin occupancy. The cruise companies are no better and no worse than others in the holiday industry in assuming that customers come in pairs. This is an issue about which there is growing concern.

Given an ageing UK population and changes in the make-up of family life it seems likely that the demand for single accommodation will grow rather than diminish. It is a shame therefore that the latest cruise ships to be built have no dedicated single cabins.

## Disabilities

The older generation of ocean liners were not wheelchair friendly, many having lips at the bottom of doorways that meant a wheelchair had to be lifted over them. The more modern ships not only have easier access into cabins and ramps where required but also have specially equipped cabins for those with a disability.

So, what is the answer to the question posed at the beginning of this section – who are the 800,000 Britons who cruised in 2002? It was almost anybody who wanted to.

## The itineraries

Research in 1999 showed that, whereas the global cruise market, dominated as it is by the USA, placed the Caribbean, the Mediterranean and Alaska as the top three cruising areas, the preference for UK cruise passengers is the Mediterranean, the Caribbean and the Atlantic Islands (Canaries and Maderia plus Morocco) in that order. To a degree this reflects the ease of getting to these places.

# Menu.

## LUNCHEON.

### Hors d'Œuvres
Salami de Milan           Sardines in Oil
Anchovies Gorgona     Asparagus Tips     Salade Bagatelle
Bismark Herrings     Eggs Ecarlate     Red Cabbage     Museau de Bœuf
Salade de Légumes     Seville Olives     Tomatoes, Fines Herbes

### Soups
Consommé Paysanne           Scotch Broth

### Fish
Fried Plaice with Lemon
Fresh Prawns, Natural

### Egg Dishes
Omelets, Savoyarde           Shirred Eggs

### Entrées
Macaroni Polonaise           Veal Sauté, Chasseur
Boiled Fowl and Rice, Suprême

### Vegetables
Dressed Cabbage           Spring Carrots
Boiled Jacket, Baked Jacket, Mashed and Fried Potatoes

---

### To Order (10-15 Minutes
Bordeaux Pigeon
Tournedos     Calves' Brains, Maître d'Hôtel     Lamb Chops

### Cold Buffet
Anglo Ox Tongue     York Ham     Melton Mowbray Pie
Prime Ribs and Sirloin of Beef
Galantine of Turkey           Roast Surrey Capon
Roast New Season's Lamb, Mint Sauce
Home-made Brawn     Norfolk Boar's Head     Derby Round of Beef
Sausages : Bath, Salami, Luncheon, Bologna

### Salads
Lettuce     Tomato     Beetroot     Potato     Cucumber
Endive     Spring Onions     Radishes
Mayonnaise and French Dressings

### Sweets
Black Currant Tart
Sago Custard Pudding
Compôte of Fruit and Cream
Eldorado Ice Cream : Raspberry     Lemon

### Cheese
Duchess Packet Cheddar     Stilton     Cheshire     Gorgonzola
Petit Gruyère     New Zealand Cheddar     Cream

### Dessert
Apples     Oranges     Bananas     Cherries

---

Coffee

---

### "ARANDORA STAR."
The World's Most Delightful Cruising Liner
All the Year
Norwegian Fjords Cruise—En route Balholm—Sat., August 10th, 1935

SL35/1

Dining 1930s-style on Blue Star Line's *Arandora Star*, the 'World's most delightful cruising liner'.

UK market cruise ships can, however, be found throughout the world. It was noted earlier that world cruises are very popular with the British but there has also been a considerable expansion in the areas covered by UK market-orientated ships.

South America, including the Amazon, has become a regular itinerary for the major UK traditional cruise companies, as has the Caribbean outside of the hurricane season (June to October). Norwegian cruises have been expanded in many cases to include Spitzbergen, Iceland and Greenland. The Baltic ports have gained in popularity since the end of the Cold War at the beginning of the 1990s.

Although much of the UK-orientated cruise market has been concentrated on the western Mediterranean, due to the ease of operating seven-day cruises out of established holiday destinations such as Majorca or the ability of a Southampton-based ship to be able to reach Venice and back on a 14–17 day cruise, there has been a growth in eastern Mediterranean, Holy Land and Red Sea cruises when the political situation has allowed it. As noted earlier Airtours have operated UK market cruises in the Far East using the *Seawing*.

As yet there has not been a UK market ship based in the Pacific or Alaska but these may well be areas that the cruise companies will consider in the future. At present those UK cruise passengers wishing to cruise Alaskan waters must do so in a US market vessel. As the numbers of Britons wishing to cruise increases so will the demand for new cruising areas.

It is often remarked by those who study culture that there are many more things that are common to all of us regardless of our race, nationality, etc. than are different. Nevertheless it is often the small differences that we notice rather than the huge similarities. The cruise industry is no different. Americans, Germans, Japanese and Britons all undertake cruises (in increasing numbers) in ships that appear at first glance or to the uninitiated to be very similar. Refitting a cruise ship from one market to another can be as simple as changing the artwork and signage to reflect national tastes. Designing a new-build cruise ship for a particular market requires a more detailed examination of the behaviour of the cruise passengers from that market. Whilst there has been a growth in what can be termed 'international cruising', with a cruise product that is designed to appeal to a variety of nationalities, a large number of cruise ships are designed and operated with a particular national group in mind. A good example of an 'international' operation is that of Festival Cruises whose ships, especially since the introduction of the *Mistral* in 1999, have catered for a general European clientele. Festival introduced the euro as the onboard currency well in advance of the replacement of national currencies by the majority of European Union members in 2002.

1. Royal Mail Steam Packet Co.'s RMS *Avon* in Southampton Water, *c.*1910.

2. The Ellerman liner *City of Nagpur* in the Suez Canal on a company-issued postcard.

# DUCHESS of RICHMOND 2000 TON

**AUGUST 1930** **SUMMER SEA CRUISES** **AUGUST 1930**

S.S. "ADRIATIC"
25,000 TONS
LARGEST STEAMER CRUISING
FROM THE BRITISH ISLES

A SEA CRUISE TO
ATLANTIC AND
BALEARIC ISLES

18 DAYS FROM £35

Routes of Cruises

S.S. "CALGARIC"
16,063 TONS
FIRST CRUISE TO
NORWEGIAN FJORDS
2 WEEKS FROM £21

SECOND CRUISE TO
NORTHERN
CAPITALS
2 WEEKS FROM £21

 WHITE STAR LINE

**WEST INDIES CRUISE 1933**
**CANADIAN PACIFIC**

3. *Above:* Kenneth Shoesmith's wonderful art deco brochure for the Canadian Pacific's *Duchess of Richmond*'s 1933 West Indies cruise from Southampton.

4. *Left:* An unusual advertising medium was the blotter, an example of which is shown here advertising White Star's August 1930 cruises on *Adriatic* and *Calgaric*.

# CUNARD WHITE STAR LINE *Cruises*

HOERTZ

## Cunard Cruising — Reproduced by courtesy of "The

**PLEASURE-CRUISE LIFE IN A LUXURY LINER: THE DELIGHTFUL NEW FORM OF HOLIDAY-MAKING BY OCEAN TOURS AT ALL SEASONS OF THE**

The vogue of ocean touring has increased enormously, and during the coming season this new type of holiday will doubtless prove even more popular. Though the great shipping concerns which run fortnightly trips to the Mediterranean, Atlantic Isles, and Norwegian Fiords do not make a large profit from them, nevertheless they are keeping ships and crews employed and ducating thousands of people to realise what a wonderful life can be enjoyed in a well-appointed British liner; moreover, the money spent goes largely into British pockets. Our illustration shows the Cunard cruising liner "Lancastria" (17,000 tons) gently steaming in the Straits of Gibraltar and affording passengers their first glimpse of the Rock. To give some idea of the amenities of this magnificent floating hotel, we illustrate the upper deck busy with sports and pastimes, organised by the expert sports officer on board known as Cruise Directors. Naturally, all these pastimes would not always be proceeding simultaneously. Besides the items there are regular fancy-dress dances on the sports deck when cruising in warm climes; bridge and whist drives, and athletic aquatic sports. For the studious there is the free library, stocked with 2000 books. Lower down in the ship are two or more ba

5. *Left:* By 1934 Cunard and White Star had merged. The steam turbine, white-hulled Cunarder contrasts sharply with the motor-ship *Britannic* of White Star Line.

6. *Below:* RMS *Lancastria*, tragically sunk during the fall of France in 1940 with the loss of over 3,500 soldiers and crew, is cut away in this Cunard brochure from the mid-1930s.

d London News" Liner "Lancastria" 17,000 Tons

**UNION-CASTLE LINE**

**SUMMER & WINTER TOURS TO AND FROM SOUTH AFRICA**

At Reduced return fares

|              | 1st   | 2nd  | 3rd  |
| ------------ | ----- | ---- | ---- |
| Capetown     | £90   | £60  | £30  |
| Algoa Bay    | £95   | £63  | £32  |
| East London  | £98   | £65  | £34  |
| Natal        | £100  | £67  | £35  |

Write for full particulars

Head Office: 3, Fenchurch St. London, E.C.3.

7. *Left:* Union-Castle Line issued this bookmark to advertise their tours to and from South Africa, many of which were undertaken on the company's line voyages.

8. *Opposite above:* Holidays could be taken closer to home too, as can be seen from this 1939 brochure for the North of Scotland & Orkney & Shetland Steam Navigation Co.'s RMS *St Clair*.

9. *Opposite below:* Canadian Pacific's RMS *Empress of Canada* was a popular ship in the 1960s.

# HOLIDAYS BY SEA

## FROM LEITH & ABERDEEN TO CAITHNESS, ORKNEY AND SHETLAND

**SAILINGS FOR JUNE · JULY AUGUST AND SEPTEMBER**

**1939**

R.M.S. "ST. CLAIR"

THE **NORTH** OF **SCOTLAND** & **ORKNEY** & **SHETLAND** **STEAM NAVIGATION CO. LTD.**
I, TOWER PLACE LEITH-PHONE 36471
67, YORK PLACE EDINBURGH-PHONE 20489
HEAD OFFICE – MATTHEWS' QUAY, ABERDEEN – PHONE 2860 (5 LINES)

EMPRESS OF CANADA

10. *Oriana* leaving Southampton, May 1978. The Orient Line ship led a long life but in June 2004, while in use as a hotel ship in China, she capsized and sank.

11. P&O's RMS *Chusan* in the early 1960s.

12. Shaw Savill's *Northern Star* was used for cruising but was early to the breaker's yard.

13. Perhaps one of the most famous cruise ships of all time is the Harland & Wolff-constructed *Canberra*, seen in San Francisco in 1997, her last year of service.

14. Every British cruise ship should have a terraced stern and pool. Here is *Carmania*'s from 1963.

15. *La Palma* in Piraeus in the final years of her career.

16. The Greek Line's *Ellenis,* looking rather the worse for wear and in need of a refit.

17. *Ausonia* in the striking floral livery of First Choice Cruises.

18. *Southern Cross*, ex-*Southward,* in her CTC livery at Gibraltar.

19. Thomson's *The Emerald* dressed overall, with *The Topaz* astern.

20. *The Topaz* in Malta.

21. Fred Olsen's *Black Watch*, one of the most popular cruise ships today, is being re-engined in 2005 for a further lease of life.

22 and 23. P&O's *Aurora* was built specifically for the ever-expanding British cruise market. Here she is seen in the Caribbean, with the lower picture showing her at Tortola.

24. Saga's *Saga Rose* was converted from Cunard's *Sagafjord*, which had originally been owned by Norwegian America Line. Here she is off Easter Island in February 2001.

25. *Vistafjord* is the sister of the *Sagafjord* and is shown here in her Cunard livery. She is leaving Cunard's service (as *Caronia*) to join her sister once again as *Saga Ruby*.

26. *Minerva*, converted from an unfinished Russian spy ship, offered timeless elegance for Swan Hellenic passengers.

27. *Minerva* was replaced by the much larger *Minerva II*, an ex-Renaissance cruise ship (*R Eight*), and Swan Hellenic used the opportunity to grow its market and take some of the passengers from its parent company, P&O, when *Victoria* was sold.

*Chapter 4*

# CRUISE BRITANNIA – THE SHIPS

The list that follows provides details of the vast majority of vessels we have been able to ascertain as operating in the UK cruise market for some part of their careers.

The gross registered tonnage (grt) is, unless otherwise stated, the tonnage at the time of building.

The building date represents the date launched.

The passenger numbers are, unless otherwise stated, those at the time of building or at the time of entry to the cruise market.

Names shown in bold e.g. Canberra refer to a ship with its own entry.

## Airtours (My Travel)

The UK package-holiday retailer Airtours (renamed My Travel in 2002) entered the UK cruise market in 1995. Adding its own dedicated cruise operation to the portfolio of products was a way in which the company could grow extra business – branding the new product as Sun Cruises. Notably, at the same time, Thomson and First Choice (Airtour's main UK competitors) also entered the cruise sector with dedicated ships. Initially Airtours employed an outside company to manage the cruise operation but later took it in house and managed it themselves.

Commencing with two ships, the Airtours operation provided a lower cost cruise holiday and was seen by many as a natural extension of the packaged, resort holidays that the company had sold for some time. Interestingly, by 2002 the My Travel operation had moved in the direction of the more traditional type of cruise. As Airtours had their own charter airline operating out of UK regional airports and an excellent relationship with resort hotels it was easy for the company to offer regional flights and cruise plus stay holidays. The initial base ports for the ships were in the Canary Islands, Majorca and Cyprus – areas that featured considerably in the Airtours package-holiday brochures.

The company is able to keep prices low by using their own airline and by using high-density ships. The cruises are designed purely for the UK market and are attracting a considerable degree of repeat business as they are judged to be excellent value for money.

In 1996, 29.6 per cent of Airtours was purchased by the Carnival Corporation and the next year Carnival and Airtours jointly acquired Costa Cruises. In 2002 Carnival bought Airtours' share in Costa and relinquished its 29.6 per cent holding in the UK company. In 1998 Airtours acquired Direct Cruises – see the entry under Direct Cruises. In late 2002 and early 2003 My Travel announced that its profits were considerably reduced. Losses have impacted on the cruise operations and in early 2004 the company announced its withdrawal from the cruise market.

Initially operating in the Mediterranean and Canary Islands, My Travel offered a portfolio of itineraries for the UK market, itineraries that included Norway, the Baltic, the Caribbean and for 2003, the Far East.

*Carousel*, one of the first Airtours ships, in 1995.

### Carousel

23,149grt (as lengthened in 1980)
637.5ft length overall (as lengthened in 1980)
79ft breadth
1,158 cruise passengers (as lengthened in 1980)
Built in 1971 by Wartsila, Finland
Powered by diesel engines

Built as the *Nordic Prince* for Royal Caribbean in 1971 and lengthened in 1980, the vessel was designed for the US cruise market. Of particular interest when built was the 'Viking Crown' lounge set half way up the funnel – this feature was removed from *Nordic Prince* and her sister ship *Song of Norway* when acquired by Airtours' Sun Cruises operation, the latter ship becoming *Sundream* in 1997.

    *Carousel* and *Seawing* became the first ships in the Airtours' Sun Cruises operation in 1995. Initially *Carousel* operated out of both the Canary Islands and Majorca on seven-day cruises with the option of a hotel holiday before or after the cruise. *Carousel* was still in service for My Travel in 2003.

### Seawing

16,710grt
536ft length overall
75ft breadth
926 cruise passengers
Built in 1971 by Cantieri del Tirreno et Riuniti, Italy
Powered by diesel engines

Designed as a more refined version of *Sunward* for Norwegian Caribbean Cruises and operated in the Caribbean for the US market as *Southward*, *Seawing* was the companion vessel to *Carousel* in beginning the Airtours' Sun Cruises operation. Acquired in 1995, she operated full time for Airtours until 2000 when she was chartered to Louis Cruise Lines as part of a deal that released Direct Cruises, after its acquisition by Airtours, from a four-year charter of the Royal Olympic-owned *Apollon*, a sister company to Louis Cruise Lines. *Seawing* was chartered back to Airtours for six months of the year and in 2003 began the company's Far Eastern cruise itineraries.

## Sunbird

37,584grt
705ft length overall
93ft breadth
1,611 cruise passengers
Built in 1982 by Wartsila, Finland
Powered by diesel engines

The largest of the Airtours fleet in 2003, *Sunbird* was built for Royal Caribbean as the *Song of America* in 1982 and acquired by Airtours in 1999. Unlike the earlier Royal Caribbean ships acquired by the company she retains the 'Viking Crown' lounge on the funnel. *Sunbird* moved Airtours up market in terms of standards – she has balcony cabins and suites with butler service and is also a more traditional cruise product.

## Sundream

22,945grt (as lengthened in 1980)
638ft length overall (as lengthened in 1980)
79ft breadth
1,257 passengers (as lengthened in 1980)
Built in 1970 by Wartsila, Finland
Powered by diesel engines

Built as the *Song of Norway* for Royal Caribbean in 1970 and lengthened in 1980, the vessel was designed for the US cruise market. Of particular interest when built was the 'Viking Crown' lounge set half way up the funnel – this feature was removed from *Song of Norway* and her sister ship *Nordic Prince* when acquired by Airtours' Sun Cruises operation, the latter ship becoming *Carousel* in 1995. *Sundream* was purchased in 1997 following the success of the initial two vessels.

# Anchor Line

First registered as a trade name in 1852, the Scottish-based Anchor Line acquired its first ship in 1854. By 1864 the majority of the company's activities were in the Scotland–USA (mainly New York) and also the Mediterranean–USA trade. There was also some activity in the UK–India trade and this was increased in 1882. Passenger services ended in 1966 with the last passenger sailing to Bombay. The passenger service to the USA had ceased in 1956.

Seasonal cruises from the UK and the USA commenced in 1926 but ceased in 1939 at the start of the Second World War, a conflict in which the company lost a number of its vessels.

## Caledonia

17,046grt
578ft length overall
70ft breadth
279 first-class, 461 tourist-class and 248 third-class passengers after 1930
Built in 1925 by Fairfield Shipbuilding & Engineering Co., Govan, Scotland
Powered by two double-reduction geared turbines

Laid down in 1922, work was suspended and the ship was not launched until 1925. A sister ship to *Transylvania* she served on the Glasgow–New York service and was altered into a single-cabin-class ship in 1929. In 1935 she began summer cruises to Bermuda out of New York and between 1937 and 1939 she undertook eight or nine cruises to the Caribbean from the UK. Requisitioned as an Armed Merchant Cruiser in 1939 she was torpedoed and sunk by U 56 off Ireland on 10 August 1940. She had been taken in tow but sank with the loss of forty-eight of her crew.

## Transylvania

16,923grt
578ft length overall
70ft breadth
219 first-class, 344 second-class, 800 third-class passengers
Built in 1925 by Fairfield, Shipbuilding & Engineering Co., Govan, Scotland
Powered by two double-reduction geared turbines

Laid down in 1922 like *Caledonia* but work was suspended and the ship was not launched until 1925. She served on the Glasgow–New York service and was altered into a single-cabin class ship in 1929. Between 1930 and 1939 she undertook seasonal cruises in addition to her line voyages. In 1930 her accommodation was altered but unlike *Caledonia* she retained three classes. She was requisitioned as an Armed Merchant Cruiser in 1939.

## Tuscania

16,991grt
573ft length overall
70ft breadth
206 first-class, 439 tourist-class, 431 third-class passengers after 1931
Built in 1921 by Fairfield Shipbuilding & Engineering Co., Govan, Scotland
Powered by two double-reduction geared turbines

Laid down in 1919 but not completed until 1921, *Tuscania* was built for the Glasgow or Mediterranean to New York services. In 1926 she was chartered to Cunard for a season. Between 1926 and 1931 she undertook a number of winter cruises in addition to some service on the route to Bombay. Her accommodation was altered in 1931, the year in

The Anchor Line RMS *Tuscania*, used for winter cruising as well as on the Bombay route.

which she commenced a series of summer cruises. She was laid up in 1938 and in April 1939 she was sold to the General Steam Navigation Company of Greece as their first ship and renamed *Nea Hellas*. She was used as an Allied troopship during the war and re-entered her owner's Mediterranean–New York service in 1947. In 1955 she was renamed *New York*. Laid up in 1959, she was scrapped in Japan in 1961.

## Aznar Line

The Spanish shipping company Naviera Aznar SA operated a network of routes from Spain to North and South America and the Caribbean. After the end of the Second World War the Spanish Government allotted important UK–Canary Island trade to the company. The Canary Islands are an important source of fruit and vegetables (especially tomatoes) and the company's ships transported these items to both London and Liverpool.

Whilst not designed as cruise ships, the company's vessels were built for cargo and passengers, from 1960 onwards the company began to offer cruises from the UK down to the Canary Islands and back. Potential cruise passengers living in the North of England especially appreciated the option of cruises from Liverpool. In the earlier ships the cruise passengers had to place their deckchairs amongst the cargo-handling machinery.

In 1977, however, the company sold their last two passenger ships, the ferries *Monte Granda* and *Monte Toledo*, and the company left the cruise industry.

## Monte Anaga

6,813grt
429ft 2in length overall
59ft 3in breadth
108 passengers
Built in 1959 by Cia. Euskalduna
Powered by single-screw, Sulzer diesel machinery

*Monte Anaga* was a refined version of the 1956-built *Monte Arucas*, which also served on the Liverpool–Canaries route but carried just thirty-six passengers. *Monte Anaga* had accommodation spread over three decks: Sun, Promenade and Lower Deck. On the Sun Deck there were single and double cabins: forward there was a lounge with a bar and a small library, and aft there was a Veranda lounge. The ship had two dining rooms, adjacent to each other, on Promenade Deck, and a bar open off the starboard side of the forward of these two rooms. Further single and double cabins were located both forward and aft of the dining rooms, and there was a group of cabins forward on Lower Deck. Most of the cabins were fitted with either private or shared bathrooms.

Monte Anaga was employed on the Liverpool to the Canary Islands service, with calls during the summer months at Vigo.

## Monte Granada (and *Monte Toledo*)

10,839grt
497ft length overall
67ft 9in breadth
800 passengers when in service as cruise ships; 1,000 passengers when operating as ferries
*Monte Toledo* entered service in February 1974; *Monte Granada* entered service in October 1975. Both were built by Union Naval de Levante SA
Powered by two 16-cylinder Bazan-MAN diesel engines driving two controllable-pitch propellers

*Monte Toledo* and *Monte Granada* replaced the conventional cargo/passenger liners that had previously been operated by the company on their United Kingdom to the Canary Islands service. They were designed as multi-purpose ships to carry passengers, general cargo and fruit between London and the Atlantic Islands during the winter and, during the summer season, passengers, cars and general cargo between Southampton and Santander. The ships were seen as ushering in a new era in sea travel between the United Kingdom and Spain. The *Monte Granada*'s summer service was between Amsterdam and Santander. With this role as ferries during the summer months the ships were a departure from what had been the practice at the time for Aznar Line.

The ships had seven decks available to passengers: Observation, Sun, Boat, Lounge, Gallery, Golden and Cinema Decks. There was an extensive sheltered lido area midships on Sun Deck. All the public rooms, with the exception of the cinema, were located on Lounge Deck. There were two large lounges, one facing forward and one aft. There were two restaurants in the central section of the ship either side of the galley. The larger of these converted into a self-service cafeteria when the ships were operating as ferries. Access between the two lounges was by a starboard side gallery, the restaurants not extending the full width of the ships. Virtually all the cabins aboard the ships had their own bathrooms. The exception being fifteen one- and two-berth cabins on Cinema Deck. These had been built to allow for modification to permit the installation of 250 reclining seats when the ships were operating on short ferry voyages.

In 1977, after only a very brief period of operation on their intended routes both ships were sold to the Libyan Ministry of Transport. *Monte Toledo* was renamed *Toletela* and *Monte Granada* was renamed *Garnata*. They were registered under the ownership of the General National Maritime Transport Co., and were used on ferry services in the Mediterranean.

## Monte Toledo

See under *Monte Granada*.

## Monte Ulia

10,123grt
487ft 4in length overall
62ft 5 in breadth
114 passengers
Built in 1952 by Soc. Española de Const. Naval
Powered by single-screw Sulzer diesel machinery

*Monte Ulia* was one of what was known as the 'Monasterio' class of ships. There were six ships of the class: four owned by Aznar and the other two owned by Compania Tranatlantica Española S.A. *Monte Ulia* gained a particularly popular reputation on her cargo and cruise service from London's Millwall Docks to the Canary Islands. Her accommodation was spread over three decks: Sun, Promenade and Main. Double cabins, all with private bathrooms on Sun Deck, while forward there was a cocktail bar and aft, a Veranda lounge. The main dining room was forward on Promenade Deck, with a lounge situated aft. Between these two public rooms were twenty-five cabins, eleven of which did not have private bathrooms. There was a further public room, a somewhat multi-function space, on Main Deck. As built this was originally another dining room, however in later years it was used as a disco, bar, cinema and games room. Aft of this room were four-berth cabins, while further forward there were cabins for four and six people. None of the cabins on this deck had private bathrooms. A swimming pool was located on the deck above Sun Deck.

## Monte Umbe

9,961grt
508ft length overall
62ft 4in breadth
300 passengers
Built in 1959 by Cia. Eskalduna
Powered by single-screw Sulzer diesel machinery

*Monte Umbe* was the flagship of the fleet. She had been designed to carry large numbers of emigrants, approximately 490, and with just four passengers in First Class and eighty-four in Tourist Class. Originally she was employed on the service between Spain, Brazil and Argentina but, in 1968, she was taken off this service and was sent to her builders to have her passenger accommodation restyled to make her more suited to the United Kingdom–Canary Islands run. Her accommodation was spread over four decks: Sun,

A deck scene from *Monte Umbe*, the Aznar line flagship.

Promenade, Main and A Deck. Although having been rebuilt to suit the UK cruise market the greater proportion of her cabins were still without their own bathrooms. The cabins on Sun Deck, and a few on Promenade Deck, were fitted with private facilities. There were sixteen cabins on Promenade Deck with shared facilities. The majority of the cabins on Main and Promenade Decks were without private bathrooms. *Monte Umbe* had a forward-facing lounge on Sun Deck, and following the pattern of her fleet mates; she had an aft-facing Veranda lounge that looked out over the swimming pool. A Nightclub was located aft on Promenade Deck. Forward on that deck was a lounge and bar built around one of her cargo hatch trunkings. On the port side this was the Marina Lounge, while on the starboard side a cinema was created. The restaurant was on Main Deck.

*Monte Umbe* entered UK service with sailings from Liverpool. However, she also spent several seasons sailing from London. She was returned to the Liverpool service in 1973 and remained based there until May 1975. She was sold to the Lebanese company Dem Line and renamed *Liban*. For barely four years, she was operated on a Black Sea and Eastern Mediterranean service. In 1979 she was sold for scrap and was broken up in Pakistan.

## *Monte Urquiola*

7,723grt
487ft 4in length overall
62ft 5in breadth
55 passengers
Built in 1949 by Soc. Española de Const. Naval
Powered by single-screw Sulzer diesel machinery

*Monte Urquiola* was the third ship to be built in the 'Monasterio' class. She had just two decks of passenger accommodation: Sun Deck and Promenade Deck. The passenger cabins on Sun Deck were fitted with private bathrooms while those on Promenade Deck were not. Forward on Sun Deck was a bar, library and a small lounge. A veranda lounge was aft on this deck, and this looked out onto a swimming pool. The restaurant was forward on Promenade Deck. *Monte Urquiola* served on both the Liverpool and the London to Canary Islands routes.

## Bergen Line

The Bergen Line was formed in 1851 and by 1890 it was operating a regular UK–Norway service in addition to its routes up and down the Norwegian coastline. The company was sold in 1984 to Kosmos who sold the Bergen Line name in 1988, by which time the company had ceased its involvement with the coastal operation. Bergen Line is still remembered as a constituent of the 'The Norwegian Coastal Voyage' or 'Hurtigruten' that carries both local and tourist traffic into Norway's ports. That service has run almost without interruption since its beginning, even during the Second World War and the German occupation, albeit in a reduced form.

Bergen Line was also one of the founders of Royal Viking Line, one of the companies that specialised in the US cruise market in the 1970s and 1980s until the Royal Viking name was acquired by Cunard in 1994 for $170. No dabbler in people pleasing, Bergen Line was one of the first companies to specialise in cruising in a specific region. The beautiful yacht-like *Stella Polaris* of 1927 was built for Bergen Line and is now preserved as the *Hotel Scandinavia* in Japan.

The cover of the 1968 Bergen Line brochure.

BY BERGEN LINE TO SUNNY MADEIRA

FOR AN AUTUMN HOLIDAY 1968

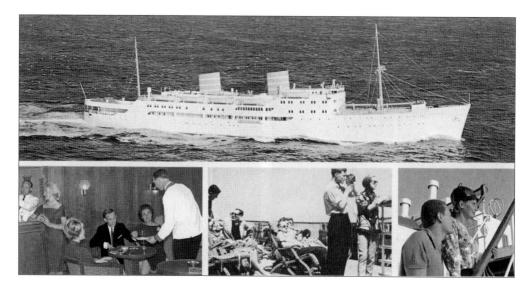

*Venus*, a popular 1950s–60s cruise ship, was scrapped at Faslane in 1968.

In the 1940s, 1950s and 1960s the company marketed cruises for the UK market, cruises that saw the Norwegian passenger ferries cruising as far as Maderia and the Mediterranean.

### Venus

6,269grt
420ft length overall
54ft breadth
259 passengers
Built in 1931 by Elsinore Shipbuilding & Engineering Co. Ltd
Powered by twin-screw Burmeister & Wain diesel engines

*Venus* was initially built for service across the North Sea, linking Newcastle and Bergen. When she was delivered, in May 1931, she was the world's fastest motorship, with a speed of over 20 knots. In 1940 she was requisitioned by German forces for conversion into a submarine depot and target ship. On 15 April 1945 she was sunk at Hamburg during an air raid.

Operations to salvage the ship began in September 1945, and she was towed back to Elsinore to be totally rebuilt. She was given a new raked bow section, which was one deck higher than the original, new funnels and new accommodation. For her service on the North Sea route she was able to accommodate 135 first-class and 278 tourist-class passengers. The new accommodation bore no relation to that of the ship as originally built. The attractiveness as well as the size of the tourist-class public rooms made them practically equal to those in first class. The decorations and furnishings throughout the ship were typically Norwegian, and she was decorated with Norwegian artworks, tapestry, glassware and paintings.

*Venus* re-entered service in May 1948 and that December made the first of her winter cruises, from Plymouth to Madeira and Tenerife. In 1953 she was fitted with stabilisers and her UK cruising terminal was changed to Southampton. In 1965 she was given a more cruise-like livery of white hull and yellow funnels. She had by this time established herself as a great favourite with the British cruising public. With the introduction of a new and larger car ferry on the UK–Norway service, in 1966 *Venus* was transferred to a weekly Bergen–Rotterdam service during the summer months. She was withdrawn from service in the autumn of 1968 after a final cruise from Southampton. She was scrapped at Faslane on the Clyde, arriving there on 19 October 1968.

*Meteor*

2,856grt
297ft length overall
45ft breadth
146 passengers
Built in 1955 by Aalborg Vaerft A/S
Powered by single-screw Burmeister & Wain diesel engines

*Meteor* was designed and built primarily to operate cruises along the Norwegian coast and to the fjords, and occasionally to the northern capitals. She also had a secondary role, to act as a substitute on the Hurtigruten service when other vessels were being overhauled. Having been designed for cruising, her accommodation was far superior to that of the usual coastal ships. She had six decks: Navigation, Boat, Upper, A, B and C Decks. The

*Meteor*, the longest lasting of the Bergen Line fleet, surviving from 1955–2002.

public rooms were mainly on Upper Deck but there was a forward-facing lounge and an aft-facing veranda on Boat Deck. All the cabins were either double or single berth and approximately half of them had private bathrooms.

Although designed with Norwegian coastal cruising in mind, *Meteor* actually cruised extensively beyond Scandinavia, to the Mediterranean and the Black Sea and to the Caribbean. During the 1950s and 1960s several of her cruises were specifically aimed at the British market. Harwich was often her UK terminal port for cruises either to Norway or into the Baltic, and in fact her very first cruise was from Harwich to Hamburg, Visby, Stockholm, Copenhagen and Oslo from 4–14 June 1955. However, she would also sail to the Mediterranean from Harwich. For example, in September 1957 she departed Harwich on a twenty-one-day cruise to the Mediterranean and Black Sea. The cruise ended in Venice, from where her passengers could return home either by air (making this one of the forerunners of the fly-cruise concept) or by train. She also sailed from other UK ports, including Southampton and Ardrossan. *Meteor* also occasionally undertook cruises to the Western Isles on behalf of the National Trust of Scotland.

After having been severely damaged by fire in May 1971, when she was on the return leg of an Alaska cruise, Bergen Line sold the ship to Epirotiki Line of Greece, who had her renamed *Neptune,* and rebuilt and refitted to their distinctive style, for Greek Island cruising. Much of her career with Epirotiki was spent in the Mediterranean, Aegean and Red Sea. The *Neptune* also undertook cruises to Scandinavia and the Baltic, recalling her days as *Meteor.* After sailing as part of the Epirotiki fleet for over twenty years she was laid up and was eventually sold to Turkish breakers, arriving at Aliaga on 2 March 2002.

# Blue Star Line

The Blue Star Line was owned by the Vestey Brothers' Union Cold Storage Company which commenced operating its own ships in 1909. The company's prime cargo was frozen produce, initially from South America and China. In 1911 Blue Star Line was formed with Union Cold Storage as the parent company. Services to Australia and New Zealand were inaugurated in 1933.

Its passenger services to South America terminated in 1972, but cargo and container services continue. The company only operated one cruise ship, but the *Arandora Star* was renowned as one of the finest cruise ships operating before the Second World War when she was lost to submarine attack. The company did not re-enter the cruise market after the war.

*Arandora Star*

15,501grt
535ft length overall
68ft breadth
420 passengers
Built in 1927 by Cammell Laird, Birkenhead
Powered by twin-screw geared steam turbines

*Arandora Star* was one of five sister ships built for the Blue Star Line's cargo and passenger service to South America. As built she was primarily a cargo ship, with accommodation for just 164 passengers, and at that time her name was *Arandora*.

In 1929 she was rebuilt as a cruise ship at the Fairfield yard at Govan: the company having realised that the competition on the South American route was such that they had no real need to maintain all five of the ships on the service. During the course of the conversion her superstructure was enlarged considerably, which resulted in a very square, and far from graceful, vessel. She was nevertheless well fitted out for her new role and was regarded as being one of the principal cruising liners of the 1930s. In 1934, 1935 and 1936 considerable sums of money were spent on the ship in order to keep her up to a luxury cruising standard.

She operated the very traditional circuit of Norway and the Baltic in the summer, the spring and autumn were spent in the Mediterranean and during the winter months she was in the Caribbean and South America.

During the war she operated as a troop transport and also was used to take prisoners of war across the Atlantic to Canada. It was on one of these latter voyages, in July 1940, that she was attacked by a submarine and sunk with considerable loss of life.

# British India Steam Navigation Co.

British India Steam Navigation was, as its name suggests, a major operator in the lucrative UK–India route and the branch trade from India to the countries and territories around the Persian Gulf in the days of the British Empire.

The parent company of the British India Steam Navigation Company Limited was the Calcutta & Burma Steam Navigation Company, formed in 1856. In 1862 the company became the British India Steam Navigation Co. Ltd. In 1914 the British India Steam Navigation Co. amalgamated with the Peninsular & Oriental Steam Navigation Company (P&O) but retained its identity until the withdrawal of the *Uganda* in 1986, at the end of her MOD contract. In 1914, in terms of number of ships, British India was the largest UK shipping company.

Many of the company ships were only 500 tons or so, but they carried passengers on coastal services round the Indian coast or from India to Zanzibar and the Persian Gulf, some carrying native passengers on deck.

The company also maintained a troopship service for the British Government. As Britain withdrew from east of Suez, and as air travel took over from the liner trade, the requirement for troopships declined. Beginning in 1932 the company began to offer educational cruises for which troopships, with their dormitory accommodation, were well suited. The last such cruises occurred before *Uganda*, the remaining educational cruise ship, was requisitioned as a hospital ship in the Falkland's conflict of 1982 – the ship only returning briefly to the educational cruise market between September 1982 and January 1983 before being re-chartered by the MOD. With her scrapping in 1986 the British India operation ceased to exist.

*Neuralia*

9,082grt
480ft length overall
58ft breadth
50 cabin-class passengers and 1,050 troops
Built in 1912 by Barclay, Curle & Co. Ltd, Glasgow
Powered by twin-screw, quadruple-expansion engines

*Neuralia* was the ship that introduced British India's educational cruises, in July 1932. After the First World War she had been placed on the London–East Africa service, but from 1925 onward she (and her sister, *Nevasa*) was given over to permanent trooping.

When they were not on trooping duties they were laid up off Southampton. However, in 1932 *Neuralia* inaugurated the school ship cruises, which would eventually become extremely popular. *Neuralia's* cruises took her up to the Baltic and the Norwegian fjords, and she continued these cruises when not on trooping duties until 1935. She sank in the Mediterranean in May 1945, having struck a mine off Taranto.

## Dunera

12,620grt
517ft length overall
63ft breadth
187 cabin passengers and 834 children
Built in 1937 by Barclay, Curle & Co. Ltd, Glasgow
Powered by twin-screw Doxford diesel engines

*Dunera* was built as a troopship and as such was able to carry 1,150 troops, as well as 3,400 tons of cargo. *Dunera* operated just one season of school cruising, during the summer of 1939. Between March 1950 and March 1951 her accommodation was modernised by her builders, and she was then employed for a further ten years in trooping duties. Released from this service early in 1961, following the decision by British India to re-enter educational cruising, she was converted into a full-time educational cruising ship, fitted with six classrooms. She made fifteen educational cruises in her first year, and the experiment was such a success that she carried 9,704 passengers in that period. The success of *Dunera* in this role was such that three further British India ships were also converted for educational cruising roles. She remained in service until November 1967, when she was scrapped in Spain.

British India's *Devonia*, originally built as *Devonshire* for Bibby Line.

## Devonia

12,796grt
517ft length overall
63ft breadth
194 cabin passengers and 834 children
Built in 1939 by Fairfield Shipbuilding & Engineering Co. Ltd, Glasgow
Powered by twin-screw Sulzer diesel engines

*Devonia* entered service as the troopship *Devonshire* for the Bibby Line, and, apart from her machinery and funnel design, was similar in most other respects to the *Dunera*. Following the success of Dunera as an educational cruise ship, British India bought the *Devonshire* at the end of 1961, after it had been announced that the Government would in future move troops by air rather than by sea. Renamed *Devonia*, she was refitted by Barclay, Curle in early 1962, entering educational cruise service in April. She sailed for British India for five years before being sold for scrap in Spain in December 1967.

## Nevasa

20,746grt
609ft length overall
78ft breadth
308 cabin passengers and 1,090 children
Built in 1956 by Barclay, Curle & Co. Ltd, Glasgow
Powered by twin-screw Pametrada turbine engines

*Nevasa* entered service as a troopship with accommodation for 220 first-class, 110 second-class and 180 third-class passengers, and 1,000 troops. She was employed in this role for six years before it was decided that future troop movements would be undertaken by air rather than by sea. After the Government cancelled their contract to use *Nevasa* she was laid up in the River Fal in October 1962 at the end of her final trooping voyage. In 1964, emboldened by the success of *Devonia* and *Dunera, Nevasa* was sent to the P&O-owned shipyard of Silley Cox & Co. Ltd, to be given a £500,000 refit, transforming her into an educational cruise ship. Before re-entering service she undertook a shakedown cruise around Britain. *Nevasa* departed Southampton on 28 October 1965 on her first educational cruise, to Madeira, Tangier and Lisbon. Although *Nevasa's* deep draft hull limited the range of ports that she could berth at she was nevertheless a very popular ship. Without doubt she was the most handsome of all the liners used in educational cruising. Sadly, her career in this role was brought to a premature end with the oil crisis of the early 1970's, and she was sold to be scrapped in Taiwan in April 1975.

## Uganda

16,907grt
539ft 8in length overall
71ft breadth
306 cabin passengers and 920 children
Built in 1952 by Barclay, Curle & Co. Ltd, Glasgow
Powered by twin-screw Parsons turbine engines

*Nevasa* was sent for conversion to a cruise ship in 1964 and successfully cruised until scrapping in 1975.

*Nevasa* at Southampton (viewed from P&O's *Himalaya*) in May 1974.

*Uganda* was requisitioned by the MoD in 1982 to serve in the Falklands and this effectively killed her cruising days. She was scrapped in the mid-1980s.

*Uganda* was built for British India's London–East Africa service, and spent fifteen years on the route with her sister, *Kenya*. Increased competition from the airlines, as well as the changes to the pattern of trading following the gaining of independence by the countries she was built to serve and the closure of the Suez Canal in 1967, brought about the demise of British India's East Africa route. Before her withdrawal from service the company had already announced that she would be rebuilt as a schools ship.

The work was undertaken at the Howaldtswerke yard in Hamburg, and took almost a year to complete: from March 1967 to February 1968. It was an extensive rebuild, incorporating classrooms and dormitories in what had formerly been cargo spaces, and creating two lido areas: one forward for the cabin passengers and one aft for the children. The original first-class public rooms remained relatively unchanged, for the use of the cabin passengers, but many of the cabins were also rebuilt. An entirely new bridge structure was also created, which, along with the forward lido area and extended after decks, totally changed her profile.

She sailed from Southampton on 27 February 1968 on her first cruise, to the Mediterranean. Her normal pattern of employment was on cruises from various British ports during the summer months to Scandinavia and the Baltic and to the Atlantic Islands. In the late summer she would then reposition to the Mediterranean and operate fly cruises throughout the winter.

*Uganda* occasionally operated cruises under charter to various organisations, and was a particular favourite with the National Trust of Scotland for cruising the Western Isles. *Uganda* became probably the most popular of the schools ships and built up a very loyal following among her cabin passengers, many of whom returned year after year. In December 1972 British India ceased to exist as a separate entity and both *Uganda* and

*Nevasa* were transferred to the ownership of P&O. From 1973 they were marketed under the BI Discovery Cruises banner, retaining the British India funnel colours.

In April 1982, she was requisitioned by the Government to become a hospital ship during the Falklands conflict. She returned to Southampton four months later, in August, and was given a refit converting her back into a cruise ship. This, however, was only a brief return to commercial service (thus bringing to an end the British India school ship concept) as she was chartered in January 1983 by the Ministry of Defence to provide troop transport between the Falkland Islands and Ascension Island. The charter was for two years, after which *Uganda* was laid up in the River Fal and was later sold to be broken up in Taiwan. While at anchor near Kaohsiung she was driven ashore by a typhoon, capsized and was gradually broken up *in situ*.

# British Rail

Even before the grouping together of Britain's railway companies into four main organisations in 1923 and the nationalisation of the whole network in 1948, the railways had operated their own ferry services. The Irish Sea, the North Sea and especially the English Channel were served by steamers, and later ferries, whose sailings were tied to the railway timetables.

Whilst the London & North Eastern Railway introduced cruises in the 1930s it was after nationalisation in 1948 that British Rail saw a new revenue-earning possibility and used a number of its vessel for cruising.

British Rail withdrew from the cruising market in 1974 – by then the old-fashioned steamers were being replaced by modern roll-on/roll-off vehicle ferries and there was no spare capacity for cruising. British Rail no longer exists, having been split up and privatised in the late 1990s.

## *Vienna*

4,218grt
366ft length overall
50ft breadth
Number of passengers carried when in cruise service unknown
Built in 1929 by John Brown & Co. Ltd, Clydebank
Powered by twin-screw geared turbines

The *Vienna* inaugurated the London & North Eastern Railway diversion into cruising. Normally she was employed on the Harwich–Hook of Holland route. However, in 1932 she undertook the first cruise. Several cruises followed, these being mainly weekend trips to Antwerp, Amsterdam, Ghent, Flushing, Zeebrugge, Hook of Holland or Rotterdam. As they were very successful, *Vienna* was modified in 1936 to create more sheltered deck space and more lounge accommodation, making her more suitable as a cruising ship. While *Vienna* survived the war, remaining in service until 1960, she made no further cruises after 1939.

*Vienna*, the London & North Eastern Railway Harwich–Hook of Holland steamer was also used as a part-time cruise ship.

## Falaise

2,416grt
310ft 6in length overall
49ft 8in breadth
216 passengers (when on cruise service)
Built in 1947 by Wm. Denny & Bros Ltd, Dumbarton
Powered by twin-screw geared turbines

*Falaise* was built for the Southampton–St Malo service, with accommodation for 1,527 passengers in two classes. However, she also operated as a part-time cruise ship, with considerable success, between 1948 and 1963. The cruises were usually two- and three-day trips run over the weekends during May and early June, and she usually operated about seven cruises each year. They generally started at Southampton but she also operated some from Folkestone. The cruises included calls at such ports as St Malo, Jersey, Le Havre and Rouen but she also made cruises up to Holland and Belgium to coincide with the bulb season.

At the end of 1963 *Falaise* was withdrawn from the St Malo service and was converted into a stern-loading drive-on car ferry.

## Duke of Lancaster

4,797grt
376ft length overall
57ft 4in breadth
350 passengers (when on cruise service)
Built in 1956 by Harland & Wolff, Belfast
Powered by twin-screw geared turbines

The *Duke of Lancaster* was the first of three sister ships, and was regarded as the flagship of the trio. All three were built to serve on the Heysham–Belfast overnight ferry service with accommodation for 600 first-class and 1,200 second-class passengers. However, when she was being built, the *Duke of Lancaster* was fitted out to enable her to carry out the alternative role as a cruise ship: cabins could be transformed into bathrooms, double cabins were convertible into singles and by the removal of fixed seating, public rooms were converted into a ballroom and more spacious lounges. The second-class cafeteria could be transformed, by the use of decorative panels, into a dining room of the same style as that in First Class. When converted she was able to carry her cruise passengers in one class. The *Duke of Lancaster* undertook her first cruise in 1958: the cruises being undertaken during what was regarded as being the 'off season' – May and June and again in September. Her first cruise was of six days duration, from Southampton to Amsterdam, Ostend and Rouen. While some of her cruises were from Heysham, she also sailed from Harwich and Plymouth, with up to six cruises being run each year, some of which were of thirteen days. She operated cruises as far south as Portugal, or up to Norway, Denmark and Belgium. In 1961, for example, she undertook two twelve-day cruises visiting Norway, Denmark and Holland as well as a six-day cruise to Holland and Belgium. Also during that year, in the spring and autumn, she undertook ten-day cruises to the Scottish Lochs and around the Western Isles. Her final cruises were in 1966. Various fleet changes required that *Duke of Lancaster* sail full time on the Irish Sea.


*Avalon*

6,580grt
405ft length overall
57ft 6in breadth
320 passengers (when on cruise service)
Built in 1963 by Alexander Stephen & Sons Ltd, Linthouse, Glasgow
Powered by twin-screw steam-turbine engines

At the time of her introduction into service, on the Harwich–Hook of Holland route, *Avalon* was British Rail's largest and most luxurious vessel. When employed on this service she had passenger accommodation for 750 passengers, in two classes. *Avalon* had six decks: Bridge, Promenade, Shelter, Upper, Main and Lower Decks. The first-class public rooms were situated forward with the second-class rooms aft. The first-class lounge and the second-class lounge were on Promenade Deck, separated by deluxe cabins and engineers accommodation. On Shelter Deck were the first-class smoking room and restaurant and the second-class cafeteria and smoking room. The remaining three decks were given over to passenger cabins. The standard of furnishing and décor throughout the ship was of such a high standard that it enabled her to be opened up as a one-class vessel when operating cruises. Her first cruise was a weekend cruise to Amsterdam, in April 1964. That autumn she made a further cruise, on this occasion an eight-day trip northward, which included a call at Copenhagen. Other similar cruises followed and became more far reaching. In 1966 her cruise programme was even more extensive than those she had previously operated with calls in Portugal, Morocco, and up to Scandinavia and into the Baltic. In 1967, with the introduction of other ferries on the Harwich–Hook service, *Avalon* was able to expand her cruise programme beyond just the spring and autumn. In 1972, she operated only three cruises, one was of five days duration, while the other two were of twelve and fourteen days. The short cruise was from Harwich to Rouen, and the twelve-day cruise took her through the Kiel Canal to Visby and then to Copenhagen and Oslo. The fourteen-day cruise called at Bordeaux, Seville, Gibraltar and

Santander, and each call was approximately a twenty-four-hour stay. During her cruises one of the lounges was converted into a nightclub and one room functioned as a cinema. Also she had a Cruise Director to co-ordinate all the usual activities found aboard full-time cruise ships.

In 1974 *Avalon* was withdrawn from the Harwich–Hook service and was converted into a stern-loading car ferry, for use on the Irish Sea. (*Avalon* had been built as a conventional ferry with limited space for the carriage of cars, which were loaded by crane into her forward hold.) This brought to a close British Rail/Sealink's cruise operations.

N.B. The 2,217 gross ton *Normannia*, built for the Southampton–Le Havre service in 1952, made two weekend cruises from Folkestone to Amsterdam and Ostend in the spring of 1961.

British Rail's *Avalon* was their most luxurious vessel when introduced in 1963. Here is her cruise brochure for 1972.

# Canadian Pacific

Canadian Pacific was an important shipping company with routes from the UK to Eastern Canada and from British Columbia across the Pacific. The thousands of miles that lie between the Atlantic and Pacific coasts were bridged by the Canadian Pacific Railway – the CPR – an operation that is still going today. The railway was completed in 1887 and two years later the company won the mail contract from Canada across the Pacific. In 1903 the company bought the Canadian interest of the Elder Demster Line and began a transatlantic service.

The company first offered cruises in 1928 and continued to offer UK-based cruises as an adjunct to the company's transatlantic trade until the last of its liners was sold in 1971. The company's shipping interests are now in containerships, although none are operated under the CP name or houseflag.

## Empress of Australia

21.833grt
615ft length overall
75ft breadth
404 first-class, 165 second-class, 270 third-class and 674 steerage passengers
Built in 1919 by Vulkan Werke AG, Stettin
Powered by twin-screw reduction-geared turbines

*Empress of Australia* came to Britain after the First World War, having been built as the Hamburg Amerika liner, *Tirpitz*. Initially she was managed by P&O but in 1921 she was purchased by Canadian Pacific, who gave her the name, *Empress of China*. The name was a reflection of the fact that she was employed on the Vancouver–Hong Kong service. Her name was changed again in 1922, to *Empress of Australia*, when Canadian Pacific proposed

Leaving Southampton for a cruise the fjords in the mid-1930s is the Canadian Pacific 'White Empress' RMS *Empress of Australia*.

using her on service to Australia. In 1927 she was transferred from the Pacific to the Atlantic, sailing from Southampton to the St Lawrence ports. It was at this time that she became very popular as a cruise ship during the 'off season'. Between 1928 and 1937 *Empress of Australia* made a total of forty-nine cruises. Nineteen of these were from Southampton (the remainder were from New York). She also made four cruises around the world. After an overhaul in 1938 she made three further cruises during 1939. Having survived the war, her remaining days were spent as a troopship until she was scrapped at Inverkeithing in May 1952.

## Empress of Britain

25,516grt
640ft length overall
85ft breadth
150 first-class and 900 tourist-class passengers (reduced capacity, in one class, when cruising)
Built in 1956 by Fairfield Shipbuilding & Engineering Co. Ltd, Glasgow
Powered by twin-screw steam turbines

*Empress of Britain* was the first liner to be built for Canadian Pacific after the war, introducing a very modern 'new look' with her low profile. Although principally designed for the UK to Montreal service she was also designed to operate as a cruise ship. Therefore her public rooms were of a very similar style and standard in each class, and some of them were shared between the classes. Her first cruises were from New York to the Caribbean during the early months of 1960, and it was not until February 1962 that she undertook her first cruise for British passengers: from Liverpool to Madeira, Canary Islands, Cape Verde Islands, Casablanca and Lisbon. Between 26 January and 1 April 1963 she operated four cruises, of similar itineraries to the Atlantic islands and North Africa, from Liverpool. On 25 October 1963 she sailed on her first cruise under charter to the Travel Savings Association, calling at La Coruña, Tangier, Villefranche, Valencia and Gibraltar. Her charter to TSA had initially been set for five years and after a further cruise out of Liverpool, to Palma and Lisbon, she sailed for Cape Town to undertake a series of cruises across the South Atlantic to Brazil, Argentina and Uruguay. Early in 1964, however, it was announced that the charter would be prematurely ended. In February 1964 she was sold for £3.5 million to the the Greek Line, for delivery later in the year. For the remaining months she was employed solely as a cruise ship, sailing from Liverpool, and sometimes from Southampton, to the Mediterranean, Atlantic islands, Norway and the Baltic. On 18 November 1964 she left Liverpool for Piraeus as *Queen Anna Maria* and did not undertake any further cruises for the British market for over thirty-three years, by which time she had passed through various owners.

## Empress of England

25,585grt
640ft length overall
85ft breadth
158 first-class and 900 tourist-class passengers (reduced capacity, in one class, when cruising)
Built in 1957 by Vickers Armstrong Shipbuilding Ltd, Newcastle
Powered by twin-screw steam turbines

*Empress of England* was a virtually identical sister ship to the *Empress of Britain*, the only noticeable external difference being in the arrangement of the windows below the bridge wings. Internally, there were differences in décor and furnishings and with minor changes to the arrangement of the public rooms. The *Empress of England* gained a good reputation as a cruise ship sailing out of New York to the Caribbean during the winter months, when she was not employed on the Canada service. Her first cruise for the British market was in January 1962, sailing from Liverpool on 13 January for the Canary Islands, Madeira, Casablanca, Tangier and Lisbon. In October 1963 she was placed under charter to the Travel Savings Association, and her first voyage under their banner departed Liverpool on 28 November for Dakar and Cape Town. From there she made several cruises to South America and into the Indian Ocean. On 19 December 1964 she made her second British market cruise, from Liverpool to Madeira, Cape Verde Islands, Canary Islands and Gibraltar. It was the first of a series of five cruises that extended through until 1 April 1965. One of the cruises was a thirty-five day trip to the Caribbean, and this became a regular feature of her winter cruise programme for the next five years, although the itinerary varied from year to year, sometimes taking her as far south as Rio de Janeiro. In 1965 her programme of voyages across the Atlantic to Canada was reduced to enable her to undertake two cruises to the Mediterranean between 24 September and 26 October. *Empress of England* became a firm favourite of British cruise passengers with her winter cruises from Liverpool. However, with reduced numbers of passengers travelling by sea across the Atlantic, Canadian Pacific decided to sell her, and try to maintain a single-ship operation with the *Empress of Canada*. In January 1970 she was sold to Shaw Savill to become their *Ocean Monarch*.


## Empress of Canada

27,284grt
650ft length overall
87ft breadth
192 first-class and 856 tourist-class passengers (reduced to 750 in one class when cruising)
Built in 1961 by Vickers Armstrong Shipbuilding Ltd, Newcastle
Powered by twin-screw steam turbines

The *Empress of Canada*, while slightly larger, resembled the earlier two 'Empresses' but had a more built-up superstructure and a more gracefully flared bow. Following the design thinking of the other ships, she was also built with a dual role of transatlantic liner and 'off-season' cruise ship. The *Empress of Canada* was mainly targeted at the American market and cruised extensively each winter from New York to the Caribbean, and in fact only ever made five cruises for the British market. The first of these was a Christmas and New Year cruise that departed Liverpool on 21 December 1962, calling at Madeira, Canary Islands, Cape Verde Islands and Casablanca, and returning to Southampton. The second cruise departed Southampton on 10 January 1963 and was a twenty-eight-day trip to the West Indies. The *Empress of Canada* did not undertake any further cruises for the British market until 2 July 1969, when she departed Liverpool on a fourteen-day cruise to Bergen, Stockholm, Helsinki and Copenhagen. The remainder of her British-based cruises were also undertaken in 1969. On 19 September she made a fifteen-day cruise to the Western Mediterranean, and on 21 October she sailed from Southampton on an eighteen-day cruise to the Eastern Mediterranean, sailing as far as Istanbul. *Empress of Canada* continued to operate on the Liverpool to Montreal service during the summer and cruising the Caribbean out of New York in the winter until she was withdrawn from service in November 1971. In January 1972 she was sold to become the *Mardi Gras*, the first ship of the fledgling Carnival Cruise Line.

## Duchess of Atholl

20,119grt
601ft length overall
75ft breadth
573 cabin-class, 480 tourist-class and 510 third-class passengers
Built in 1928 by William Beardmore, Glasgow
Powered by geared turbines, twin screw

The *Duchess of Atholl* was built for the service from Liverpool to the St Lawrence ports. However, before entering into this service she undertook a short cruise from Liverpool to the Hebrides. (There is no record of her making any further cruises.) In December 1939 she was converted into a troop transport and on 10 October 1942 she was torpedoed and sunk 200 miles east of Ascension Island.

## Duchess of Richmond

20,022grt
600ft length overall
75ft breadth
580 cabin-class, 480 tourist-class and 510 third-class passengers
Built in 1928 by John Brown's, Clydebank
Powered by twin-screw geared turbines

The *Duchess of Richmond* was launched in June 1928 and was completed just six months later. On 26 January 1929 she departed Liverpool on a six-week cruise to the Canary Islands and North Africa. She did not begin Atlantic service to Canada, for which she had been built, until March of that year. In January 1935 she undertook a cruise to the West Indies and among her passengers were the Duke and Duchess of Kent, who were on their honeymoon. She had made a similar cruise in 1933. In January 1940 she made her first voyage as a troop transport. Having survived the war she was restored to peacetime service by Fairfield, Glasgow, during the spring of 1946, re-entering service in July as the *Empress of Canada*. During a refit in Liverpool in 1953 she was severely damaged by fire and sank. A year later she was refloated and was towed to Italy where she was broken up.

## Montcalm

16,418grt
575ft length overall
70ft breadth
542 cabin-class and 1,268 third-class passengers
Built in 1921 by John Brown's, Clydebank
Powered by twin-screw geared turbines

*Montcalm* departed Liverpool on her maiden voyage to Canada in January 1922, having been completed in the previous month. Over the winter months of 1928–29 she was fitted with new geared turbines, and was then switched to Canada sailings from Southampton. She later made sailings from both Antwerp and Hamburg to Canada. From July 1932 onwards *Montcalm* was used almost exclusively as a cruise ship. In 1939 she was rebuilt as the armed merchant cruiser, *Wolfe*, but in 1941 she was converted into a troop transport and then later to a submarine depot ship, having been sold to the Admiralty. In 1950 she was laid up and in November 1952 she was towed to Faslane where she was broken up.


## Montrose

16,402grt
575ft length overall
70ft breadth
542 cabin-class and 1,268 third-class passengers
Built in 1922 by Fairfield, Glasgow
Powered by twin-screw geared turbines

Originally intended to be named *Montmorency* and was launched as such, her name was changed to *Montrose* before she was completed. On 5 May 1922 she departed Liverpool on her first voyage to Montreal. In 1929 she was transferred to the Hamburg–Montreal service and in 1931 was fitted with new geared turbines. In 1932 *Montrose* was used almost exclusively as a cruise ship. In 1939 she was renamed *Forfar* and fitted out as an Armed Merchant Cruiser. She was torpedoed and sunk in December 1940 off the west coast of Ireland.


## Montclare

16,314grt
575ft length overall
70ft breadth
542 cabin-class and 1,268 third-class passengers
Built in 1922 by John Brown's, Clydebank
Powered by twin-screw geared turbines

It was originally planned that *Montclare* would be named *Metapedia*. Her first voyage departed Liverpool for the St Lawrence ports on 18 August 1922. In 1929 she was fitted with new geared turbines and was then transferred to the Antwerp–Montreal service but she later made sailings from Hamburg. In 1933, like her sisters, she was used mainly as a cruise ship. In 1939 she was converted to an Armed Merchant Cruiser and then in 1942 to a submarine depot ship. In June of that year she was sold to the Admiralty. Having survived the war she remained in their service until 1955 when she was laid up. In February 1958 she arrived at Inverkeithing to be broken up by T.W. Ward.


## Melita

13,967grt
546ft length overall
67ft breadth
550 cabin-class and 1,200 third-class passengers
Built in 1918 by Harland & Wolff, Belfast
Powered by triple-expansion engine plus a low-pressure turbine, triple screw

The hull of the *Melita* was launched in April 1917 at the Barclay, Curle yard in Glasgow and was then towed to Belfast for the ship to be completed by Harland & Wolff. This was

Dressed overall, Canadian Pacific's *Montclare* is somewhere in Norway.

done by January 1918 and she made her first voyages as a troop transport. In 1920 she was placed on the Liverpool–Canada service and from 1922 to 1927 she operated from Antwerp to Canada. *Melita* was refitted by Palmers at Jarrow in 1925, and in 1926 her passenger accommodation was reconfigured into three classes. Between 1932 and 1934 she was used mostly as a cruise ship but was placed in lay-up in September 1934. The following April she was sold to be broken up in Italy, however she was then re-sold to the Italian government. Re-named *Liguria* she was used as a troop transport. In 1940 she was badly damaged at Tobruk and was consequently laid-up. The following year she capsized after a bomb attack and it was not until 1950 that she was raised and then towed away to be broken up.

## Chandris Line

The first Chandris Line vessel, the sailing ship *Dimitros*, was bought by the company's owner John D. Chandris in 1915, rapidly followed by three steam cargo vessels. The company traded around the Greek Islands and in 1922 began to operate passenger services. In 1936 it began to operate a combination passenger/cruise service out of Venice.

John Chandris died soon after the end of the Second World War and his sons took over the business. Under the operating title of the Greek Australia Line they began a service between Greece and Australia via the Suez Canal. This service was extended to Southampton and catered mainly for the emigrant trade between the UK and other parts of Europe and Australia.

Chandris increased the scope of its Greek cruising operation but also introduced cruises for the UK market operating out of Southampton. By 1976 the company could boast the largest cruise liner fleets in the world, carrying 500,000 cruise passengers a year, of which a fair proportion were from the UK. Interestingly, none of the ships was acquired new.

By the early 1980s the company had withdrawn from the UK cruise market. In 1990 the first ships of a new Chandris operation, Celebrity Cruises, came out. The Celebrity ships have all been designed for the top end of the premium cruise market in North America. Celebrity Cruises became part of Royal Caribbean Cruises in 1997. The clue to the Chandris involvement in Celebrity is the fact that the ships retain a large X on the funnel – X being the Greek symbol for C; C for Chandris.

## Australis

34,449grt
720ft length overall
93ft 6in breadth
2,000 passengers in one class (reduced to 1,500 when cruising)
Built in 1940 by Newport News Shipbuilding & Drydock Co.
Powered by twin-screw geared turbines

*Australis* entered service as the *America* for the United States Line, but, because of the war, her first voyages were cruises from New York to the West Indies rather than the transatlantic crossings that she had been designed for. After extensive war service as the USS *West Point*, she was restored to peacetime splendour and entered transatlantic service in 1946. She remained in service with United States Line until withdrawn and bought by Chandris in September 1964. She underwent a considerable conversion to make her suitable for the round-the-world service to Australia and New Zealand, and it was on this service that she was mainly employed. However, she also operated occasional cruises for the UK market from Southampton to the Mediterranean. She was withdrawn from service in 1977. The following year she was sold to America Cruise Lines, which was later restyled as Venture Cruise Lines, and briefly operated out of New York on short cruises under her original name, *America*. The operation was not a success, with the ship in a poor state of repair. Chandris bought the ship back again and during 1979 operated her on Mediterranean cruises as the *Italis*. These cruises were not, however, marketed only to British passengers, but throughout Europe. By the end of the year she was withdrawn from service and laid up. There were many plans for her future use but they came to nothing until, after almost twelve years in lay-up and name changes to *Noga* and *Alferdoss*, she was sold to become a floating hotel in Thailand. After a lengthy dry docking, renamed *American Star*, she was towed out of the Mediterranean and into the Atlantic. The intention was to tow the liner to Thailand via South Africa. However, caught by violent weather off the Canary Islands in January 1994, the towline broke and she was driven ashore and wrecked on the coast of the island of Fuerteventura.

## Ellinis

24,351grt
642ft length overall
79ft breadth
1,668 passengers (1,100 when cruising)
Built in 1932 by Bethlehem Steel Corp., Quincy, MA, USA
Powered by twin-screw steam turbines

Built as the *Lurline* for Matson Line's San Francisco–Hawaii service, she became the most popular and beloved liner on the run. One of three sister ships, she was the only one to be reconditioned and put back into the service after the war. She was withdrawn from service in 1963 after developing mechanical problems, and in September of that year she was sold to Chandris for the booming emigrant trade to Australia. She was restyled by Smith's Dock Co., at North Shields for this new role, increasing her passenger capacity from 760 to over 1,600. She was also given a more modern profile, with more streamlined funnels and a more raked bow, and was given the name, *Ellinis*. By the early 1970s she was interspersing her liner voyages with cruises from Sydney, and for the UK market from Southampton. She undertook many cruises from Southampton up to Scandinavia and to the Atlantic Islands and the Mediterranean. Some of her cruises, however, did include a call at Amsterdam, where continental passengers could be embarked. So while *Ellinis* was not exclusively aimed at the British market, British passengers were generally in the majority and her cruises were aimed at British tastes, which earned her considerable popularity. However, she had to adopt a broader appeal when in the late 1970s she was operating cruises out of Genoa to a wider market. Nevertheless, she was still marketed strongly in Britain at this time. In October 1980 she was withdrawn from service and laid up in Eleusis Bay in Greece. In 1987 she was towed to Taiwan to be scrapped.

*Britanis*

25,245grt
642ft length overall
79ft breadth
1,750 passengers
Built in 1932 by Bethlehem Steel Corp., Quincy, MA, USA
Powered by twin-screw steam turbines

The Chandris liner *Britanis* at Tilbury on the Thames, May 1975.

*Britanis* originally entered service as the *Monterey* in April 1932, on the trans-Pacific route for the Matson Line subsidiary, Oceanic Steamship Company, sailing with her sister vessels, *Lurline* and *Mariposa*. After war service as a troopship, *Monterey* was placed in lay-up, the cost of refitting her for commercial service being prohibitively expensive. She was, however, reactivated in the mid-1950s, and returned to service in 1957 as *Matsonia*. When her sister, *Lurline*, was sold in 1963 to become *Ellinis*, she adopted that more popular name. She remained on the San Francisco–Honolulu route until 1970, when she was also sold to the Chandris Line. Renamed *Britanis*, she was refitted in Piraeus, her former 760 passenger capacity being increased by a thousand. She re-entered service in February 1971, on a seventy-five-day round-the-world route to Australia. In 1975 she was diverted to full-time cruise service, with the summers spent in Europe and the winters in the Caribbean. Her first series of summer cruises were to Norway, North Cape and Spitzbergen, with one late summer cruise down to Dakar and the Canary Islands. While these cruises were in most cases based on sailings from Tilbury, they also included a call at Amsterdam to embark continental passengers. Future summer itineraries were also organised this way, however some of her cruises were based on Amsterdam with British passengers flying there to join the ship. Thus, she was not an exclusively British market ship. Nevertheless, as most of her passengers were British, and having gained experience of British tastes when operating their ships on the Australia service, *Britanis*, like *Ellinis*, catered very well to the British market. In 1981 *Britanis* was repositioned to the Caribbean permanently and remained in service until 1994.

## Regina Magna

32,336grt
697ft length overall
90ft breadth
1,120 passengers
Built in 1939 by Penhoet, St Nazaire, France
Powered by quadruple-screw geared turbines

The career of *Regina Magna*, under the Chandris flag, was very brief. However, she had already enjoyed a remarkable and successful career before they acquired her in 1971. Built as *Pasteur* for France's Compagnie Sud-Atlantique, she would have been the fastest and most luxurious liner on the France–South America service. However, her completion coincided with the outbreak of the Second World War, so instead of entering commercial service she was at first laid up, and then, in August 1940, she made a voyage to Canada carrying France's gold reserves. She was then converted into a troopship, mainly sailing on the North Atlantic. After the war she remained on trooping duties between France and her troubled south-east Asian colonies. In January 1957 her trooping career came to an end and there was some consideration to her being converted as an Atlantic liner for the French Line. This never materialised and instead she was sold to Norddeutscher Lloyd for use on their North Atlantic service. Renamed *Bremen*, she was extensively rebuilt, though essentially retaining her original profile except for a more modern-styled funnel. She re-entered service in July 1959 and became most popular, both on the Atlantic and operating cruises, usually based out of New York.

For ten years *Bremen* was a most successful ship but by 1970 she was beginning to suffer from mechanical problems and NDL decided to sell her instead of becoming involved in expensive repairs. At the end of 1971 she was sold to Chandris Cruises, a division of Chandris Line, and re-named *Regina Magna*. From May 1972 *Regina Magna* was based in Northern Europe for cruises to Scandinavia and the Baltic. The late summer was spent

operating cruises from Genoa to Mediterranean ports and the winter months in the
Caribbean. A similar cruise programme was operated during 1973, with some of her
cruises being based from Tilbury. The company obviously capitalised on their already
well-established reputation created by *Ellinis*. While many of her cruises also began and
ended at Amsterdam they were extensively marketed in the UK. However, *Regina Magna*
never had the opportunity to build up any loyal following of passengers: she was
expensive to run (particularly as a consequence of the 1973 fuel crisis) and she continued
to suffer from mechanical problems. At the end of the summer, in 1974, she was laid up
in Perama Bay. In 1977 she was sold for use as an accommodation ship, to house workers
at a construction project in Saudi Arabia, and was re-named *Saudi Phil 1*. The following
year her name was changed to *Filipinas Saudi 1*. She served in her static role until 1980
when she was sold for scrap. Whilst under tow for Taiwan she sank in the Indian Ocean.


## Queen Frederica

21,329grt
582ft length overall
83ft breadth
950 passengers
Built in 1927 by William Cramp & Sons, Shipbuilding & Engineering Co.
Powered by twin-screw geared turbines


Right up until the very end of her career the *Queen Frederica* was a most popular ship.
Although she was forty-six years old when withdrawn from service she could boast all
the amenities of more modern cruise ships, being fully air-conditioned, with an attractive
lido deck and an extensive array of public rooms (some of which still retained the elegant
features that were the fashion at the time of her Matson Line career). As built, she was
named *Malolo,* and served on Matson's San Francisco–Hawaii service. She proved to be
highly successful, and following the introduction of other large liners into the Matson
fleet, she was modernised and renamed *Matsonia* in the late 1930s. She had a successful
wartime career, transporting many thousands of servicemen. She was briefly returned to
the Hawaiian service but in 1948 was withdrawn and sold to Home Lines. As built, she
had been given accommodation for 700 passengers. Refitting her for transatlantic service
Home Lines increased her passenger capacity to 1,178, in three classes, and renamed her
*Atlantic*. At the end of 1954 she was again renamed, this time to *Queen Frederica*, and was
transferred to the Home Lines subsidiary, National Hellenic American Line, for their
Piraeus–New York service. In 1965 the National Hellenic American Line, and the *Queen
Frederica*, were sold to Chandris Line. They operated the ship for part of the year on the
Southampton–Australia and New Zealand service, and for the remainder of the year
between Mediterranean ports and New York.
   In 1970 she was placed under charter to the British-owned tour operator, Sovereign
Cruises, operating seven-day western Mediterranean cruises from Palma. She was given
their funnel markings of a white Maltese Cross in place of the Chandris 'X'. The cruises
were marketed heavily in the UK, and passengers were given the opportunity to extend
their holidays with four days in a hotel either at the beginning or end of their cruise. It
was, however, only for a brief time that the *Queen Frederica* was aimed solely at the British
market, for in 1971 she was laid up in the River Dart. The following year she was moved
to Piraeus, and in 1973 she was chartered to a Chandris subsidiary company, Sun Cruises,
to operate a series of seven-day western Mediterranean cruises. Her funnels were again
repainted, this time with a stylised sun design over white wavy lines to represent the sea.
While these cruises were also extensively marketed in the UK, they were also sold

elsewhere in Europe and America. She was scheduled to undertake thirty-three similar cruises during 1974. However, having been placed in winter lay-up in November 1973, she was never to sail again; the increasing cost of fuel, as much as anything, being the deciding factor. She was sold for scrap in 1977, and was gutted by fire before the work was really underway, in February 1978.

# Clarkson Holidays

Clarkson's were a budget tour operator, which gained brief prominence in the early 1970s, operating former French liners, under charter from the Greek ship owner, Efthymiadis. Clarkson Holidays collapsed in 1974, unable to operate in the face of steeply rising fuel costs.

## Delphi

10,881grt
492ft length overall
64ft breadth
700 passengers (approximately)
Built in 1952 by Forges Chantiers de la Gironde, Bordeaux
Powered by twin-screw Burmeister & Wain diesel engines

*Delphi* was built as the *Ferdinand de Lesseps* for Messageries Maritime's Marseilles–M auritius service. She was a cargo liner with accommodation for nearly 500 passengers in three classes, one of four identical sister ships. In 1968 she was sold to Efthymiadis, and following considerable refitting she began cruising, as *Delphi*, in the Mediterranean under charter to Clarkson Holidays. Following Clarkson's collapse she initially found employment under charter to Canadian-based company, Strand Cruises. After the Efthymiadis company collapsed, the ship went to other owners and was once again briefly marketed to British holidaymakers. (See under Perlus Cruises.)

## Delos and *Melina*

4,500grt
373ft length overall
49ft breadth
450 passengers
Built in 1949–1951 by Ateliers et Chantiers de Bretagne, Nantes
Powered by single-screw steam turbine engines

*Delos* and *Melina* entered service as the *Azzemour* and *Azrou,* respectively, for Paquet Lines' service between Marseilles and Casablanca. In 1968 *Azrou* was sold to Efthymaides, and the following year she was joined by her sister, *Azzemour.* They were extensively rebuilt from three-class passenger/cargo ships into quite stylish cruise ships, and were subsequently placed under charter to Clarkson Holidays, operating seven-day cruises around the Greek islands. Following the collapse of Clarkson's, the ships remained in service until 1977 and the collapse of Efthymaides. Both *Delos* and *Melina* had been troubled by mechanical problems and were laid up. *Melina* was sold for scrap but her engines were removed and replaced those aboard *Delos*, which was sold in 1980.

However, on only her second cruise for her new owners these engines failed, and she was withdrawn from service.

A similar passenger/cargo vessel, *Djebel-Dira*, owned by Compagnie de Navigation Mixte, was sold to another Greek operator, Spyros P. Billinis, in 1970, and she also underwent a very similar rebuild to *Delos* and *Melina*. She was given the name *Phoenix* and was chartered to the British holiday company, Horizon, to operate Aegean cruises. As with the Clarkson Holidays venture, this appears to have been short lived. She later sailed as *Melody*, and as such was badly damaged during a storm in the Mediterranean in 1980. She then passed through several owners, without having sailed for any of them. The damage sustained in the storm was not repaired until 1990, and while this was underway the ship caught fire and began to sink. She was abandoned off a small island outside Piraeus harbour.

# Classic International

Classic International Cruises has been offering cruises to the UK market since 1986. The company's ships tend to be chartered out to various holiday companies so that the ship may be operating in the UK market for one set of cruises and in the German or French market for another.

## *Arion*

6,000grt
381.5ft length overall
54ft breadth
340 passengers
Built in 1965 by the Brodgradiliste, Yugoslavia
Powered by diesel engines

Built as the *Istra* for cruising along the Dalmatian coast, she was acquired by Caravella Shipping in 1993 and renamed *Astra*. As *Astra* she cruised for the German and the emerging Russian markets. Classic International acquired her in 1999 and renamed her *Arion*. Often under charter to a variety of European (including UK) holiday companies she provides a relaxed, small-ship ambience and is able to visit ports that larger cruise ships cannot enter. She has been chartered by Voyages of Discovery, the UK operator of educational cruises.

## *Funchal*

9,847grt
501ft length overall
63ft breadth
440 passengers
Built in 1961 by the Elsinore Shipbuilding Co., Denmark
Powered by diesel engines

When *Funchal* entered service she was the flagship of Portugal's Empresa Insulana fleet, operating a service from Lisbon to Madeira, the Canary Islands and the Azores. At that time she accommodated 500 passengers in three classes in very fine and attractive

*Funchal* is regularly operated under charter and is a frequent sight at British ports.

surroundings. She was designed with the idea that she should also be used in cruise service. In 1972 she was withdrawn from regular liner service and underwent extensive refitting, which included the replacement of her original turbines by diesel engines.

She was increasingly employed in both Europe and South America, often under charter. Her ownership changed in the mid-1970s to Companhia Portuguesa de Transportes Maritimos. In 1985 she was acquired by Arcalia Shipping, who more recently has marketed her under the Classic International Cruises banner. Over the years, and particularly since her ownership by Arcalia, she has been regularly upgraded and refurbished. One of the things that was unusual was the fact that for a number of years a small number of cabins shared one set of toilet facilities between two cabins with a light indicating whether or not the facilities were in use.

During the summer months she is regularly operated under charter to various British tour companies who operate her on cruises to Scandinavia and the Atlantic islands, and she has developed a very loyal following. Despite her somewhat international ownership she remains a distinctly Portuguese ship and still operates cruises for the Portuguese market. She has been chartered by Voyages of Discovery, the UK operator of educational cruises, as well as several other UK travel companies.

## Princess Danae

10,501grt
533ft length overall
69ft breadth
560 passengers
Built in 1955 by Harland & Wolff, Belfast
Powered by twin-screw diesels

*Princess Danae* was built as the refrigerated cargo vessel, *Port Melbourne*, to operate on a regular service between Europe, Australia and New Zealand. In 1972 she was sold, along with her sister *Port Sydney*, to the Greek ship-owner, John C. Karras, for rebuilding into luxury cruise ships. They emerged with radically different profiles from their days with Port Line, but their hull shapes remained unchanged. While the former *Port Melbourne* was given the name *Danae, Port Sydney* was renamed *Daphne*. In 1979 the ships were placed under charter to Costa Line, and in 1985 they purchased them outright. Both ships acquired a very good reputation with Costa, often operating very long exotic cruises, sometimes around the world. In 1996 Arcalia Shipping acquired *Danae*, changing her name slightly to *Princess Danae*. As she had spent the previous four years under a variety of owners she was no longer of luxury standard. Arcalia spent over $10 million refurbishing her before placing her in service in August of that year. She undertook some cruises under charter to British tour companies in Scandinavian waters and around the British Isles. However, in more recent times she has been regularly chartered by a French company.

Originally owned by Port Line, *Princess Danae* was converted from a refrigerated cargo vessel into this handsome cruise ship in 1972. She is viewed here at Lisbon.

# CTC Lines

CTC Lines – the Charter Travel Club – was formed in 1966, not as a cruise operator but as an operator of liner voyages, mainly for the benefit of Australians wanting an inexpensive sea voyage to the UK. The ships they used were those belonging to the Black Sea Steamship Company, which were part of the vast Soviet fleet. The *Shota Rustaveli* was the first ship to operate for them, on a round-the-world voyage, in 1968. By the early 1970s the passenger ships of the Baltic Steamship Company, another part of the Soviet fleet, had become such dominant players in the cruise market that by 1972 they were the largest users of the Tilbury Landing Stage (now known as the London International Cruise Terminal) with twenty-three cruises being offered to British holidaymakers. That year was particularly significant for it was the first time that Russian ships had operated a year-round cruising programme from the UK. At that time the vessels operating these cruises were the *Alexandr Pushkin*, the brand new *Mikhail Lermontov, Nadezhda Krupskaja, Baltika* and the recently refitted *Estonia*.

The *Mikhail Lermontov* started her cruise programme on 22 April 1972 and undertook twelve cruises between then and early December. These cruises ranged between Scandinavia, Iceland and the Baltic to the Mediterranean, West Africa and the West Indies. By 1974, with several significant British liners having been withdrawn from service, the Baltic Steamship Company increased their number of cruises to forty-one, offering close on 12,000 berths to British holidaymakers. Again, the *Mikhail Lermontov* undertook the bulk of these cruises.

At this time Royal Mail Lines operated as the UK agents for the Baltic Steamship Company, with CTC marketing just the liner voyages to and from Australia and New Zealand. However, following Royal Mail's demise from passenger liner operations, CTC Lines took the role of marketing both the liner voyages and the cruises, and during the remainder of the 1970s and the 1980s they were a significant player in the UK cruise market. Other ships, such as *Mikhail Kalinin, Leonid Sobinov, Kareliya* (later renamed *Leonid Brezhnev*) and *Odessa* were all operating cruises for the British market at one time or another, under the CTC Lines banner. With the fall of the Soviet Union, the huge fleet was no longer underwritten by the State, and the CTC Lines operation folded, no longer able to hold its competitive edge.

The following are the principal Russian cruise ships that served the U.K. market at that time.

*1. Mikhail Lermontov*
*2. Alexandr Pushkin*
*3. Taras Shevchenko*

20,000grt
578ft length overall
77ft breadth
650 passengers
Built (1) 1972; (2) 1965; and (3) 1966 by Mathais Thesen Werft, Wismar
Powered by twin-screw Werkspoor-Sulzer diesel engines

The *Alexander Pushkin* is still in service as the *Marco Polo* for Orient Lines. The *Mikhail Lermontov* sank in New Zealand waters in 1986. *Taras Shevchenko* was renovated in 1988 for the French/Italian cruise market before being laid up in 2001.

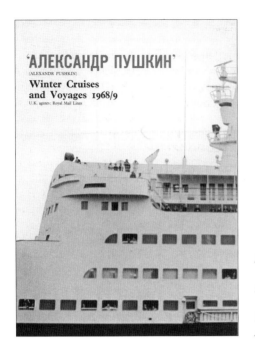

'АЛЕКСАНДР ПУШКИН'
(ALEXANDR PUSHKIN)

**Winter Cruises
and Voyages 1968/9**
U.K. agents: Royal Mail Lines

*Left:* The 1968 brochure for the *Alexandr Pushkin.*

*Below: Mikhail Lermontov* at Tilbury, June 1975.

*Bottom:* About to cast off at Tilbury, May 1976, is *Alexandr Pushkin.*

One of the most commonly seen of the Russian cruise ships in British waters was *Mikhail Kalinin*, seen here at Lisbon, October 1987.

*1. Mikhail Kalinin*
*2. Nadezhda Krupskaja*
*3. Estonia*

4,900grt
401ft length overall
53ft breadth
300 passengers
Built (1) 1958; (2) 1963; and (3) 1960 by Mathais These Werft, Wismar
Powered by twin-screw DMR diesel engines

The *Mikhail Kalinin* was the vessel used most frequently by CTC for the UK market. She was withdrawn from the UK market in 1984 but survived as a cruise ship for Soviet Bloc countries until she was broken up in India in 1994.

*1. Kareliya/Leonid Brezhnev*
*2. Gruziya*

16,700grt
513ft length overall
71ft breadth
504 passengers
Built (1) 1976; and (2) 1975 by Wartsila A/B, Abo
Powered by twin-screw Pielstick diesel engines

These were two of the members of a quintet of ships originally designed as large car ferries.

The *Kareliya* was renamed *Leonid Brezhnev* in 1982 and then reverted to *Kareliya* in 1989. She left the cruise market in 1997.

After a number of name changes (*Odessa Sky* and *Club 1*) the *Gruziya* entered the French cruise market as the *Van Gogh* in 1999.

## Baltika

7,494grt
445ft length overall
60ft breadth
437 passengers
Built in 1940 by NV Nederlandsche Schps. Maast., Amsterdam
Powered by twin–screw Stork steam-turbine engines, with electric drive

*Baltika* at Tilbury, 1974.

One of the earliest vessels used by the Russians in order to gain hard currency by offering cruises to the UK market after aircraft removed the need for the direct London–Leningrad (St Petersburg) in which she operated up to the 1960s. She was broken up in Pakistan in 1987.

*Leonid Sobinov*

For statistics see *Saxonia*, Cunard Line.

# Cunard Line

One of the great names of the shipping world, Cunard was formed in 1840 by a Canadian, Samuel Cunard, to operate between the UK and North America. The company has had more Blue Riband holders than any other. Names like *QE2*, *Mauretania*, *Queen Mary* and *Queen Elizabeth* still stir the imagination. Cunard was a fairly early entrant into cruising for both the UK and the US markets.

Merged with White Star in 1934, Cunard was acquired by Trafalgar House Investments in 1971 and, after a series of acquisitions including Norwegian America Cruises and the Royal Viking Line, the Cunard name passed to Kvaerner when that company bought Trafalgar House. The *Caronia* of 1948 operated in the US Cruise market.

Calculating the day's run on board a 1930s Cunarder on cruise service.

In 1998 the Cunard brand was purchased by the Carnival Group – the largest cruise group in the world. Carnival has continued to invest in Cunard as evidenced in 2004 by *Queen Mary 2* and the 85,000grt *Queen Victoria* which enters service in 2007.

## Samaria

19,597grt
624ft length overall
74ft breadth
350 first-class, 340 second-class and 1,500 third-class passengers
Built in 1921 by Cammell Laird, Birkenhead
Powered by twin-screw double-reduction geared turbines

*Samaria* was mainly employed on the Liverpool to Boston and New York service. However, in January 1923 her accommodation was rearranged to carry approximately 600 passengers in 'one class' on a world cruise out of New York. The cruise proved to be a great success and consequently was repeated the following year. *Samaria* continued to be employed on the Boston and New York service but was also used as a cruise ship. She made a large number of cruises from both New York and from British ports, and developed considerable popularity.

During the war she was converted into a troop transport. Immediately after the war she divided her time between trooping voyages and transporting war brides to Canada. She also made a number of voyages transporting refugees to Canada. In 1950 *Samaria* was refitted for her return to regular Atlantic service, from Liverpool to Montreal. She was never again employed as a cruise ship and was sold for scrap in December 1955.

## Franconia

20,175grt
625ft length overall
73ft breadth
331 first-class, 356 second-class and 1,266 third-class passengers
Built in 1923 by John Brown & Co., Clydebank
Powered by twin-screw double-reduction turbines

*Franconia* was built for the Liverpool–New York service but was also designed with cruising in mind, and during the 1920s and 1930s she earned a legendary reputation for her long cruises, some of which took several months. She sailed from New York on 4 November 1923 on her first world cruise, and most of her long-haul cruises were geared to the American market, attracting the very cream of American society. Apart from her lengthy winter cruises, *Franconia* also undertook cruises to the Caribbean at other times in the year. However, not all of her cruises were aimed at the American market. For example, she sailed from Southampton on 26 December 1931 on a cruise around the world lasting six months. In late 1932 *Franconia* was given an extensive refit that changed her passenger capacity to 350 in both first and second classes and 930 in third class. She was also given a white hull, which better suited her cruising role. She continued to cruise extensively from both American and British ports but two cruises in particular from Southampton were notable for their length. In 1935 she departed that port on a cruise of 163 days, and on Christmas Eve 1938 she sailed from Southampton on what would be her final world cruise. It took 170 days, returning on 12 June 1939.

*Franconia*, in cruising white, sometime in the mid-1930s.

She was converted into a troopship during the war but is most famous for her role as the headquarters for the British delegation that attended the Yalta Conference in 1945. After further trooping duties she was returned to Cunard in June 1948 and returned to North Atlantic service the following June, on the Canada route. She was withdrawn from service in 1956 and arrived at Rosyth in December to be broken up.

## Carinthia

20,277grt
624ft length overall
73ft breadth
330 first-class, 420 second-class and 1,500 third-class passengers
Built in 1925 by Vickers, Barrow
Powered by twin-screw double-reduction-geared turbines

*Carinthia* was almost an identical sister to *Franconia*, and like her, acquired an enviable reputation as a cruise ship. She entered service in August 1925 and was employed on the Liverpool–New York service until the end of the year when she departed on her first world cruise, lasting 142 days. Almost every year, from then until 1933, she undertook a similar circumnavigation. Her 1932/33 world cruise was so fabulous that it was known as 'the millionaire's cruise'. Although her cruises were almost always for the American market there were occasions when, during some summers, she operated some short cruises from Southampton for the British market. She became particularly well known for her cruises to the Norwegian fjords and up to North Cape. In 1932 she also adopted an all-white cruising livery.

At the outbreak of war *Carinthia* was converted to an Armed Merchant Cruiser. In June 1940 she was torpedoed off the Irish coast.

An artist's impression of the *Carinthia*, dressed overall.

## Lancastria

16,243grt
572ft length overall
70ft breadth
580 cabin-class and 1,000 third-class passengers
Built in 1922 by William Beardmore, Glasgow
Powered by twin-screw double-reduction-geared turbines

*Lancastria* began life as Anchor Line's *Tyrrhenia*. However, she was taken over by Cunard, while still under construction, when they acquired Anchor Line. She entered service in June 1922 on the Liverpool to Quebec run but also made voyages to New York, Boston and Halifax. In December she undertook a Mediterranean cruise from New York, and during the following year undertook several other cruises. In 1924 Cunard decided to convert the ship to make her more suited to a cruising role. Her passenger accommodation, which had been built for 1,175 in three classes, was redesigned for just Cabin and Third Class. Two swimming pools were constructed aft on her promenade deck, and it was at this time she was given the name *Lancastria*. She was then employed on various Atlantic routes, and in the winter months sailed as a cruise ship, making cruises from both New York and from Liverpool. In October 1932, at the beginning of a fourteen-day Mediterranean cruise from Liverpool, she rescued the crew of a cargo vessel that was in difficulties in a gale in the Bay of Biscay. *Lancastria* spent the whole of the summer and autumn of 1938 operating a series of cruises to the Mediterranean and the Atlantic Islands, from Liverpool and London. Then in the spring of 1939, after a refit, she sailed for New York. The following six months were spent operating four- and five-day cruises to Bermuda and Nassau.

*Lancastria* was a popular cruising liner. She met her fate at the hands of a German bomber pilot in 1940 and sank with the loss of at least 3,500 soldiers, civilians and crew being evacuated from France.

At the outbreak of war she sailed for London and was converted into a troop transport. In June 1940, having embarked over 5,500 troops at St Nazaire, she was attacked in a raid by German bombers and sank in just twenty minutes. The sinking of *Lancastria*, with the loss of over 3,000 men, is regarded as one of the worst maritime disasters of the war.

## Mauretania

35,655grt
772ft length overall
89ft breadth
470 first-class, 370 cabin-class and 300 tourist-class passengers
Built in 1939 by Cammell Laird, Birkenhead
Powered by twin-screw single-reduction-geared turbines

*Mauretania* left Liverpool on her maiden voyage to New York on 17 June 1939. She spent the first few months of the war laid up at her Manhattan berth until she was converted into a troopship. She maintained this role until 1946 and was then given an eight-month overhaul to return her to her pre-war splendour. During the summer months she helped maintain Cunard's transatlantic service to New York. In the winter months, with her passenger capacity reduced to just 600 she operated a programme of twelve- and eighteen-day cruises from New York to the Caribbean. This pattern of operation continued until the early 1960s, by which time *Mauretania* had become outclassed by newer ships. In an attempt to make her more profitable, Cunard scheduled a programme of four cruises for her from Southampton during the winter of 1964. The first of these departed on 14 January, a thirty-six-day cruise to the Canary Islands, the Caribbean, Port

The Cammell Laird-built *Mauretania* leaving Southampton for New York. She was a popular cruise ship from the mid-1950s, serving both the American and British markets.

Everglades, the Bahamas and the Azores. This was followed by a thirteen-day cruise to Madeira, the Canaries, Casablanca, Tangier and Lisbon, and the next cruise, departing Southampton on 7 March, was a repeat of this itinerary. On 24 March, she departed on a twenty-day Mediterranean cruise calling at Tangier, Malta, Alexandria, Piraeus and Gibraltar. *Mauretania* then returned to New York for a further series of Caribbean cruises. However, by this time Cunard were in dire financial difficulties, and in September 1965 it was announced that she was to be withdrawn from service. She was broken up later that year at Inverkeithing.

## Queen Mary

81,235grt
1,019ft length overall
118ft breadth
711 first-class, 707 cabin-class and 577 tourist-class passengers
Built in 1936 by John Brown & Co., Clydebank
Powered by quadruple-screw single-reduction-geared turbines

*Queen Mary* at Las Palmas on one of her 1960s cruises.

CRUISE BRITANNIA – THE SHIPS

*Queen Mary* is one of the legendary ocean liners: she was designed purely to operate a year-round service between Southampton and New York, a role as a cruise ship was never considered. Her service as a troopship during the war was heroic. She remained in government service for many months after the end of the war, transporting war brides across to North America. In September 1946 she was returned to her builders and was given a ten-month refit that restored her to her pre-war splendour. *Queen Mary* resumed her commercial transatlantic service in August 1947 and, along with her near sister, *Queen Elizabeth*, maintained this successfully throughout the 1950s. By the early 1960s, even though the numbers of passengers carried, particularly during the winter months, were seriously declining, Cunard envisaged the ship would remain in service until 1969. In an attempt to offset the heavy losses that the company were incurring during the winter, a short programme of cruises was planned for the ship. On 23 December 1963 *Queen Mary* departed Southampton on her first ever cruise, six days to Las Palmas. On 30 December she repeated the itinerary, and then on 26 March she departed on an eight-day cruise calling at both Las Palmas and Lisbon. Other cruises were scheduled, taking her into the Mediterranean. She also operated some cruises from New York to the Bahamas. Nevertheless, Cunard continued to lose money and in early 1967 it was announced that *Queen Mary* would be withdrawn from service that autumn. In August she was sold to the city of Long Beach and her delivery voyage, via Cape Horn, was sold as a thirty-nine-day cruise. While this of course departed from Southampton, on 30 October 1967, it was in fact marketed through the American travel company, Fugazy. *Queen Mary* remains in Long Beach, as a hotel and museum and as a monument to the great ocean liners of the past.

## Queen Elizabeth

83,673grt
1,030ft length overall
119ft breadth
823 first-class, 662 cabin-class and 798 tourist-class passengers
Built in1940 by John Brown & Co., Clydebank
Powered by quadruple-screw single-reduction-geared turbines

*Queen Elizabeth*'s design was a refinement of that of the *Queen Mary*, and it was planned that her entry into service would coincide with the centenary of the Cunard Line, in 1940. The war interrupted these plans and, instead of a gala maiden voyage, the barely completed liner's first voyage was a secret dash across the Atlantic to the safety of New York. Along with the *Queen Mary* her transportation of American and Canadian troops across the Atlantic to Europe is said to have made a significant contribution in bringing the war to an end. The *Queen Elizabeth* was the first of the two giant liners to be released from war service in March 1946. Refurbishment work took place first at her builders and was completed in Southampton. She made her commercial entry into service on 16 October 1946, and was joined by the *Queen Mary* the following August. At last Cunard's envisioned two-ship express service across the Atlantic was established. For the remainder of the 1940s and throughout the 1950s the liners were popular and profitable. However, by the early 1960s more and more people were turning to aircraft for transatlantic travel and both the 'Queens' began to suffer as a result, particularly during the winter months. Cunard announced that the *Queen Elizabeth* would undertake her first-ever cruises beginning in February 1963. These were of between three and five days, from New York to Nassau, and most of the cruises made by *Queen Elizabeth* would be for the American market. However, she did undertake some cruises from Southampton

*Queen Elizabeth* was converted at Greenock for cruising in the early 1960s, with air conditioning and a lido pool added.

including, in 1964, a Mediterranean cruise, and also an Atlantic Islands cruise. In 1966 she was given an extensive overhaul that gave her more cabins with private bathrooms, redecorated public rooms and the creation of a lido deck with an open-air swimming pool. All of these features were to make her more attractive as a cruise ship and as a suitable running mate to the new Cunard liner then under construction, and due to enter service in 1968. The devastating seamen's strike of 1966 was such a serious blow to the already ailing company that when in 1967 it was announced that the *Queen Mary* would be withdrawn later that year, the *Queen Elizabeth*'s retirement in 1968 was also announced. She completed her final transatlantic crossing in November 1968, having been sold to become a tourist attraction in Port Everglades. The project lost money and she sailed from there in February 1971for Hong Kong, having been sold to the Chinese shipping tycoon, C.Y. Tung. His aim was to have her rebuilt as a cruise ship and floating university and she was renamed *Seawise University*. In January 1972, with the work almost completed, she was destroyed by several fires, undoubtedly the work of an arsonist.

## Carmania

22,592grt
608ft length overall
80ft breadth
117 first-class and 764 tourist-class passengers
Built in 1954 by John Brown & Co., Clydebank
Powered by twin-screw double-reduction-geared turbines

*Carmania* was built as *Saxonia*, the lead ship of a quartet designed for the Liverpool–St Lawrence service. As originally built, no facilities for use as a cruise ship had been incorporated into the design. With extensive cargo-carrying capacity it was imagined that they would maintain a year-round service (to coastal Canadian ports during the winter when the ice made the St Lawrence impassable). Therefore, as *Saxonia*, she never operated any cruises, but by the early 1960s Cunard was faced with mounting losses and a fleet of liners totally unsuited to the demands of the expanding cruise market. In 1962 it was announced that both *Saxonia* and *Ivernia* would be rebuilt in order to make them more attractive as dual-role cruise ships and Atlantic liners. The work was done by John Brown's. The work involved dispensing with cargo holds in order to create an attractive lido, remodelling cabins and restyling the public rooms. She was also renamed, *Carmania*. Initially, her cruising duties were concentrated on the American market, sailing from New York to the Caribbean during the winter months. It was not until October 1966 that *Carmania* undertook a cruise from the UK, and this was her first voyage into the Mediterranean. A further Mediterranean cruise, of nineteen days, was made from Southampton in the autumn of 1967. Unlike the previous year's cruise, which had been concentrated on the western Mediterranean, this one ventured as far as Istanbul. Up until this time she had maintained her dual role of cruise ship and Atlantic liner. However, from 1968 she was employed fully as a cruise ship. Cunard had scheduled an extensive programme of Southampton-based cruises. In June she made her first cruise up the Norwegian coast as far as Hammerfest. Other cruises included calls in Spain, Portugal and Morocco. At the end of September *Carmania* began a programme of Mediterranean fly cruises based on Naples. The series of cruises ended back in Southampton in November

An aerial view of *Carmania*, which had been converted and renamed from the Liverpool–Canada route RMS *Saxonia*.

1968, and she was then repositioned to the Caribbean. The following year she returned to Southampton operating a similar programme of cruises, including her first voyage to the Baltic capitals. The programme ended with another round of Naples-based fly cruises. During the summer of 1970 *Carmania* undertook a full programme of cruises from Southampton, and the following summer she returned and also resumed her Mediterranean fly-cruise programme. This was her last season operating for Cunard. The line had decided to make her available for sale. She and her sister, *Franconia*, were in need of expensive refitting, and the company were finding the ships increasingly costly to operate. Also, they had taken delivery of the new flagship, *Queen Elizabeth 2* and were poised to take delivery of two new, purpose-built cruise ships, *Cunard Adventurer* and *Cunard Ambassador*. *Carmania* was laid up in the River Fal and in August 1973 was sold to Panamanian interests, Nikreis Maritime. (See *Leonid Sobinov*, CTC Lines).

## Franconia

22,637grt
608ft length overall
80ft breadth
119 first-class and728 tourist-class passengers
Built in 1955 by John Brown & Co., Clydebank
Powered by twin-screw double-reduction-geared turbines

*Franconia* entered service as *Ivernia*, the second ship in the Canadian quartet. Like *Saxonia* she was designed to carry over 900 passengers and a large quantity of cargo year-round on the service to Canada. Rebuilt in 1962, and renamed *Franconia*, she was much more suited to the demands of cruising. Initially she divided her time between summers on the Atlantic service and winters sailing from New York to the Caribbean. However, on 25 September 1965 she made her first cruise from the UK: the itinerary included calls at ports in Spain and Portugal and her call at Malaga was her first visit into the Mediterranean. A similar cruise followed but called at Casablanca instead of Malaga. *Franconia* was, however, mainly the 'American market' ship, and she really made her name on the regular New York–Bermuda run. Nevertheless, she occasionally operated cruises from the UK and in the early months of 1968, before returning to the Bermuda service, she cruised from Liverpool down to Portugal, North Africa and the Atlantic Islands. She returned to Southampton at the close of the Bermuda season and undertook a Christmas cruise to the Atlantic Islands and Dakar. She was back in Southampton to operate the 1969/70 Christmas and New Year cruise, and that year was in Madeira on New Year's Eve. *Franconia* was withdrawn from Cunard's service, along with *Carmania*, and after a period of lay-up in Southampton they were moved to the River Fal awaiting sale. *Franconia* was sold, with *Carmania*, in August 1973 to Nikreis Maritime.

## Carinthia

21,947grt
608ft length overall
80ft breadth
154 first-class and 714 tourist-class passengers
Built in 1956 by John Brown & Co., Clydebank
Powered by twin-screw double-reduction-geared turbines

*Carinthia* on her flying mile speed trial off Arran, when built.

Although *Carinthia* was of almost an identical design to her earlier sisters, it had been announced at the time she entered service that she would undertake a 'dollar-earning' cruise out of New York during December 1956. This was the first cruise to be operated by one of this class of ships. *Carinthia*'s first cruise from the UK was not until 7 January 1966, when she departed Liverpool for Madeira, Tenerife, Las Palmas, Casablanca and Gibraltar. This was followed by a thirteen-night cruise of a similar itinerary, and she also undertook a fourteen-night Christmas cruise that year from Liverpool. Early in 1967, after having completed one round-trip Atlantic crossing, she sailed from Southampton on an Atlantic Islands cruise. Then in mid-summer, on 20 July, she departed Liverpool on the first of two cruises to Spain, Portugal and Morocco. These were to be her final cruises under the Cunard flag. In October 1967 it was announced that she would be withdrawn from service. On 23 November she departed Southampton on her final transatlantic voyage and early in December was laid up in Southampton.

At the end of January 1968 it was announced that *Carinthia* had been sold to the Fairland Shipping Corporation, a subsidiary of the Sitmar Line, and would be rebuilt and renamed *Fairland*. Plans for her future employment went through several changes before she eventually left for Italy to be rebuilt. She emerged, totally transformed, as *Fairsea*, and operated from various American ports to the Caribbean, Mexico and Alaska. In 1988 Sitmar Cruises was absorbed into the P&O empire and *Fairsea* was renamed *Fair Princess*, as part of their Princess Cruises fleet. While her cruises were available to the British market she was principally aimed at American passengers and never sailed from the UK again. In 1997 she was repositioned to Sydney to serve the Australian market but this was relatively short-lived and at the end of 2000 she was sold to become a gambling ship for the growing Chinese market.

## Sylvania

21,989grt
608ft length overall
80ft breadth
154 first-class and 724 tourist-class passengers
Built in 1957 by John Brown & Co., Clydebank
Powered by twin-screw double-reduction-geared turbines

*Sylvania* was the last of the Canadian quartet, her design closely following that of her sisters. However, by the time she entered service, transatlantic travel by sea had reached its peak and soon after began its steady decline. Just six months after her entry into service, *Sylvania* departed New York on 17 December 1957 on her first cruise, to the Caribbean and the Bahamas. By the mid-1960s the directors of Cunard had decided that as the demand for mid-winter transatlantic sailings had declined so much both *Sylvania* and *Carinthia* would be better employed on a series of winter cruises. *Sylvania*'s first cruise for the British market departed Liverpool on 10 February 1965. This was a twenty-seven-day trip to Mediterranean ports. At the end of the year she made a Christmas cruise from Liverpool to Madeira and the Canary Islands, and following this she was repositioned to Southampton from where she departed on 28 January 1966 on another Atlantic Islands cruise. This was followed by three further cruises: one a month-long trip around the Mediterranean, then two shorter cruises again to the Atlantic Islands and then a further Mediterranean cruise. In December 1966, during a refit, *Sylvania* was repainted with a white hull to emphasise her increased cruising role. (It had also been planned to paint *Carinthia* with a white hull but her delayed return to the UK due to a severe storm meant that there was not enough time to carry this out. She therefore retained her black hull to

*Sylvania* cruising in the Mediterranean in 1967, here seen at Ajaccio, Corsica.

Cunard's SRN6 hovercraft being raised onto the deck of *Sylvania* in 1967 at Southampton just before her departure on a series of Gibraltar-based cruises in conjunction with British European Airways.

the end of her Cunard career.) *Sylvania*'s cruise programme continued after the December 1966 refit through until May 1967. On 13 January she sailed from Southampton on a thirty-six-day cruise to the Caribbean. On her return from this cruise, as an experiment, she was fitted with a Hovercraft on her foredeck. This was to be used to take passengers on sightseeing excursions. It was probably not very successful as no other ship was fitted with one and *Sylvania*'s SRN6 was returned to her owners in April 1968. In February 1967 she cruised to the Mediterranean, the cruise ending in Gibraltar and the passengers flown home from there. A further four Mediterranean cruises were undertaken with passengers being flown out to join the ship at Gibraltar using British European Airways flights. Despite this real move towards cruising Cunard were unwilling to invest more money to make *Sylvania* and *Carinthia* suitable for the task in hand, and in October 1967 they announced that the ships would be withdrawn and sold. *Sylvania* remained in their service until May 1968. At the end of her 1967 Atlantic season she sailed from Southampton on a Christmas cruise to Lisbon, Madeira, Tenerife, Casablanca, Gibraltar and Cadiz. This was followed by a month-long cruise to the Caribbean. Then from February to early May she operated a series of cruises, the first of which ended in Gibraltar. The remaining six cruises were again operated from there on a fly-cruise basis and were mainly to Mediterranean ports. On 7 May 1968 *Sylvania* joined her sister in lay-up in Southampton.

The sale of both ships to the Sitmar Line had been announced earlier in the year, and *Sylvania* was renamed *Fairwind*. It was not until January 1970 that she left Southampton for Trieste, where she was to be rebuilt. (See *Albatros*, Phoenix Reisen.)

*QE2* tendering at Guernsey, a perennial short cruise favourite of Southampton-based cruise lines.

## Queen Elizabeth 2

70,327grt
963ft length overall
105ft breadth
1,756 passengers (double-occupancy basis)
Built in 1969 by Upper Clyde Shipbuilders Ltd, Clydebank (formerly John Brown & Co.)
Powered by twin-screw MAN B&W diesel–electric engines. Originally powered by double-reduction-geared turbines

The *Queen Elizabeth 2*, or *QE2* as she is more commonly known, is arguably one of the most famous liners ever built. Unlike her predecessors she was built with a dual role of transatlantic liner and cruise ship, and as such she has sailed far further than the previous two 'Queens'. While she has maintained a somewhat regular service between Southampton and New York, this has often been interspersed with cruises. Until recently it was not possible to categorise the *QE2* as a 'British market' ship, for although during the summer months, between some of the Atlantic voyages, she operated cruises from Southampton to Scandinavia, the Atlantic Islands and the Mediterranean, these cruises more generally attracted an international mix of passengers; even if the British passengers were often in the majority. In fact, many of her Atlantic voyages were marketed as part of an extended cruise, thus, British passengers could board the ship in Southampton, voyage across to New York and remain aboard while she cruised up to either New England and Canada, or to Bermuda, or down to the Caribbean, and then return in the ship to Southampton. Likewise, similar packages were available for North American passengers to join the ship in New York, and remain aboard for one of the European cruises, and then return home aboard the ship. On 4 January 1975 the *QE2* departed Southampton on her very first cruise around the world, a voyage of ninety-two days. This has been a regular feature almost every year since then, although in 1978, for example, she undertook a ninety-day 'Great Pacific Cruise' instead. With the introduction of the new Cunard liner, *Queen Mary 2*, in 2004, the *QE2* ceased her role as a transatlantic liner and is now based in Southampton as a full-time cruise ship. Having developed an almost legendary status, she will, however, doubtless still attract an international mix of passengers all seeking to travel on the 'greatest ocean liner in the world'.

## *Cunard Countess* and *Cunard Princess*

17,495grt
537ft length overall
75ft breadth
950 passengers (*Countess*) 947 passengers (*Princess*)
Built in 1975 by Burmeister & Wain Skibsbyggeri A/S, Copenhagen, internal fitting by Industria Navali Mechaniche Affini
Powered by twin-screw Burmeister & Wain–Hitachi geared diesels

The *Cunard Countess* and *Cunard Princess* were built primarily to cruise the Caribbean, replacing an earlier, smaller and somewhat less than successful pair of ships, *Cunard Adventurer* and *Cunard Ambassador*, the latter of which had been lost to fire. While far from being the luxury ships that people generally associated with the name Cunard, the *Countess* and *Princess* did establish a degree of popularity. They were mostly based in the Caribbean on seven-day alternating itineraries, which could be combined into a fourteen-day cruise that was particularly attractive to the British market. Sometimes the ships were employed in other cruising areas, such as Alaska or the Mediterranean. While

*Cunard Countess* cruising the Caribbean.

*Cunard Countess* was generally regarded as being the ship that was aimed at the British market (in fact Cunard actually marketed her as 'Britain's favourite Caribbean cruise ship') between November 1990 and October 1991 *Cunard Princess* was repositioned to the Mediterranean. These cruises, marketed heavily in the UK, took the ship into the Black Sea, the Aegean and to Madeira and the Canary Islands – all the traditional cruising areas beloved of British passengers.

*Cunard Countess* was sold to Epirotiki Line in 1995. Briefly she sailed as *Awani Dream* for the Indonesian company Awani Cruises, but she was returned to Epirotiki, which had been restyled as Royal Olympic Cruises, and sails as *Olympia Countess*. *Cunard Princess* was sold to Starlauro Cruises/Mediterranean Shipping Cruises in 1995 and was renamed *Rhapsody*. In their new guises both ships still attract British passengers but are aimed at a broad international market.

## Vistafjord / Caronia

24,292grt
627ft length overall
82ft breadth
670 passengers
Built in 1973 by Swan Hunter Shipbuilders, Wallsend
Powered by twin-screw Sulzer diesel engines

*Vistafjord* was the last ship to be built for the prestigious Norwegian America Line. While designed to operate for at least part of the year on the Oslo to New York run she in fact made very few such voyages, and almost from the very outset of her career was operated

Inherited from Norwegian America Line, *Caronia* was originally called *Vistafjord*. Her last season with Cunard is 2004 and she sails under the Saga flag from 2005 as *Saga Ruby*.

Everyone's idea of a Caribbean cruise is of seeing their ship pictured against a sandy beach and palm trees. In the 1920s it was no different, as this view of the Cunarder *Laconia* at St Vincent shows.

as a cruise ship. She was operated by Norwegian America primarily on cruises from European ports, attracting mainly German and British passengers. Her near sister ship, *Sagafjord*, which had been built in 1965, was meanwhile mainly aimed at the American market. In 1983 both ships were sold, along with the goodwill of what had by this time become Norwegian America Cruises and the right to retain their names, to Cunard. Cunard continued, to some extent, to operate the ships in the same way, with *Sagafjord* more generally aimed at the US and *Vistafjord* aimed at Europe. However, both ships were marketed on both sides of the Atlantic. *Sagafjord* was sold from the fleet in 1996. (See Saga Cruises.) In December 1999, following a major refurbishment, *Vistafjord* was re-launched into the Cunard fleet as *Caronia*. From 2001 she was based full time at Southampton with her cruises focussed exclusively on the British market, sailing extensively to the Mediterranean and Scandinavia. She has now been sold to Saga as *Saga Ruby*, to rejoin her older sister.

## DFDS *(Det Forenede Dampskibsselskab A / S)*

DFDS began their passenger service between Harwich and Esbjerg in Denmark in 1880. Cruises aimed at the UK market commenced in 1987 using the ferry *Winston Churchill* and continued until 1993.

*Winston Churchill*

8,657grt
461.5ft length overall
67ft breadth
400 cruise passengers
Built in1967 by Cantieri Navali del Tirreno e Riuniti, Genoa, Italy
Powered by diesel engines

An extremely stylish car ferry for her time, the *Winston Churchill* was employed on the Harwich–Esbjerg service carrying 462 passengers and up to 180 cars (or an equivalent number of lorries, coaches, etc.).

Made obsolete by the introduction of newer ferries, she was used on a series of experimental cruises to Norway from Denmark in 1987 with the British contingent arriving via the night ferry from the UK. The experiment was deemed a success and extra accommodation was added in 1989. She continued as a part-time cruise but also as a relief ferry until 1993 when she made her last cruise, being used thereafter on charter to other ferry operators. Her small cabins and lack of a swimming pool reduced her appeal as a cruise ship although the lack of a pool may not have been an issue on Norwegian cruises. She did, however, build up a reputation for friendliness and comfort. In this respect she shared some of the attributes of Fred Olsen's *Black Prince*.

## Direct Cruises

Direct Cruises were perhaps the most unsuccessful UK market cruise operation. Direct Holidays were and remain well known in the UK (especially Scotland) as a major package-holiday company.

In 1997, Direct Cruises was set up by the UK-based Direct Holidays to operate the 32,700 *Eugenio Costa* as the *Edinburgh Castle*. Although slightly smaller than P&O's *Canberra*, the ship had something of the looks of the much-loved favourite.

In many respects the Direct Cruise operation resembled that of the *Reina del Mar*, being aimed a particular UK segment, in this case particularly at ex-*Canberra* cruise passengers.

Unfortunately for Direct Cruises, whilst their initial uptake was enough to need a second ship for the first season, the *Apollo*, they had a difficult start. Press reports indicated that the *Edinburgh Castle* was not fully complete in time for the first cruise, although this was related to only a few cabins. The *Apollo* was late out of refit and cruises had to be cancelled. Then, in the summer of 1998, the *Edinburgh Castle* was the subject of a Legionnaires Disease scare. Later in the summer of 1998 Direct Holidays sold the Direct Cruise operation to Airtours (now My Travel). The cruises continued to be operated and branded separately throughout 1999 with an extensive 2000 itinerary being planned. However, the cruise operation was wound up at the end of 1999.

*Apollon*, Direct Cruise's second ship was also the first for Carnival. She sailed for them as *Mardi Gras* and helped create the cruise industry of today.

## Apollon

28,574grt
650ft length overall
87ft breadth
1,256 cruise passengers when in Direct Cruise's service
Built in 1961 by Vickers Armstrong Shipbuilding Ltd, Newcastle
Powered by twin-screw steam turbines

For the early career of this ship please see *Empress of Canada* under Canadian Pacific. Although referred to as *Apollo* in the Direct Cruise literature the formal name of the ship was *Apollon*.

As *Mardi Gras* she was the first ship of the now huge Carnival Group. By 1998 she had been sold to the Royal Olympic Cruise Line and renamed *Apollon*. A classic and beautiful ship she was leased to Direct Cruises following the early rush of bookings for the new cruise line. Direct Cruises anglicised her name from *Apollon* to *Apollo* for marketing purposes. Following the demise of Direct Cruises she was returned to Royal Olympic. After operating some cruises for them in the Mediterranean, she was withdrawn from service in 2000 and sold to be broken up in Alang, India, in late 2003.

*Edinburgh Castle* was used for a short time by Direct Cruises. As *Big Red Boat II*, she lies at Freeport, Bahamas with an uncertain future.

## Edinburgh Castle

33,753grt
713ft length overall
96ft breadth
1,418 passengers
Built in 1966 by Cantieri Riuniti dell' Adriatico, Italy
Powered by steam turbines

Built in 1966 as the three-class *Eugenio C*, she was designed for the Costa Line's Genoa–South America liner route on which she operated on a regular basis for over ten years. Modernised in 1987 as a single-class cruise liner she was renamed *Eugenio Costa* and spent much of her career cruising for the Italian market.

She was leased to Direct Cruises in 1997 as their start-up ship but gained notoriety as mentioned above by having some of her accommodation incomplete at the start of her first cruise for Direct Cruises. Within a few months Direct Cruises was no longer operating and *Edinburgh Castle* was under arrest as a result of the failure of the owners who had leased her to Direct Cruises. In 2000 she became Premier Cruise Line's *Big Red Boat II* operating in the US cruise market. However, Premier Cruises folded in 2000 and their vessels were put up for sale. At the time of writing the ship was still laid up.

# Ellerman Line / Wilson Line

A well-known UK shipping operation, cruises were undertaken during the 1930s.

## City of Nagpur

10,136grt
490ft length overall
59ft breadth
226 first-class and 92 second-class passengers
Built in 1922 by Workman Clark & Co. Ltd, Belfast
Powered by single-screw quadruple-expansion engines

## City of Paris

10,902grt
504ft length overall
59ft breadth
230 first-class and 100 second-class passengers
Built in 1922 by Swan Hunter & Wigham Richardson Ltd, Newcastle
Powered by single-screw geared-turbine engines

Initially, the *City of Nagpur*, and her sister *City of Paris*, were employed on the UK–Japan service, then being transferred to the run to Bombay. In 1933 the *City of Nagpur* was moved to the South African service, and in 1936 she was joined by the *City of Paris*. Both ships occasionally operated cruises.

In 1925 the *City of Nagpur* undertook a cruise to the northern capitals: calling at Stockholm, Copenhagen, Oslo and Gothenburg. During 1934 and 1935 she made

Ellerman & Bucknall's *City of Paris* was a favourite cruise ship on the long haul to South Africa. A sixty-three-day cruise in 1933 was 65 guineas.

cruises to the Mediterranean, and in 1936, under the management of the Wilson Line, she made cruises to Scandinavia.

The *City of Paris* undertook a series of cruises in 1923 and 1924. She also operated under the Ellerman Wilson Line in 1934; sailing from Hull on a series of Scandinavian cruises.

The *City of Nagpur* was sunk in a submarine attack in April 1941. The *City of Paris*, however, survived the war, having served as a troopship, and was returned to the South Africa service. She was finally scrapped at Newport, Mon., in 1956.

## *Calypso*

3,820grt
354ft length overall
44ft breadth
100 passengers (approximately) when cruising
Built in 1898
Powered by single-screw triple-expansion engines

*Calypso* was acquired by Ellerman's Wilson Line in November 1920 from the Shipping Controller. She had been built for Belgian owners as the *Bruxellesville* but on completion she was operated on the Antwerp–Congo service under the ownership of the Woermann Line – controlled by the Soc. Maritime du Congo. In 1901, having been transferred to full Woermann ownership, she was renamed *Alexandra Woermann* and used on the Hamburg–West Africa route.

Her usual employment for Ellerman's Wilson Line was on the Hull–Oslo service but in 1933 she inaugurated a series of ten-day cruises from London (Millwall Docks), to Copenhagen, Oslo and Kristiansand. Such was the success of these cruises that they were continued until the autumn of 1936. *Calypso* was then briefly laid up, and was then sold to be scrapped in Belgium.

The 8,331grt *City of Canterbury* also operated cruises under the Wilson Line flag, from Hull to Kristiansand and Oslo during 1933.

# First Choice Holidays

The entry of Airtours, Thomson and Direct Holidays into the UK cruise market with ships chartered solely for the use of their customers was soon followed by the other major UK travel company – First Choice. Initially operating with chartered vessels, in 2001 the company announced a partnership with Royal Caribbean to form Island Escape Holidays using the Royal Caribbean vessel *Viking Serenade* as the *Island Escape* from 2002. Described as 'aspirational cruising' the ship is marketed to young families as an alternative to or in conjunction with resort stays. In this respect it has a similarity to P&O's *Ocean Village* operation. Many of the on-board services are provided by well-known UK retailers – Costa Coffee, Oddbins and Holmes Place.

The *Island Escape* was the subject of a 2002–2003 UK television 'docusoap' in which many of the operation's teething problems were seen by a large audience. At the time of writing it is uncertain as to whether the publicity gained from the TV series will aid or hinder the company.

## Ausonia

12,609grt
522.5ft length overall
70ft breadth
701 cruise passengers
Built in 1957 by Cantieri Riuniti dell' Adriatico, Italy
Powered by steam turbines

An old, but well-kept, classic ship, *Ausonia* was designed for the Trieste–Beirut service of Adriatica Line Spa. She was converted into a one-class cruise ship in 1978–1979 and operated in the Italian and general European cruise market. Sold to Louis Cruise Lines in 1998 she was chartered by First Choice in 2000 and cruised for them until *Island Escape* entered service in 2002.

The refurbishment by Louis Cruise Lines was excellent and the ship provided a good value-for-money product for the UK cruise passenger with some interesting itineraries including some sailings from the UK.

Since the end of the charter she has rejoined the fleet of Louis Cruise Lines.

## Bolero

15,781grt
526ft length overall
75ft breadth
984 cruise passengers
Built in 1968 by AG Weser, Germany
Powered by diesel engines

Originally Kloster's *Starward*, and one of the ships to kick-start cruising in the USA in the late 1960s, *Bolero* operated for First Choice.

Built as the *Starward* for Kloster, she was designed for Caribbean cruising out of the USA. In 1995 she was purchased by the European cruise market operator Festival Cruises and renamed *Bolero*. Prior to 2000 she was chartered to First Choice and operated the First Choice cruise itineraries out of Majorca. Returned to Festival Cruises she was transferred to the Spanish Cruise Line (one-third owned by Festival) to operate in the Spanish cruise market.

*Island Escape*

40,132grt
623ft length overall
88.6ft breadth
1,863 cruise passengers
Built in 1982 by Dubigeon-Normandie, France
Powered by diesel engines

Entering service in 1982 as the *Scandinavia* she began her career as a cruise/ferry taking cars and passengers between the USA and the Bahamas before being transferred to ferry operations in the Baltic. In 1985 she was sold to the Sundance Cruise Corporation and refitted before being renamed *Stardancer* for cruising on the West Coast of Canada and the USA. She was acquired by Royal Caribbean in 1990, renamed *Viking Serenade* and had her car deck removed and replaced by cabins. In this guise she operated on the West Coast of North America. In 2001 it was announced that, as the *Island Escape*, she would introduce the new Royal Caribbean/First Choice cruise service out of Majorca.

# Fred Olsen

Fred Olsen Cruises has gained a very loyal UK following for its cruises since it entered the UK market in the 1960s. Fred Olsen Cruises are unashamedly British.

For reasons connected with family ties, the Olsen shipping group has had interests in both Norway and the Canary Islands for a number of years.

In conjunction with the Bergen Line, in 1966 Fred Olsen introduced two very modern ferries on the North Sea route between the UK and Norway and on the UK–Canaries run. Sailing as *Black Prince* and *Black Watch* for Fred Olsen in winter down to the Canaries, the ships then operated as *Venus* and *Jupiter*, respectively, for the Bergen Line summer service across the North Sea.

The ships not only provided a ferry service from the UK to the Canaries but also offered cruises with passengers staying on board when the islands were reached and then returning to the UK.

So successful were the Canary cruises that *Black Prince* was converted into a full-time cruise ship and was for many years one of the few cruise ships operating out of UK ports. In the 1990s and early years of this century, Fred Olsen has expanded to a three-ship operation with cruises to an increasing number of global destinations. The company has specialised in small–medium-sized ships that are targeted at the traditional UK cruise market, a philosophy that had gained considerable repeat business.

Olsen's *Black Prince* is often chartered out to organisations such as the National Trust for Scotland, which runs cruises for members on a regular basis.

## Black Prince and Black Watch (1966)

11,209grt
470ft length overall
66.6ft breadth
472 cruise passengers
Built in 1966 by Fender Werft, Germany
Powered by diesel engines

In 1966 Fred Olsen and the Bergen Line entered into a twenty-year agreement to share ships on their respective routes. Bergen Line operated a summer service from the UK to Norway whilst Fred Olsen ran from the UK to the Canary Islands in winter. Sailing as *Black Prince* and *Black Watch* for Fred Olsen in winter down to the Canaries, the ships then operated as *Venus* and *Jupiter*, respectively, for the Bergen Line summer service across the North Sea. When built they were the largest ferries in the world. The service to the Canary Islands was often used as a cruise by many passengers.

At the end of the twenty-year agreement, *Black Prince* was retained by Fred Olsen for conversion to a full-time cruise ship, whilst *Jupiter* went to the Bergen Line. In 1991 *Jupiter* was sold to become the ferry *Crown M* in the Mediterranean and then in the late 1990s sold again to Lebanese interests as the *Byblos*. Laid up since the sale her future appears bleak.

*Black Prince*, however, became a very successful and well-loved cruise ship. Although small and somewhat old-fashioned the ship has a friendly ambience and some extremely well-furnished public rooms. All of the cabins have been refurbished, although the facilities in some are not as sophisticated as those in modern cruise ships. Part of her old car deck and the stern doors are used as a portable marina for watersport activities when at anchor – a facility found on few other cruise vessels.

In recent years *Black Prince* has been available for charter, Page & Moy have used the ship on a regular basis, and also to pioneer new itineraries such as Cuba and South America. Despite her small size she has proved to have excellent seakeeping qualities and is quite capable of an Atlantic crossing.

## Black Watch (1996)

28,492grt as lengthened
674ft length overall as lengthened
82.5ft breadth
843 cruise passengers
Built in 1972 by Wartsila, Finland
Powered by diesel engines

Built as the 22,000grt *Royal Viking Star* for the Royal Viking Line (a consortium that included the Bergen Line) and designed for long-distance cruising, the vessel was lengthened in 1981 by 90ft in order to increase her carrying capacity. There were two other sister ships and all three have found gainful employment over the years.

Norwegian Cruise Line (NCL) acquired Royal Viking Line in 1984 and renamed the vessel *Westward*. Another change of name occurred in 1994 when she became the *Star Odyssey* of the Royal Cruise Line.

In 1995 she was purchased by Fred Olsen but did not enter service at once as she was chartered back to the Royal Cruise Line for her final season with them.

Since her entry into Olsen service as *Black Watch* she has proved a popular addition to the fleet and has allowed the company to expand its itineraries as well as offering enhanced cabin facilities to its customers.

## Braemar

19,089grt
537ft length overall
74ft breadth
821 cruise passengers
Built in 1993 by Union Navale de Levante, Spain
Powered by diesel engines

To cope with a growing demand for UK market cruises, Olsen purchased the *Crown Dynasty* from the failed Crown Cruise Line in 2001, renaming her *Braemar*. *Crown*

*Braemar* helped expand the Olsen operation to three vessels, a result of their marketing good-value cruises and gaining much repeat business with loyal customers.

*Dynasty* and *Crown Jewel* were ordered by the Commodore Cruise Line. In 1993 Cunard and Crown Cruise Line entered into a ten-year agreement to operate the ships (plus *Crown Monarch*) under the Cunard Crown Cruises name. The agreement did not last for anywhere near ten years and in 1997 the Crown Dynasty was transferred to Majesty Cruise Lines but by 1999 was again operating under the Crown Cruise Line name.

The ship slotted in neatly in terms of size between *Black Prince* and *Black Watch* and appears to be gaining a loyal following. Recognising the needs of the UK cruise market Fred Olsen converted a number of double cabins into ones for single cruise passengers. Internally the ship is well appointed and has a five-deck high atrium and a good selection of public rooms.

## Blenheim

10, 420grt
490ft length overall
65.5ft breadth
396 cruise passengers
Built in 1970 by Upper Clyde Shipbuilders, Scotland
Powered by diesel engines

A slightly larger version of *Black Prince*, *Blenheim* operated to Norway in the summer (when she could accommodate 995 passengers and 300 cars) on the scheduled ferry service from the UK and on the scheduled cruise/liner service to the Canary Islands in the winter.

She was disposed of to DFDS in 1981 and in 1982 entered service in the US cruise market as the *Scandinavian Sea* on the ferry/cruise route between Florida and the Bahamas.

She caught fire on 9 March 1984 whilst on a day cruise. No lives were lost but the ship was declared a total loss. Notwithstanding the status of the ship as a loss, she was purchased firstly by a Greek and then a US buyer, becoming *Discovery 1*, under which name she operated day cruises out of Florida. Fire struck again in May 1996 and she was scrapped later that year.

# Fyffes

Fyffes bananas were once a household name in the UK. The Fyffes Group (known as Elders & Fyffes prior to 1969) was a subsidiary of the United Fruit Company of the USA. Elders & Fyffes were not only involved in the growing and wholesaling of bananas but also provided their own ships to bring the perishable product from the Canaries and West Indies to the UK. Before the advent of commercially-viable air freight operations the shipping of bananas required fast ships with insulated cargo holds.

Elders & Fyffes' ships used a series of cargo/passenger ships on the banana run between the West Indies and the UK and after the Second World War placed in service two brand new ships that had accommodation for 103 passengers, many of whom used the ship's twenty-six-day out and back voyage to the West Indies as a cruise experience. With white hulls to reflect the heat the ships provided a leisurely cruise experience with a high degree of traditional comfort.

The huge increase in air freight and air travel from the 1960s onwards, and the huge increases in oil prices, drove Elders & Fyffes out of the passenger ship trade in 1972.

*Golfito*, built by Alexander Stephen and Sons at Linthouse, is shown here leaving Southampton in July 1960.

### Camito and Golfito

8,687grt
447.5ft length overall
62ft breadth
103 passengers
Built in 1949 (*Golfito*) and 1956 (*Camito*) by Alexander Stephen & Sons, Scotland
Powered by double-reduction turbines

Virtually sisters, although built seven years apart, the ships provided very comfortable accommodation and facilities for 103 passengers. As built neither had air-conditioning, an omission that the company remedied in 1966, at which time the accommodation was slightly reduced to 99. It was hoped that the provision of air-conditioning and improved accommodation would allow both the ships to compete with the airlines and attract new cruise passengers.

The rise in the price of fuel oil and changes to the means of packing and storing bananas saw the ships become more and more unprofitable. *Golfito* was sold for scrap in 1972 with *Camito* following her to the breakers' yard in 1973.

## Greek Line

The Greek Line decided to add cruising for the UK market to its portfolio of operations in the early 1960s.

Firstly, the company operated the *Arkadia*, acquired in 1958, and then in 1962 the Netherland Line vessel *Johan Van Oldenbarnevelt* was purchased and renamed *Lakonia*. The vessel entered service in 1963 and operated out of Southampton but whilst on a Christmas cruise in 1963 she caught fire off Maderia and sank with serious loss of life. To replace the *Lakonia* the Norwegian America Line *Oslofjord* was chartered for a short period. As far as the UK cruising market was concerned the company never really recovered from the loss of the *Lakonia*.

## Arkadia

20,265grt
550ft length overall
83.5ft breadth
1,583 cruise passengers
Built in 1931 by Vickers Armstrong, Newcastle-upon-Tyne; rebuilt by Thorneycroft, Southampton, 1948
Powered by four turbo-electric engines

She was launched in 1931 as the *Monarch of Bermuda* for the weekly New York–Bermuda service of the Furness Bermuda Line. Built to the highest standards of elegance, both the *Monarch of Bermuda* and her near sister, the *Queen of Bermuda*, were extremely popular with the Americans who made up the majority of the company's customers.

Following war service, the *Monarch of Bermuda* was being refitted to her pre-war glory when she caught fire and was gutted in March 1947.

The hulk was purchased by the UK government and converted into the emigrant ship *New Australia* for the traffic to Australia from the UK and Europe. With only a single funnel in place of the original three (two and a dummy) plus a strange bipod exhaust/mast forward of the funnel, she presented a very unbalanced appearance. Shaw Savill managed the *New Australia* until 1958 when she was sold to become the Greek Line's *Arkadia*. As *Arkadia* she operated in the UK and the more international cruise market until 1968 when she was withdrawn and broken up. The ship had had an interesting career and bore little resemblance to the elegant three-funnelled original design by the end of her service.

*Arkadia* was broken up in 1968 after a career that involved her sailing with a combination of three, two or one funnels.

*Lakonia* at Lisbon, shortly before the fire on board that killed 128 passengers and crew.

## *Lakonia*

20,214grt
608ft length overall
74ft breadth
1,186 cruise passengers
Built in 1930 by the Netherlands Shipbuilding & Dry Dock Co., Amsterdam
Powered by twin diesel engines

Built in 1930 as the *Johan Van Oldenbarnevelt* for the Netherlands Line service between the Netherlands and the Dutch East Indies, the ship served as a troopship during the war and was modernised in 1959.

She operated the company's round-the-world service with the *Oranje* and the *William Ruys*. The three ships were expensive to operate and could not compete with the Greek and Italian ships on such a service. She was sold in 1962 to the Greek Line and refitted as a 1,186 one-class cruise ship for the emerging UK market.

Her career as a cruise ship was short-lived as she caught fire off Madeira on 22 December 1963. Attempts were made to tow the hulk into port but after six days she sank. Tragically 128 passengers and crew were killed. The *Lakonia* disaster was the worst disaster to befall a cruise ship operating in the UK market.

The Norwegian America liner *Oslofjord* was chartered by the Greek Line for a year in 1967 for Southampton-based cruises.

## Oslofjord

16,884grt
577ft length overall
72ft breadth
179 first-class and 467 tourist-class passengers
Built in 1949 by the Netherlands Shipbuilding Co., Amsterdam
Powered by twin Stork diesel engines

*Oslofjord* was chartered by the Greek Line in 1967–1968 to operate cruises from Southampton. The charter only lasted for a single year and the vessel remained in Norwegian America Line livery. In 1968 she began a two-year charter to Costa Cruises and was renamed *Fulvia*. On 20 July 1970 she caught fire off the Canary Islands and sank, fortunately without any loss of life.

## Kloster's Sunward Ferries

The name of Norwegian Knot Kloster is best known in the US cruise market where the *Sunward* is often referred to as the most important ship in the growth of the US market from the middle of the 1960s onwards. The *Sunward* pioneered the mass-market cruise business out of Florida. The Kloster family were well-established Norwegian cargo and ferry operators.

What is less well known is that *Sunward* was a UK market cruise ship, albeit for a very short period before she went to the USA. She was introduced on a new Southampton–Vigo–Lisbon–Gibraltar cruise/ferry service in June 1966.

Whilst prospects for the new venture looked good, offering as it did both a cruise and a ferry service, it was not in fact successful and closed after only nineteen weeks.


*Sunward*

8,666grt
457ft length overall
68ft breadth
558 cruise passengers
Built in 1966 by Mekanisker Verksted, Bergen
Powered by diesel engines


One of the first cruise/ferries, *Sunward* was intended for the new Kloster car ferry service from Southampton to Gibraltar via Vigo and Lisbon in June 1966. She introduced new standards of comfort to the UK ferry market and the intention was that the service could be as much a cruise as a ferry operation. Unfortunately, due to British government restrictions on currency for foreign travel and continued tension with Spain regarding Gibraltar, the service came to an end after just nineteen weeks. The ship was transferred to the USA, where she operated as the first ship of Norwegian Caribbean Lines offering 3 to 7-night cruises. Norwegian Caribbean Lines grew rapidly and as new, larger ships based on her design were introduced she became surplus to requirements. Sold in 1972 she reverted to the ferry trade as the *Ile De Beauté* of Cie Générale Transméditerranée operating between France and Sardinia. In 1976 she was sold again to become a floating hotel in the Persian Gulf with the name *Grand Flotel*. She returned to ferry service in 1978 as *Saudi Moon 1*, on the Suez–Saudi Arabia service. She continued to pass between owners becoming a cruise ship for diving enthusiasts in 1988 with the name *Ocean Spirit*. This career lasted until 1990 when she entered the one-day cruise market out of Florida with the name *Scandinavian Song*. The UK–Gibraltar service was not the only failed cruise/ferry service that she operated and which failed after a very short time. In 1994 she was chartered out, bearing the name *Santiago de Cuba*, to operate cruises out of Cuba. This venture failed within a few short weeks. Later that year she went to the Far East to operate day cruises out of Penang, being renamed *The Empress*. She was scrapped in 2004.


## Lamport & Holt Ltd

A long-established UK shipping company, Lamport & Holt entered the cruise market briefly in the 1930s.

## Vandyck

13,241grt
559ft length overall
64ft breadth
300 first-class, 150 second-class and 230 third-class passengers
Built in 1921 by Workman, Clark & Co. Ltd, Belfast
Powered by twin-screw geared turbines

## Voltaire

13,301grt
559ft length overall
64ft breadth
300 first-class, 150 second-class and 230 third-class passengers
Built in 1923 by Workman, Clark & Co. Ltd, Belfast
Powered by twin-screw quadruple-expansion engines

Both ships entered service between New York and the River Plate, remaining on this
route until 1930 when they were withdrawn and laid up; the *Vandyck* in Southampton
and the *Voltaire* on the River Blackwater. In 1932, Lamport & Holt took advantage of
the sudden boom in cruising, converting first the *Vandyck* and then *Voltaire*, which joined
her in the following year. Both ships became very popular, operating cruises out of

Lamport & Holt's *Vandyck* in a Norwegian fjord.

Southampton until 1939. *Vandyck* was converted into a troop transport, and was sunk in June 1940 off the coast of Norway. *Voltaire* was converted into an Armed Merchant Cruiser, and in April 1941 engaged the German auxiliary cruiser *Thor* in the mid-Atlantic. After an exchange of fire lasting one hour, *Voltaire* was destroyed and sank.

# North of Scotland & Orkney & Shetland Steam Navigation Company

The company, as its name suggests, was formed to operate the passenger and cargo ferry services between the mainland of Scotland and the islands of Orkney and Shetland. Originally founded as the Leith & Clyde Shipping Company in 1760, by the 1880s it had adopted its new name and was usually referred to as the North Company.

In the early summer of 1886 the *St Rognvald* undertook the first of the company's Norwegian cruises with ninety passengers paying £10 each for a nine-day cruise. So successful was the first cruise that the company instituted a regular summer cruise schedule using the *St Rognvald*. In 1887 the company ordered the first ever purpose-built cruise ship – the *St Sunniva* – to operate alongside the *St Rognvald*. By 1889 cruises were being offered to the Baltic and the Mediterranean in addition to the Norwegian coast. *St Sunniva* was often chartered in the Mediterranean area, thus bringing in additional revenues for the company. By the start of the twentieth century, however, competition was beginning to grow and with the loss of the *St Rognvald* in 1900 the company began to withdraw from the cruise market to concentrate on its core ferry business, the final cruises being in 1908. The company was taken over by Coast Lines in 1961, Coast Lines itself becoming part of P&O in 1971. In the 1990s, however, P&O (who operated the services from Scrabster and Aberdeen to Orkney and Shetland until 2002 when the contract was awarded to Northlink) offered mini-cruises aboard their *St Sunniva*. The mini-cruises used the regular ferry sailings from Aberdeen but included all meals and there were also optional excursions that could be purchased.

## *St Rognvald*

984grt
241ft length overall
31ft breadth
100 cruise passengers
Built in 1883 by Hall Russell & Co., Aberdeen
Powered by a triple-expansion, coal-fired steam engine, single screw

She was built for the weekend Leith–Aberdeen–Kirkwall (Orkney)–Lerwick (Shetland) service in 1883. The ship operated the earliest North Company cruises in 1886 with berths for 100 cruise passengers. Her schedule included cruising in summer and the ferry service in winter and it was on the latter that she was wrecked on Burgh Head, Stronsay, on 24 April 1900.

## St Sunniva

864grt
235ft length overall
30ft breadth
142 passengers
Built in 1887 by Hall Russell & Co., Aberdeen
Powered by a triple-expansion, coal-fired steam engine, single screw

Important as the first ever purpose-built cruise ship, the *St Sunniva* was built as a result of the cruises undertaken by the *St Rognvald*. Of yacht-like appearance she was a very handsome vessel. She operated to the Norwegian fjords, the Baltic and the Mediterranean where she also undertook a number of charters. When the company left the cruise market in 1908 she was placed on the direct service to Lerwick with cargo space added and some passenger accommodation removed. She served until 1930 when she ran aground on the island of Mousa on 10 April. Salvage was impossible and she was declared a total constructive loss.

## My Travel

See under Airtours.

## Orient Line

The entries in this section refer to the Orient Line of the UK, a company in which P&O held the majority shareholding from 1919 and with whom Orient Line merged in 1965.

The Orient Line was formed by Anderson, Anderson & Company in 1878 in conjunction with the Pacific Steam Navigation Company (PSNC) to operate between the UK and Australia. Four PSNC ships – *Chimbozaro*, *Cuzco*, *Garonne* and *Lusitania* – were chartered and then bought outright. This explains the South American origin of three of these vessels, *Lusitania* being the exception. PSNC was acquired by the Royal Mail Steam Packet Company in 1906. In 1919 P&O acquired a majority shareholding in Orient Line and the two companies merged in 1960 with the outstanding minority shares in Orient Line being acquired by P&O in 1965.

Orient Line were amongst the early pioneers of cruising for the UK market, the Norwegian fjords being an area cruised by many of the company's ships.

A number of the ships listed below only cruised for a short period due to both the First and Second World Wars. Orient Line lost 50 per cent of its ships in each conflict. The vessels are included, however, as it was the company's intention to use them for both line and cruise voyages if war had not intervened.

## Chimborazo

3,847grt
384ft length overall
41.5ft breadth
72 first-class, 92 second-class and 265 third-class passengers
Built in 1871 by John Elder & Co., Glasgow
Powered by a coal-fired compound engine driving one screw

A near sister to *Garonne* and *Lusitania*, *Chimborazo* was designed for the PSNC South American service but was chartered in 1877 and then bought outright by Orient Line in 1878 for the Australia service. From 1891 she was used in the summer for cruising in Norwegian waters and the Mediterranean. She was sold in 1894 to a shipbroker and renamed *Cleopatra*. In 1895 she was sold to the Ocean Cruising & Highland Yachting Company who only owned her until 1897 when she was broken up at Preston, Lancashire.

## Cuzco

3,898grt
384ft length overall
41.5ft breadth
70 first-class, 92 second-class and 228 third-class passengers
Built in 1871 by John Elder & Co., Glasgow
Powered by a coal-fired compound engine driving one screw

A near sister to *Garonne* and *Lusitania* and a sister of *Chimborazo*, *Cuzco* was designed for the PSNC South American service but was chartered in 1877 and then bought outright by Orient Line in 1878 for the Australia service. She was switched to full-time cruising in 1902. In 1905 she was withdrawn and sold to Italian shipbreakers.

## Garonne

3,876grt
382ft length overall
41.5ft breadth
60 first-class, 100 second and 320 third-class passengers
Built in 1878 by Napier & Sons, Glasgow
Powered by a coal-fired compound engine driving one screw

Built for PSNC in 1871, *Garonne*, an elegant ship complete with auxiliary sails and a bowsprit, was chartered from PSNC for the London–Melbourne service in 1877 and purchased outright for £71,570 in 1878. By 1897 the ship had completed twenty-five mail voyages to Australia and forty-one cruises. Since 1889 she had been employed almost exclusively in the cruise market.

She was considerably outdated by 1897 and she was sold firstly to John Porter of Liverpool and then almost immediately re-sold to the F. Waterhouse Company in Seattle. Under the US flag she carried prospectors to the Klondike for the gold rush and served the US Government as a troopship in the Spanish–American War of 1898. She was scrapped in Genoa in 1905.

## Lusitania

3,877grt
380ft length overall
41ft breadth
85 first-class, 100 second-class and 270 third-class passengers
Built in 1878 by Laird Brothers, Birkenhead
Powered by a coal-fired compound engine driving one screw

Similar in appearance to the *Garonne*, the Orient Line *Lusitania* is less well known than the Cunard liner of 1907 of the same name that was torpedoed with great loss of life in 1915.

*Lusitania* was designed for the PSNC South American service but like *Garonne* was chartered and then bought outright by Orient Line for the Australia service. In 1882 and again in 1884 she was chartered by the Government, firstly as a troopship and latterly as an Armed Merchant Cruiser (AMC). Following her military service she was refitted in 1886 and was then chartered to PSNC until 1893. Returned to Orient Line she made her last mail sailing in 1897.

From 1897 until 1889 she cruised exclusively, until in August of 1899 she collided with a jetty in Copenhagen. Orient Line desired to replace the ship and she was sold to Elder Dempster Line for £15,000 and placed on the Beaver Line service to Canada.

She ran aground on 27 June 1901 near Cape Race, Newfoundland. There were no casualties but the ship was declared a total loss.

## Ophir

6,814grt
482ft length overall
53.5ft breadth
230 first-class, 142 second-class and 520 steerage-class passengers
Built in 1891 by Robert Napier & Sons, Glasgow
Powered by two triple-expansion engines

Built as the first twin-screw vessel on the Australian mail service, *Ophir* was refitted as a Royal Yacht for the visit of the Duke and Duchess of Cornwall and York (later King George V and Queen Mary) for their visit to Australia and New Zealand in 1901. The ship called at a number of other British possessions on both the outward and homeward journeys. From the summer of 1902 onwards she made regular cruises from the UK to the Norwegian fjords. A thirteen-day cruise to Norway in 1907 cost from 13 guineas.

In 1914, on the outbreak of war she was chartered by the Admiralty, initially as a mail steamer (her normal role) but then as an Armed Merchant Cruiser (AMC) from 1915 onwards. After service in the Far East she returned to the UK to pay off. She was retained by the Admiralty and finally sold for a mere £6,000 in 1922 for scrapping at Troon, Scotland, after lying idle since 1919.

## Orama

19,840grt
632ft length overall
75ft breadth
582 first-class and 1,244 third-class passengers
Built in 1924 by John Brown & Co., Clydebank
Powered by twin single-reduction-geared turbines

The *Orama* was the first of a group of five ships launched between 1924 and 1929 for the Australia mail service. She followed a pattern of line voyages to Australia and UK-based cruises to the Mediterranean and the Norwegian fjords. Her accommodation was changed to 484 First Class and 498 Tourist Class in 1935, making her more acceptable as a cruise ship.

Her last pleasure cruise was out of Sydney in the summer of 1939 and by 12 December she was in government service as a troopship. On 6 June 1940 she was in company with the hospital ship *Atlantis*, proceeding to Narvik in Norway to evacuate troops, when the German cruiser *Hipper* spotted them and her escorting destroyers. Respecting the conventions governing hospital ships, the *Atlantis* was allowed to proceed but the *Omara* was attacked in the belief that she was an Armed Merchant Cruiser. Fortunately, she had no troops on board or else the carnage would have been horrific. As it was twenty members of her crew were killed whilst the rest were rescued by the German ships and spent the war in Stalag XIIIA.

## Orcades (1937)

See under *Orion*.

## Orcades (1948)

28,472grt
708.5ft length overall
90.5ft breadth
770 first-class and 742 tourist-class passengers
Built in 1948 by Vickers Armstrong, Barrow in Furness
Powered by twin double-reduction-geared turbines

It was fitting that the first post-war ship for the Orient Line should take the name of the last ship built before the war and so tragically lost – *Orcades*. The first of three similar vessels, *Orcades* had a similarity with her pre-war namesake with just one funnel and one mast, but she was of much sleeker appearance – gone were the old style, cowled ventilators and her bridge was much further back near the funnel. Her cruise career started in 1951 and in the early 1950s she was given a black steampipe to the top of the funnel (its resemblance was to the hats worn as part of Welsh national dress) in an attempt to alleviate the problem of smut falling on her open decks.

In 1959 she became the first Orient Line ship to be fitted with what is now the norm for cruise ships – air-conditioning. As a result of the merger with P&O she joined the combined fleet and carried out regular cruises not only for the UK market but also for the Australian one. She was refitted as a one-class ship in 1964 with accommodation for 1,400 passengers. Her final years were spent solely cruising from Southampton where she decommissioned in October 1972, reaching the breakers yard in Taiwan in February 1973.

## Orford

19,941grt
658ft length overall
75ft breadth
520 first-class and 1,162 third-class passengers
Built in 1928 by Vickers, Barrow in Furness
Powered by twin geared turbines

The fourth ship of the *Orama* type to enter service, she followed the pattern of line voyages to Australia and UK-based cruises to the Mediterranean and the Norwegian fjords. Like her sisters, her accommodation was changed to 468 First Class and 515 Tourist Class in 1935, making her more acceptable as a cruise ship.

Her career was cut short in 1940. She had been loaned to the French government as a troopship together with *Otranto* and was tasked to transport troops from Madagascar to Marseilles. She arrived at the French port and, whereas *Otranto* was sent to a secure base in the port, *Orford* was directed to an exposed anchorage. The Luftwaffe found her on 1 June 1940 and the subsequent bombing and sinking cost the lives of fourteen crew, together with twenty-five injured. She was the first Orient Line vessel to be lost in the war.

## *Oriana* (1960)

See under the P&O list.

## *Ormonde*

14,981grt
580.5ft length overall
66.5ft breadth
278 first-class, 195 second-class and 1,000 third-class passengers
Built in 1917 by John Brown & Co., Clydebank
Powered by four single-reduction-geared turbines

An Orient liner at Algiers in the 1930s.

*Ormonde* was laid down in 1913 but due to the war she was not completed until 1917, and then only because the need for ships was so great. Initially she was fitted out as a troopship and did not leave government service until 1919.

She was the largest Orient Line vessel to date. Her maiden voyage for the company was on the Australia mail service on 11 November 1919. Her first cruise for the Orient Line was to the Norwegian fjords in the summer of 1922. In 1923 she was converted to a two-class ship and continued her series of Norwegian cruises. From the 13 guineas minimum fare in 1907 in *Ophir*, the same cruise was now 20 guineas.

She spent much of the time between 1924 and 1939 on the Australia service, being converted to a one-class tourist ship in 1933 with accommodation for 700 passengers. By that time passengers were demanding more room!

In the late spring and early summer of 1939 she spent the season cruising the Norwegian fjords, leaving for Australia on 12 August. On her arrival back in the UK she was requisitioned as a troopship, a role she carried out with distinction throughout the war.

In 1920 she was converted to an 'austerity' liner carrying 1,050 emigrant passengers from the UK to Australia. She undertook this work until the number of emigrants began to decline (although it was to pick up again later) and was withdrawn in 1952 to be scrapped at Dalmuir, Scotland, only a few miles from where she had been launched thirty-five years before.

## *Ormuz*

14,588grt
550ft length overall
67ft breadth
292 first-class and 828 third-class passengers (no second-class accommodation)
Built in 1914 by Bremen Vulkan, Germany
Powered by two quadruple-expansion engines

*Ormuz* was one of three German liners handed over to the British Government as war reparations and purchased by Orient Line. Many British shipping companies had their sunken tonnage replaced with German vessels. The other two vessels which were slightly smaller and not used for cruising were the *Omar* (ex-Königin Luise) and the *Orcades* (ex-*Prinz Ludwig*).

As the *Zeppelin*, *Ormuz* had been launched by Count Zeppelin (of airship fame) himself on 9 June 1914 and was intended to be one of a series of vessels for a Norddeutscher Lloyd (NDL) service to Australia. She was still not completed when war broke out but was fitted out by 1915 and then laid up, as there would have been no chance of her breaking the blockade the Royal Navy was maintaining against German commerce.

Initially, after being handed over to Britain, she was owned by the Shipping Controller and managed by the White Star Line. After a refit in 1920 she was purchased by the Orient Line and given her new name.

Her first role was to resume the Norwegian cruises, the first of which was undertaken in June 1921. She continued a mix of mail voyages to Australia and cruises from the UK until 1926 when she was withdrawn, no longer being suitable for Orient Line service.

She eventually ended up back in the hands of her original owners (NDL) in 1927 and they paid a mere £25,700 for her. Renamed *Dresden*, she became one of the pioneer 'Strength through Joy' cruise ships initiated by the Nazi government and organized by Dr Robert Ley, the leader of the Labour Front in Germany. These cruises were designed as a low-cost opportunity for German workers to undertake cruising and next to the 'booze cruises' out of the USA in the 1920s were an example of early mass-market cruising.

In June 1934 she struck an uncharted rock in Norwegian waters and sank. Fortunately all bar three of her passengers and crew were saved.

## Oronsay (1925)

20,001grt
633ft length overall
75ft breadth
600 first-class and 1,120 third-class passengers
Built in 1925 by John Brown & Co., Clydebank
Powered by twin high-reduction-geared turbines

Launched three months after *Orama*, *Oronsay* followed the usual pattern of line voyages to Australia and UK-based cruises to the Mediterranean and the Norwegian fjords. Her accommodation was changed to 501 First Class and 482 Tourist Class in 1935, making her more acceptable as a cruise ship.

Requisitioned as a troopship she was enroute to the UK with only 50 passengers, mainly civilians, when she was torpedoed and sunk by the Italian submarine *Archimede* on 9 October 1942. Days later the Royal Navy picked up 266 survivors (passengers and crew) with another boatload of survivors being picked up by another merchant ship. Within 48 hours of her loss, the *Orcades* of 1937 was also lost.

*Oronsay* (1925) and *Otranto* at Copenhagen, *c*.1930.

## Oronsay (1951)

28,136grt
708.5ft length overall
93.5ft breadth
688 first-class and 833 tourist-class passengers
Built in 1948 by Vickers Armstrong, Barrow in Furness
Powered by twin double-reduction-geared turbines

The second new ship for the company after the war, *Oronsay's* entry into service was delayed by a fire whilst fitting out – a mishap that has occurred to a number of other vessels. Undertaking a similar liner and cruise schedule to her sister *Orcades* she was fitted with air-conditioning in 1959. She was formally transferred to P&O in 1964 and by 1972 she was operating solely as a one-class cruise ship, although more from Australia than the UK. Her final UK cruise was from the UK to Maderia, the Canaries, Morocco, Gibraltar and Northern Spain in July–August 1975. She made one more trip to Sydney and then a final cruise to Hong Kong where she remained before sailing to the breaker's yard in October 1975.

## Orsova

29,091grt
722.5ft length overall
90.5ft breadth
685 first-class and 800 tourist-class passengers
Built in 1954 by Vickers Armstrong, Barrow in Furness
Powered by six sets of double-reduction-geared turbines

*Orsova* late in her career just before scrapping in 1974.

The last ship to come out as a pure Orient Line vessel (the *Oriana* of 1960 was ordered by Orient Line but entered service after the merger with P&O), *Orsova* had a similar appearance to *Orcades* and *Oronsay* but dispensed with the mast altogether. *Orsova* was fitted with air-conditioning in 1960 and was in refit when the company merged with P&O, although it would be 1965 before she was registered to the new concern. The ship operated summer cruises from Southampton but was never converted to one class. Even in 1972 there were first-class inside cabins with bunk beds and no toilet facilities!

Late in 1973 it was announced that *Canberra* was to be withdrawn and that *Orsova* and *Oriana* would operate the UK market cruises for P&O. *Canberra's* draft was slightly greater than that of *Oriana* and it was believed that the latter would be able to enter more ports. The conversion of *Orsova* to a one-class ship was, however, deemed too costly and *Canberra* was reprieved, refitted as a one-class ship in 1974 with accommodation for 1641 cruise passengers and gave over twenty years more service in the UK cruise market. *Orsova* was withdrawn in 1973 and scrapped in Taiwan in early 1974.

## *Otranto (1909)*

12,124grt
554ft length overall
64ft breadth
300 first-class, 140 second-class and 850 third-class passengers
Built by Workman, Clark & Co., Belfast
Powered by two quadruple-expansion engines

The *Otranto* was one of five similar ships built in 1909 to compete with P&O on the Australia service, the others being *Orsova, Osterley, Otway* and *Orvieto*. Of the five, only *Otranto* made a significant number of cruises. Things might have been different but for the war, which only *Orsova, Orvieto* and *Osterley* survived, and they were needed for the mail service until new ships could be commissioned. *Osterley* did cruise to the Norwegian fjords but only for the US market in 1922 under charter to a US company based in New York.

Even before her maiden voyage to Australia, *Otranto* made a series of cruises to the Norwegian fjords and the Baltic. Between 1910 and 1914 she was used during the summer months for cruises to both the Mediterranean and the Norwegian fjords. In fact, for the whole of the summer of 1911, she was employed on cruises to Norway.

In 1914 she was commissioned as HMS *Otranto* – an Armed Merchant Cruiser (AMC). On 6 October 1918, while on a voyage from New York as a troopship, she collided with the P&O liner *Kashmir. Otranto* was almost cut in two and was run aground off Islay. With the ship in grave peril her consorts stood by to aid the evacuation. Over 600 soldiers and crew were saved, but nearly 400 were lost, including the Captain. There is a cemetery for those lost on the *Otranto* at Kilchoman on Islay and a monument erected by the American Red Cross on the southernmost tip of the island. *Kashmir* reached the Clyde with no casualties.

## Otranto (1926)

20,026grt
658ft length overall
75ft breadth
572 first-class and 1,114 third-class passengers initially
Built in 1926 by Vickers Armstong, Barrow in Furness
Powered by twin single-reduction-geared turbines

The third ship of a class of five, *Otranto* was preceded by her sisters *Orama* (1924) and *Oronsay* (1925). Like them she interspersed her mail runs to Australia with summer cruises to the Mediterranean and the Norwegian fjords. She survived her service as a troopship during the Second World War and was refitted for the carrying of emigrants from the UK to Australia during 1948. She stayed in this trade until 1957 when she was withdrawn and broken up at Faslane in Scotland.

Stewards await the arrival of the Boat Train at Immingham just before one of *Otranto*'s cruises from there in the late 1920s. Immingham was a favoured starting point for Norwegian cruises.

*Otranto* at Balholm on one of her successful 1930s Norwegian fjord cruises.

The boat train has just arrived at Immingham to discharge *Otranto*'s next complement of cruisers.

Photographed at Venice in 1935, this was *Orion* on the cruise on which she rescued the passengers of the White Star liner *Doric*, which had just been rammed while cruising in the Mediterranean.

## *Orion* (and *Orcades* 1937)

23,371grt
665ft length overall
84.5ft breadth
486 first-class and 653 tourist-class passengers
Built in 1934 by Vickers Armstrong, Barrow in Furness
Powered by two sets of single-reduction turbines

*Orion* was quite revolutionary, being the model for many subsequent liners with her single funnel and single mast. Her launch was also unique at the time, as she was launched by HRH the Duke of Gloucester who was in Australia and carried out the ceremony by radio.

With splendid interiors designed by the architect Brian O'Rorke the ship moved away from the trend of making ships like land-based hotels and instead used the ship itself to create the ambience. The huge French liner *Normandie* also moved thinking away from copying what was on land. Interestingly, in the US cruise market especially, this trend has been reversed and it is often difficult to realise that one is in a ship at all.

*Orion* was also the best protected of all British liners of the time against fire, being the first vessel to use the Grinelli sprinkler system together with extensive use of fire-resistant paint.

Like earlier Orient Line ships, her Australia runs were punctuated with cruising from the UK in summer. In 1939, however, like so many other liners, she was requisitioned for war duties as a troopship. She was in Singapore when the Japanese attacked in September 1941 but after embarking wounded troops and civilian evacuees she arrived safely in Fremantle on 6 January 1942.

Refitted at Barrow in 1947, she resumed her Australia sailings but without her sister the *Orcades* of 1937. That ship, also built in Barrow, had undertaken a series of cruises in 1938 but only one in 1939. She arrived back from the Mediterranean in April with an engine defect and was sent up to Barrow for repairs. She was requisitioned as a troopship after her repair and on the morning of 10 October 1942 she was torpedoed by U 172 whilst on passage between Cape Town and Freetown in West Africa with 1,300 service personnel and civilians on board. She survived the first attack but lowered her boats, one of which capsized with the loss of thirty-eight lives. The remainder of her passengers and many crew members were safely picked up by the Polish steamer *Narvik* and she then attempted to limp back to Cape Town. The captain and a skeleton crew of fifty-one volunteers were endeavouring to make port when the U-boat attacked again and three more torpedoes hit *Orcades*. Luckily the *Narvik* was still in the vicinity and, despite being a cargo vessel with a crew of only forty-seven, she brought nearly 1,700 survivors back to Cape Town. They had been very lucky, as the attack had occurred 300 miles from port. *Narvik* survived the war but the US Air Force sank U 172 in December 1943.

In June 1951, *Orion* commenced her first post-war cruise – thirteen nights to that favourite Orient Line destination – the Norwegian fjords. Fares ranged from £39 to £65. In 1953 she was placed on an Australia–Vancouver–San Francisco service but in 1958 she was converted to a one-class tourist ship for the emigrant trade from the UK to Australia.

With the merger with P&O in 1960, *Orion* was withdrawn from service in May 1963 flying an 84ft-long paying-off pennant as she steamed into the Thames Estuary. After a brief charter to a German company as a hotel ship she sailed for the breaker's yard in Antwerp in October 1963.


## *Orontes*

20,186grt
663ft length overall
75ft breadth
463 first-class and 1,123 third-class passengers
Built in 1929 by Vickers, Barrow in Furness
Powered by twin single-reduction-geared turbines

The last of the *Orama* type, she followed the pattern of line voyages to Australia and UK-based cruises to the Mediterranean and the Norwegian fjords with occasional trips to the Caribbean. Her accommodation was changed to 463 First Class and 418 Tourist Class in 1935, making her more acceptable as a cruise ship.

Requisitioned as a troopship, she survived the war and resumed her commercial sailings in 1948, and for the next five years she sailed on the Australia run. In 1953 she became a one-class tourist ship and until 1960 she also cruised out of Australian ports for the Australian cruise market.

In December 1961 she was withdrawn and sold for scrapping in Spain, where she arrived in March 1962.

## Oriental Steam Yachting Association/Polytechnic Touring Association/Viking Cruising Co.

There are few details about these apparently linked organisations based in London.

The first ship to be operated by this group was the *Ceylon*, purchased in 1881 from P&O. The *La Plata* was acquired from Royal Mail in 1908, renamed *The Viking* and used for cruising the Norwegian fjords before being broken up in 1913. The organisation had acquired the *Atranto* (5,366grt) in 1912, the vessel taking the name *The Viking* in 1913, following the scrapping of the *Viking* ex-*La Plata*. The outbreak of war saw the vessel being requisitioned by the Admiralty as the Armed Merchant Cruiser HMS *Vikbor*. A mine sank her in 1915.

## Pacific Steam Navigation Company

*Orbita and Orduna*

15,678 grt
569ft length overall
67ft breadth
190 first-class, 221 second-class and 476 third-class passengers
Built in 1914 by Harland & Wolff, Belfast
Powered by a triple-expansion engine plus a low-pressure turbine

*Orbita* was completed in 1915 as an auxiliary cruiser and troop transport during the First World War and it was not until 1919 that she was completed as a passenger liner.

The Pacific Steam Navigation Co.'s *Orbita* entering Havana harbour, having just passed Morro Castle.

*Orduna* was chartered throughout the war by Cunard Line to operate on the Liverpool–New York service.

*Orbita* was initially employed in the Liverpool to the west coast of South America service but, as trading conditions were difficult, from 1921 she and her sister vessel were chartered to Royal Mail Line and used on the Hamburg–New York service instead as cabin-class liners. Royal Mail took ownership of the vessels in 1923 but in 1927, following the closure of the service, they were returned to PSNC. They were converted to oil burners and returned to carrying passengers in three classes on the run to Valparaiso. However, both ships would occasionally also operate cruises between these long voyages. Both ships saw service as troopships during the Second World War but at the end of the war they were deemed to be too old to justify reconditioning for further peacetime service and they were scrapped in 1950.

### Reina del Pacifico

17,707grt
574ft length overall
76ft breadth
280 first-class, 162 second-class and 446 third-class passengers
Built in 1931 by Harland & Wolff, Govan
Powered by Burmeister & Wain diesels, quadruple screws

*Reina del Pacifico* was built for the company's Liverpool–Valparaiso service. However, before her first sailing on this route she undertook one cruise from Liverpool, thereafter being employed on the South America service. She was employed during the war as a troop transport and in 1946 was sent to the Harland & Wolff yard to be reconditioned for her return to commercial service. During a trials voyage she suffered an engine-room explosion, which killed twenty-eight of her crew. She was returned to the Valparaiso service at the end of 1948 and remained thus employed until she was sold for scrap ten years later.

## Page & Moy

The UK holiday company of Page & Moy have been regular charterers of cruise ships in order to provide dedicated cruises for their customers. In this way they have some control over the operation of the vessel and the standards of food and entertainment, etc.

The *Black Prince* of Fred Olsen (details under Fred Olsen) has been a regular feature of their portfolio that has also included the *Enrico Costa* and the *Ocean Majesty*.

### Enrico Costa

13,607grt
176.5ft length overall
73ft breadth
750 cruise passengers from 1972
Built in 1951 by Swan Hunter & Wigham Richardson, Newcastle-upon-Tyne
Powered by twin geared turbines

The *Enrico Costa* was built as the *Provence* for Soc. Générale de Transports Maritimes à Vapeur of Marseilles for the Marseilles–Argentina service. The ship was built as a

Scrapped in 2002, the *Enrico Costa* during a Page & Moy charter cruise.

three-class vessel but when she was sold to the Costa Company as the *Enrico C* in 1965 the number of classes was reduced to two. Her service route changed little, although the start point became Genoa rather than Marseilles. In 1972 she was refitted as a single-class cruise ship being renamed *Enrico Costa* in 1987. It was during her Costa service that Page & Moy chartered her for cruises to Scandinavia.

In 1994 she was sold to Starlauro Cruises and renamed *Symphony*, a name she retained when Starlauro Cruises was re-branded as MSC (Mediterranean Shipping Company). In May 2000 she became the *Aegean Spirit* of Golden Sun Cruises, who later chartered her to Cruise Holdings as the *Ocean Glory*. As such she was detained at Dover in 2002 due to safety and sanitary violations. The ship never re-entered service and was scrapped in India in November 2002.

## Ocean Majesty

10,417grt
443ft length overall
63ft breadth
621 cruise passengers
Built in 1966 by Union Naval de Levante, Valencia
Powered by twin diesel engines

The *Juan March* was built for the Spanish ferry operator Compañia Trasmediterránea as one of four side-loading passenger/car ferries for the Barcelona–Majorca and

Barcelona–Canaries service plus some services from Valencia. She was sold in 1985 to become the *Sol Christina*, operating on the Piraeus–Crete–Rhodes–Cyprus–Israel service of Sol Mediterranean Services. Within a year she became the *Kypros Star* of Health Shipping Co and was placed on the Piraeus–Rhodes–Cyprus–Alexandria route. In 1987 and 1988 she undertook a series of cruises for the Adriatic Line.

In 1991, the ship was taken in hand for refitting as a cruise vessel, although her first cruise in the guise did not occur until 1994 when she was renamed *Ocean Majesty* and registered under the Greek flag. The reconstruction raised her tonnage from 8,983grt to 10,417grt. Her owners do not operate cruises in their own name but charter the vessel to other cruise operators. In 1994 and 1995 she was chartered to the Epirotiki Line, being temporarily renamed *Olympic* for the 1994 season and *Homeric* for the 1995 season.

Page & Moy, the UK travel operator has chartered the ship each year since 1995 for a series of spring/summer cruises and she retains a very loyal UK following. For the rest of the year the ship is available for charter to other cruise operators.


# Perlus Cruises

*La Perla*

For dimensions see under *Delphi*, Clarkson Holidays.

Following the collapse of her owners, Efthymiadis, *Delphi* was sold to a Limassol-based company, Perlus Cruises SA and was renamed *La Perla*. Initially she was used in Mediterranean cruise service, then in late 1979 she was chartered by a British travel company, The Cruise Club, for a series of winter cruises mainly out of Liverpool (three cruises were also planned from Southampton) down to the Canary Islands, North Africa, Spain and Portugal. The Cruise Club was an operation aimed at the lower end of the market, and the first of the cruises was a fourteen-day Christmas and New Year cruise from Liverpool. The cruise generated a great deal of adverse publicity, much of it due apparently to the fact that the charter company had not set an adequate budget for food per passenger per day. There were, however, other complaints regarding the general condition of the ship. As a result, on her return to Liverpool, at the end of the cruise, she was placed under arrest and the remainder of the cruise programme was abandoned. *La Perla* sailed from Liverpool one night before the differences between her owners and the cruise operators had been sorted out. On her return to the Mediterranean, she was renamed *La Palma* and was registered under the ownership of Intercruise Ltd. She returned to the UK several years later; in 1987 she operated some cruises from Plymouth but did not return to UK waters after the end of the 1989 season. In 1996 she was withdrawn from service.


# Peninsular & Oriental Steam Navigation (P&O)

At some time or other nearly every P&O ship has undertaken a cruise voyage as opposed to a liner voyage. The ships detailed below are those which undertook regular cruises.

Immediately before and during the First World War, P&O took over the operations of a number of UK shipping companies, including British India. The companies retained their original names and thus British India cruise ships will be found listed under British India.

In 1919 P&O became the majority shareholder of Orient Line, the two companies merging formally in 1960 with P&O acquiring the remaining minority shares in Orient Line in 1965. Orient Line ships are listed under Orient Line with a reference in this section. The exception is the *Oriana* of 1959 as, whilst that vessel was ordered by Orient Line, she spent the majority of her life as a P&O ship.

Ships of Swan Hellenic will be found listed under that name.

P&O was founded in 1837 when Arthur Anderson and Brodie McGhie Wilcox (who had been trading as Wilcox & Anderson since 1825) set up the Peninsular Steam Navigation Company, the peninsula in question being the Iberian Peninsula, to offer a regular steamship service to Portugal and Spain.

The company was a success and as its routes became extended to India, the Far East and Australia the word Oriental was added to its title, the company becoming the Peninsular & Oriental Steam Navigation Company – P&O.

By 1920 P&O had acquired the British India Company, the Union Steamship of New Zealand and the New Zealand Steam Ship companies, as well as holding a majority shareholding in the Orient Line.

P&O policy was for acquired companies to continue operating under their own name and house flag. In 1960 there was a formal merger between P&O and Orient Line (the last of the minority shares in Orient Line were finally acquired in 1965). The last cruise ship to sail under the British India house flag was the *Uganda* in the early 1980s.

In 1974 P&O bought the growing US cruise line – Princess Cruises – and in 1983 acquired the cultural cruise operation of Swan Hellenic (to be found in its own section later). In 2000 P&O set up a separate company, P&O Princess to operate the cruise business that by 2002 included P&O Cruises in the UK, Princess Cruises, P&O Cruises (Australia), Swan Hellenic, and Seetours, Aida Cruises and A'ROSA Cruises in Germany. In 2001 P&O nearly acquired Festival Cruises and in that same year announced a merger proposal with Royal Caribbean Cruises in which P&O would hold 51 per cent of the shares in the new company. The Carnival Corporation (owners of Carnival Cruises, Cunard, Holland America and a number of other cruise lines, and the largest cruise company in the world) made a counter bid for P&O Princess (i.e. the cruise operation of P&O and not the ferries, etc.). The concept that was adopted in 2003 was for a dual-listed company, whereby Carnival and P&O would retain their identities and brands.

P&O were one of the earliest entrants to the UK cruise market and today are the largest operator of UK market cruises.

## *Adonia*

77,499grt
857ft length overall
106ft breadth
2,272 cruise passengers
Built in 1998 by Fincantieri, Italy
Powered by diesel–electric engines

With the disposal of *Victoria*, and the re-branding of *Arcadia* as *Ocean Village*, the *Sea Princess* was transferred from the US to the UK P&O Princess operation in May 2003 and renamed *Adonia*. *Adonia*, and the slightly newer *Oceana* (ex-*Ocean Princess*), form the two new 'White Sisters', reintroducing a term used for the *Strathaird* and the *Strathnaver* in the early 1930s.

Refitted to appeal to UK rather than US cruise passengers, the *Adonia* and her sister feature the latest in cruise ship interior design with large atriums and glass-walled lifts.

With the rebranding of *Arcadia* as *Ocean Village*, *Adonia* took on the role of adults-only ship and undertook a world cruise in 2004. Due to be returned to the Princess Cruises fleet and resume the name *Sea Princess*, she will still ber marketed specifically to British passengers.

## Arcadia (1954)

29,871grt
721ft length overall
90ft breadth
675 first-class and 735 tourist-class passengers
Built in 1953 by John Brown, Clydebank
Powered by geared steam turbines

Intended for the UK–Australia service, the *Arcadia*, and her near sister *Iberia*, began to cruise more intensively in the late 1950s and early 1960s. They not only operated cruises for the UK market but were also based in San Francisco for cruises intended for the US market. In 1963, *Arcadia* was modernised in order to undertake more cruising. Between 1975 and her scrapping in Taiwan in 1979, *Arcadia* was employed solely on cruising.

## Arcadia (1997)/Ocean Village

63,524grt
810ft length overall
105ft breadth
1,549 passengers
Built in 1989 by Chantiers de L'Atlantique, France
Powered by diesel–electric motors

Ordered as the *Sitmar Fairmajesty*, she was launched as *Star Princess*, as Princess Cruises (owned by P&O) had acquired Sitmar in 1988 just after the ship was laid down. *Arcadia* is a ship that has a striking profile that was quite revolutionary at the time.

*Ocean Village* at Villefranche; she is slowly revolutionising P&O's cruise activities.

She was transferred from Princess Cruises to P&O Cruises in the UK in December 1997 as the replacement for the much-loved *Canberra* and renamed *Arcadia*. In her first season the ship carried a superb collection of US contemporary art, but this was removed and works of art from the UK were substituted. The majority of standard cabins on *Arcadia* were somewhat larger than the norm and this gained her the nickname of 'the spaceship'!

In 2002 *Arcadia* was designated as an 'adults only' ship, a role that was taken on by *Adonia* when *Arcadia* was renamed *Ocean Village* in 2003.

In 2003 P&O Princess Cruises announced a new venture – *Ocean Village*. Designed for the 'thirty-something, dress-down Friday set', *Ocean Village* offers a resort cruise experience with a very relaxed ambience. Meals are buffet style and there are plenty of dining options. Shore activities include a number of sporting opportunities – cruise passengers can even rent a mountain bike direct from the ship. Port stays are longer than the traditional norm of arriving early morning and leaving just before dinner. The cruise passengers on *Ocean Village* have the opportunity of sampling local nightlife.

Whilst *Ocean Village* may not appeal to the more traditional cruise passenger, the philosophy behind the venture is that there is a large potential market that requires a more relaxed cruise experience dedicated to a younger age group.

### Aurora

76,152grt
886ft length overall
106ft breadth
1,875 cruise passengers
Built in 2000 by Meyer Werft, Papenburg, Germany
Powered by diesel–electric engines

So successful was *Oriana* and so buoyant was the UK cruise market in the late 1990s that P&O ordered a second vessel from the Meyer Weft yard. Slightly larger than *Oriana* but designed to the same philosophy of a quintessentially British ship, *Aurora* made her debut in May 2000. Only a few hours into her maiden cruise a bearing went and the ship had to return to Southampton and the cruise was cancelled. It is a measure of the way P&O handled the situation by keeping passengers informed and offering full refunds and an alternative cruise that the mishap was turned from a potential public relations disaster into a triumph.

*Aurora* introduced the concept of alternative dining options to the UK ships of the P&O Princess fleet – a product enhancement that has been applied retrospectively to *Oriana*. *Aurora* was also the first UK market ship to be fitted with a sliding 'Magrodome' that can enclose the midships section of the lido deck in inclement weather. *Aurora* has balconies not only on staterooms, mini-suites and suites but also on a number of standard cabins, as have *Adonia* and *Oceana*. Like the Cunard vessel *Caronia* (ex-*Vistafjord*) she also has two double-storey penthouse suites.

*Aurora* undertakes a world cruise during the early months of each year and has proved to be a very successful ship that is both modern and traditional.

## Canberra

44,807grt
733ft length overall
92.5ft breadth
556 first-class and 1716 tourist-class passengers, 1,641 cruise passengers from 1974
Built in 1961 by Harland & Wolff, Belfast
Powered by twin Thomson Houston turbo-electric engines

Of all UK market cruise ships *Canberra* is possibly the vessel that defined today's British cruise market.

*Canberra* and her running mate, the *Oriana* of 1960, looked very different and yet were intended to operate in the same service. Whilst P&O had held a majority shareholding in Orient Line since 1919 it was not until 1960 that the two companies merged formally. *Oriana* was ordered as an Orient Line ship and *Canberra* as a P&O new build. Dredging of the Suez Canal in the 1950s meant that 40,000grt ships could transit the Canal.

Canberra was the more revolutionary design and was undoubtedly influenced by the Shaw Savill vessels *Southern Cross* and *Northern Star*. Like those two ships her machinery was aft, leaving ample space for lido and sun decks and removing the need for funnel trunkings that encroached on the public rooms.

*Canberra* also reverted to turbo-electric drive, a system of propulsion that had not been fitted to a new P&O liner for over thirty years. A popular ship from her first voyage, *Canberra* had her share of mishaps, one of the most notable being on 4 January 1963 whilst she was off the Southern Italian coast. A fire put the main engines out of action but there were no injuries amongst her 2,200 passengers. *Stratheden* was in the vicinity and provided assistance. In June 1967 she narrowly avoided being trapped in the Suez Canal at the outbreak of the Six-Day War. The ship was approaching Port Said when the Staff Captain heard a commercial radio report that Israeli aircraft were bombing Port Said. *Canberra* turned around and proceeded to take the long way around the Cape of Good Hope to Australia.

In 1973, *Canberra* commenced a series of cruises for the US market but she was not a success, in part due to her two-class nature; a division of facilities that was unacceptable to the US market.

Late in 1973 it was announced that *Canberra* was to be withdrawn and that *Orsova* and *Oriana* would operate the UK market cruises for P&O. *Canberra*'s draft was slightly greater than that of *Oriana* and it was believed that latter would be able to enter more ports. The conversion of *Orsova* to a one-class ship was, however, deemed too costly and *Canberra* was reprieved, refitted as a one-class ship in 1974 with accommodation for 1,641 cruise passengers and gave over twenty years more service in the UK cruise market.

*Canberra* was allocated to the slowly re-emerging UK market where, throughout the 1970s, she built up a loyal following both for her normal two-week cruises out of Southampton and her annual world cruise that commenced in January and took her lucky cruise passengers south to the sun.

In the Spring of 1982, following the completion of her world cruise and a hasty survey on the final Gibraltar–Southampton leg of that cruise, 'The Great White Whale', as the Royal Navy nicknamed her, was hastily converted to a troopship to carry 3 Brigade comprising Royal Marines and elements of the Parachute Regiment to San Carlos Water in the Falkland Islands. Equipped with extensive medical facilities and helicopter landing pads, *Canberra* was in the first wave of the assault to recapture the Falkland Islands from the Argentineans. Despite her conspicuous white appearance (she was never repainted grey) and her vast bulk, she was not hit, despite intensive Argentinean Air Force activity and having spent three nerve-wracking days in the confined anchorage.

The British public had watched as *Canberra* had sailed out of the Solent on 9 April 1982 and they had cheered when she returned undamaged; the ship had entered the history books and possibly the psyche of the nation. The *QE2* also sailed south but later and only to South Georgia. *Canberra* went in harms way. At that time the QE2 was regarded as the flagship of the British Merchant Marine and the Government were unwilling to risk losing her. She transferred her troops to both the *Canberra* and the P&O ferry *Norland* on 28 May and back to the war zone went *Canberra*.

*Canberra* became a quintessential British experience. Douglas Ward, the author of the *Berlitz Guide to Cruising and Cruise Ships*, described her in 1994 as providing a cruise package in very comfortable surroundings, at an affordable price, in good British floating holiday-camp style, but with every strata of society around one.

*Canberra* built up a tremendous loyalty amongst many of her passengers and by 1987 the ship had captured 20 per cent of all cruises sold in the UK and a massive 45 per cent of all cruises that originated in UK ports. Despite the fact that she still had many inside cabins, no balconies and a proportion of cabins without en-suite facilities, *Canberra* was still holding market share well into the early 1990s with a regular 60 per cent repeat business complement of cruise passengers.

As a brand P&O Cruises was launched in 1988 based on *Canberra* and the smaller *Sea Princess* (later re-named *Victoria*). Also in that year, P&O decided to investigate either a new running mate or a replacement for *Canberra*. As it turned out, *Canberra* operated for a short period with the new ship, the *Oriana* before being replaced by the 63,500 ton *Star Princess*, which was transferred from the Princess operation and renamed *Arcadia*.

There was nothing intrinsically wrong with the *Canberra* product other than she was an old ship that had seen much service. P&O Cruises was keen to retain the success of *Canberra* and went to great lengths to analyse why the ship had such a loyal following. This information was fed into the design of the *Oriana* of 1995.

*Canberra*'s last cruise in the Autumn of 1997 was an emotional event and the crowds thronged vantage points overlooking Southampton Water and the Solent to witness the last arrival and final departure of this much-loved and highly-influential ship. *Canberra* was broken up in Pakistan late in 1997 but her memory lingers on in the design of *Oriana* and *Aurora* and in the loyal *Canberra* passengers, who can still be found on nearly every P&O cruise today. A common remark from passengers is that they sailed on *Canberra* twenty times or more. That sort of loyalty is unheard of almost anywhere else.


*Chusan*

24,318grt
673ft length overall
84ft breadth
475 first-class and 551 tourist-class passengers
Built in 1949 by Vickers Armstrong, Barrow in Furness
Powered by geared turbines

Only two years old, *Chusan* was used as an advertising poster for P&O's cruise operation in 1952. In the foreground is an oxen-powered sledge together with a native of Maderia (a favourite port of call then and now for UK cruise passengers). *Chusan* with her white hull and yellow funnel sits majestically in the background bathed in sunlight.

By the 1950s ships were being built as dual-purpose liner voyage and cruise vessels.

*Chusan* spent her whole career with P&O both on the liner routes to the Far East and Australia and as a popular cruise vessel for the UK market. In 1959 she undertook P&O's first world cruise covering 32,000 miles in eighty days and making stops at twenty-four

*Chusan* at speed on her builder's sea trials in 1949.

ports. In 1970 Chusan operated the final P&O voyage to India severing a link that had lasted over 100 years. Like so many other fine ships she was broken up in the early 1970s – in *Chusan's* case in Taiwan in 1973.

## Himalaya

28,047grt
709ft length overall
90ft breadth
1,416 tourist-class/cruise passengers (from 1963)
Built in 1948 by Vickers Armstrong, Barrow in Furness
Powered by twin geared steam turbines

P&O's first post-war ship, the *Himalaya* operated as a two-class ship on the UK–India–Australia liner service. In 1963 she was refitted as a tourist-class vessel and, as air travel began to eat into the liner trade, *Himalaya* undertook more and more cruises. Her cruising career paralleled that of ships like the *Orcades*, whom she was built next to in the same yard, and the *Reina Del Mar*. She was broken up in Taiwan in 1974.

## Minerva and Minerva 2

See under the Swan Hellenic heading.

## Moldavia

16,436grt
573ft length overall
71ft breadth
830 tourist-class/cruise passengers (from 1931)
Built in 1921 by Cammell Laird, Birkenhead
Powered by twin geared steam turbines

Like her sister *Mongolia*, *Moldavia* was given a new lease of life in 1931 by being refitted as a tourist-class/cruise ship. She spent her year either cruising or on the intermediate (as opposed to the express) service from the UK to Australia. Being a tourist-class-only ship, her cruise fares were more affordable. She was broken up in the UK in 1938.

## Mongolia

16,385grt
568ft length overall
71ft breadth
800 tourist-class/cruise passengers (from 1931)
Built in 1922 by Armstrong Whitworth, Walker-on-Tyne
Powered by twin geared steam turbines

*Mongolia* was a long-lived ship. When she and her sister left P&O service she was not broken up like *Moldavia*. In 1938 she was chartered to the New Zealand Steamship

*Moldavia* at Funchal, Madeira in the early 1930s.

Company for whom she traded as the *Rimutaka* until 1950. She was then sold to the Incres Line and renamed *Europa* and placed on the Incres Line service from Europe to the USA. In 1951 she was renamed *Nassau* and refitted as a cruise ship for the North American market. A single funnel replaced her twin funnels and she was painted white. In 1961 she was purchased by Mexican interests and renamed *Acapulco* but was scrapped in Japan in 1963.

## Ocean Village

See *Arcadia* (1997) / *Ocean Village*

## Oceana

77,499grt
857ft length overall
106ft breadth
2,272 cruise passengers
Built in 2000 by Fincantieri, Italy
Powered by diesel–electric engines

With the disposal of *Victoria*, and the re-branding of *Arcadia* as *Ocean Village*, the *Ocean Princess* was transferred from the US to the UK P&O Princess operation in November 2002 and renamed *Oceana*. *Oceana*, together with the slightly older *Adonia* (ex-*Sea Princess*), form the two new 'White Sisters', reintroducing a term used for the *Strathaird* and the *Strathnaver* in the early 1930s.

Refitted to appeal to UK rather than US cruise passengers, the *Oceana* and her sister feature the latest in cruise ship interior design with large atriums and glass-walled lifts.

In the autumn of 2002 *Oceana* commenced her operations for the UK cruise market with a series of Caribbean cruises based on Fort Lauderdale in the USA before making her maiden entry to the UK in the spring of 2003.

### Orcades

See entry under Orient Line.

### Oriana (1960)

41,920grt
804ft length overall
97ft breadth
638 first-class and 1,496 tourist-class passengers, 1,700 cruise passengers from 1973
Built in 1960 by Vickers Armstrong, Barrow in Furness
Powered by twin geared steam turbines

The last ship ordered by Orient Line before the whole of the company's shares were acquired by P&O. *Oriana* was intended, like *Canberra*, for the UK–Australia liner service. Dredging of the Suez Canal in the 1950s meant that 40,000grt ships could transit the Canal.

*Oriana*, a popular liner. Here she is at Lisbon in 1973.

Her original livery retained the corn-coloured Orient Line hull before she was repainted with a P&O white hull. From the outset she was also used for cruising and from 1973 onwards she was employed purely in the cruise trade, alternating between UK and Australian market cruises.

Of a striking design, *Oriana* was instantly recognisable. Considerable use of aluminium was made in her superstructure and she was one of earliest ships to be fitted with 'transverse propulsion units' (now known as bow thrusters) to aid docking manoeuvres.

Elegant throughout, the *Oriana* was very popular with her passengers and crew alike. The accommodation for the latter was the best that had ever been seen in a UK-registered ship up to that time. Her most dramatic moment was on 11 August 1970 when she left berth 106 in Southampton Docks bound for Australia with 1,500 passengers on board. Only an hour into the voyage there was a serious boiler fire and the ship lost all power. Passengers were called to their emergency stations, although an evacuation proved unnecessary. The fire burned for over an hour and, with no power and in danger of grounding, it might have taken hold and the ship could have been lost.

By the early 1970s it was clear that the market for cruise passengers was moving rapidly in the direction of one-class ships. The US market led the field and UK operators were forced to follow suit. In 1973 *Oriana* was refitted as a one-class ship reducing her capacity to 1,700 cruise passengers. This was so successful that in 1974 it was announced that all P&O cruise ships would be one class.

In 1976 the scrapping of *Oronsay* meant that *Oriana* was the last of the Orient Line ships. By the 1980s much of her cruising was in the Australian market but, in 1986, she was sold to Japanese buyers for use as a museum ship in Beppu Bay, Japan. Later she was sold to China as a floating hotel and conference centre in Shanghai, where she retained both her P&O livery and the name *Oriana*. In 2002 she was sold to the Port of Dalian in northeast China. She remains there at the time of writing but broke free from her mooring in 2004 and partially capsized.

## *Oriana (1995)*

69,153grt
853ft length overall
105ft breadth
1,975 cruise passengers
Built in 1995 by Meyer Werft, Papenburg, Germany
Powered by diesel engines

In 1972 P&O introduced their first purpose-built cruise ship, the 17,370grt *Spirit of London*. The ship was designed for the US market as a replacement for *Arcadia* and *Iberia*. In 1974 P&O acquired Princess Cruises and *Spirit of London* was transferred to the Princess fleet as the *Sun Princess*. Since then the ship has had a number of owners and has been named *Starship Majestic*, *Southern Cross* (see the entry for the CTC Company), and latterly *Flamenco* of Festival Cruises. In 2001 P&O very nearly acquired Festival Cruises and had they done so the ship would have re-entered the P&O fleet.

By 1991 it was clear that *Canberra* would not be suitable for service into the latter years of the decade and an order was placed for the first ever purpose-built cruise liner for the UK cruising market. Whilst it was popularly believed that *Oriana* was a straight replacement for *Canberra*, this was not the case and the ships operated alongside each other until September 1997 when *Canberra* was withdrawn and replaced by the *Arcadia* (ex-*Star Princess*).

No British yard felt able to compete for the order and it was gained by the experienced cruise liner building yard of Meyer Werft in Germany.

The first purpose-built P&O cruise ship primarily for the British market, *Oriana* made her maiden voyage in 1995.

Robert Tillberg, who was responsible for much of the design work, spent a great deal of time on *Canberra* assessing the needs of the UK cruise passenger. His design was elegant yet in many ways traditional. *Oriana*'s single funnel is designed to have a resemblance to the twin funnels of *Canberra* and the positioning of the lifeboats also reflects the design of *Canberra*.

*Oriana* is an extremely elegant ship and brought new standards of accommodation to the UK cruise market, including a whole deck of staterooms and suites with balconies. Unlike the US market ships where all cabins are referred to as staterooms, on *Oriana* and the later *Aurora* the term stateroom is reserved for a class of accommodation priced between that of standard cabins and mini-suites.

A ship entering the huge US cruise market needs to gain 2 per cent of the market share to be a success. In the UK market success requires 10 per cent of the market share. So successful has *Oriana* been in stimulating market growth that by 2003 she was both the oldest and smallest ship in the P&O Princess Cruises UK fleet, having gained a half sister in the larger *Aurora* and the company of the two 'White Sisters' the *Adonia* and *Oceana* (ex-*Sea Princess* of 1998 and *Ocean Princess* of 2000, respectively).

*Oriana* has also undertaken annual world cruises in addition to her regular series of cruises to the traditional P&O destinations and the newer ones such as South America. From 2004, however, the world cruises were handled by *Aurora* and *Adonia* with *Oriana* joining *Oceana* in the Caribbean and South America during the UK winter season.

## Orion

See entry under Orient Line.


## Oronsay

See entry under Orient Line.


## Orsova

See entry under Orient Line.


## Rajputana

16,644grt
568ft length overall
71ft breadth
307 first-class & 288 second class passengers
Built in 1925 by Harland & Wolff, Greenock
Powered by steam quadruple-expansion reciprocating engines (turbines added in 1930)

One of the four 'R' class ships built for P&O's London–Bombay service. The other ships were *Ranchi*, *Ranpurna* and *Rawalpindi*.

During the low season for travel to India the ships operated Mediterranean cruises for UK cruise passengers in the years up to the Second World War. *Rajputana*, like the other 'R' ships, was converted to an Armed Merchant Cruiser (AMC) in 1939 and was sunk by U 108 on 13 April 1941.


## Ranchi

16,738grt
570ft length overall
71ft breadth
308 first-class and 282 second-class passengers
Built in 1925 by Hawthorn Leslie, Newcastle
Powered by quadruple-expansion reciprocating steam engines (turbines added in 1931)

One of the four 'R' class ships built for P&O's London–Bombay service. The other ships were *Rajputana*, *Ranpurna* and *Rawalpindi*.

During the low season for travel to India the ships operated Mediterranean cruises for UK cruise passengers in the years up to the Second World War.

*Ranchi*, like the other 'R' ships, was converted to an Armed Merchant Cruiser (AMC) in 1939 and then to a repair ship for the Royal Navy in 1944. Returned to P&O in 1948, her accommodation was altered and she became a one-class ship carrying up to 970 emigrants from the UK to Australia. She was withdrawn from service in 1953 and scrapped at Cashmore's Newport shipbreaking yard in South Wales.

Venice, 1933, with the *Ranchi* on one of her low-season cruises to the Mediterranean.

## *Ranpurna*

16,688grt
570ft length overall
71ft breadth
310 first-class and 280 second-class passengers
Built in 1924 by Hawthorn Leslie, Newcastle
Powered by quadruple-expansion reciprocating steam engines (turbines added in 1930)

One of the four 'R' class ships built for P&O's London–Bombay service, *Ranpurna*, like the other 'R' ships, was converted to an Armed Merchant Cruiser (AMC) in 1939 and was purchased outright by the UK government in 1942 to become a fleet repair ship. She kept her name, although adding HMS, and was broken up in Italy in 1961.

## *Rawalpindi*

16,644grt
570ft length overall
71ft breadth
307 first-class and 288 second-class passengers
Built in 1925 by Harland & Wolff, Greenock
Powered by quadruple-expansion reciprocating steam engines (turbines added in 1931)

*Rawalpindi* was converted to an Armed Merchant Cruiser (AMC) in 1939. On 23 November 1939 she was attacked and sunk by the German battlecruisers *Scharnhorst* and *Gneisenau* whilst patrolling off Iceland. 275 of her mainly reservist crew were lost, there being twenty-six survivors picked up by the German ships and another eleven by the *Chitral*, another P&O ship also serving as an AMC.

## Strathallan

23,722grt
668ft length overall
82ft breadth
530 first-class and 450 tourist-class passengers
Built in 1938 by Vickers Armstrong, Barrow in Furness
Powered by geared turbines

Sister to *Stratheden*, and half sister to *Strathmore*, and included for completeness, the single-funnelled *Strathallan* is reported to have undertaken a number of cruises before her career was cut short off Oran. She was supporting 'Operation Torch', an operation that also saw the loss of the *Viceroy of India*. *Strathallan* was torpedoed and sunk by U 562 on 21 December 1942.

## Strathaird

22,270grt
664ft length overall
80ft breadth
498 first and 668 tourist-class passengers
Built in 1932 by Vickers Armstrong, Barrow in Furness
Powered by twin screw, turbo-electric engines

The second of the 'Strath' ships and sister to *Strathnaver*, she was the second of the 'White Sisters'. These vessels introduced the white hull and yellow funnel to the P&O fleet. The term 'White Sisters' was reintroduced in 2003 for the *Adonia* and *Oceana*.

The two ships gained a loyal cruise following in the 1930s, offering a series of UK-based cruises in addition to their regular UK–Australia liner service.

Like *Strathnaver*, she had her dummy first and second funnels removed after the war, being rebuilt with just a single funnel. From 1954 onwards, *Strathaird* operated a tourist-class-only service from the UK to Australia. She was broken up in 1961 at Hong Kong.

## Stratheden

23,732grt
665ft length overall
82ft breadth
577 first-class and 453 tourist-class passengers from 1947 (1,200 tourist-class passengers from 1961)
Built in 1937 by Vickers Armstrong, Barrow in Furness
Powered by geared turbines

Sister to the short-lived *Strathallan* and half sister to *Strathmore*, the single-funnelled *Stratheden* undertook a number of pre-war cruises. After the war she resumed her liner service, being sold in 1964 to become the *Henrietta Latsis*, and being renamed *Marianna Latsis* in 1966. She was broken up in Italy in 1969. Just prior to her withdrawal from P&O service she was charted in 1963 and 1964 (together with *Strathmore*) to the Travel Savings Association, the company that also operated the *Reina Del Mar*.

## Strathmore

23,428grt
665ft length overall
82ft breadth
445 first-class and 665 tourist-class passengers
Built in 1935 by Vickers Armstrong, Barrow in Furness
Powered by geared turbines

Half sister to *Strathallan* and *Stratheden*, *Strathmore* reverted to steam turbines (as did her two half sisters). She also had only one funnel instead of the three funnels of the two preceding 'Strath' ships.

She undertook a number of pre-war cruises. After the war she resumed her liner service, being sold in 1963 to become the *Marianna Latsis*, being renamed *Henrietta Latsis* in 1966. Just prior to her withdrawal from P&O service, she was charted in 1963 and 1964, together with *Stratheden*, to the Travel Savings Association, the company that also operated the *Reina Del Mar*.

She was broken up in Italy in 1969.

## Strathnaver

22,547grt
548ft length overall
80ft breadth
500 first-class and 668 tourist-class passengers
Built in 1931 by Vickers Armstrong, Barrow in Furness
Powered by twin screw, turbo-electric engines

The first of the 'White Sisters', she was a sister ship to the *Strathaird*. These vessels introduced the white hull and yellow funnel to the P&O fleet. The term 'White Sisters' was reintroduced in 2003 for the *Adonia* and *Oceana*.

The two ships gained a loyal cruise following in the 1930s, offering a series of UK-based cruises in addition to their regular UK–Australia liner service. *Strathnaver* had her dummy first and third funnels removed after the war, being rebuilt with just a single funnel.

From 1954 onwards *Strathnaver* operated a tourist-class-only service from the UK to Australia. She was broken up in 1962 in Hong Kong.

## Vectis

5,627grt
160 cruise passengers
Built in1881 by Caird & Co., Glasgow

*Strathnaver* was the first ship to introduce the white hull and buff funnel so familiar to P&O cruisers today.

Built for the UK–Australia mail service of P&O, the ship was originally named the *Rome* and was converted for cruising in 1904 and renamed *Vectis*. As the *Rome* she had accommodation for 187 first and 46 second-class passengers, but for cruising she carried only 160, making her extremely spacious in her cruising guise. She marked P&O's entry into the cruise market but was sold to the French government in 1912. She saw little service under the French flag, however, as she was sold for scrapping to an Italian company in 1913.

## *Viceroy of India*

19,648grt
612ft length overall
76ft breadth
415 first-class and 258 second-class passengers
Built in 1928 by Alexander Stephen & Sons, Glasgow
Powered by twin screw, turbo-electric engines

Designed for the UK–India service, *Viceroy of India* (the original intention had been to name her *Taj Mahal*) was only the third vessel in the world to be fitted with turbo-electric machinery, the use of which made her a fast ship compared with others in the fleet – 19kt compared with the 16/17kt of ships that entered P&O service during the 1920s. *Viceroy of India* brought a new standard of luxury to the UK–India service.

Beautifully appointed, she made regular cruises from Southampton throughout the 1930s, venturing as far as the Caribbean and the South Atlantic.

*Above: Viceroy of India* and the two 'White Sisters', *Strathnaver* and *Strathaird*, at Tilbury docks in the mid-1930s.

*Left:* The Moorish Café on board *Viceroy of India*.

Deck sports on board *Viceroy of India*.

Acting as a troopship for the 'Operation Torch' landings in North Africa in November 1942, *Viceroy of India* was returning from the landings empty of troops when she was torpedoed and sunk off Oran by U 407 on 11 November 1942 with the loss of four lives.

## *Victoria / Sea Princess*

28,891grt
660ft length overall
86ft breadth
778 cruise passengers in one class.
Built in 1966 by John Brown, Clydebank
Powered by twin diesel engines

Originally named *Kungsholm* and operated by Swedish–American on both transatlantic voyages and cruises, the ship was sold to Flagship Cruises in 1975 and operated out of New York. She was acquired by the Princess Cruises operation of P&O in 1978 from Flagship Cruises and renamed *Sea Princess*. An extensive refit saw the removal of her forward funnel and the remodelling of the after one, plus extensive alterations to her fittings – to the detriment of her appearance according to many purists.

In 1982 she was transferred to the UK P&O fleet as the running mate to *Canberra*. In 1995 she was given an 'ia' ending name to fit in with the naming of the ships of the UK P&O Cruises fleet. As *Victoria* she operated alongside *Oriana* and *Aurora* until her sale into the German cruise market in 2002 as the *Mona Lisa*.

In 1999/2000 *Victoria* was chartered by a resurrected Union-Castle Line to operate a round Africa millennium cruise. For this cruise her funnel was painted in the red and black of Union-Castle, although the hull remained white.

*Above: Victoria*, now the German *Mona Lisa*, at Malaga during her 2001 season.

*Left:* Contrasting with *Viceroy of India*'s Moorish Bar, this is the Riviera Bar on *Victoria*, little changed since her days as Swedish America's *Kungsholm*.

# Phoenix Reisen

*Albatros*

21,989grt
608ft length overall
80ft breadth
906 passengers
Built in 1957 by John Brown, Clydebank
Powered by twin-screw Pametrada geared turbines

*Albatros* was built as *Sylvania* for Cunard Line (see Cunard Line for early career details).

Between 1988 and 1993 the vessel had been part of the P&O Princess fleet, following their takeover of Sitmar Cruises, and had sailed as *Dawn Princess*. She was then sold to Happy Days Shipping, a company affiliated to the Vlasov group of Monte Carlo, and in August 1993 she adopted the new name, *Albatros*. She was placed under charter to the German tour company, Phoenix Reisen. While principally employed in the German market, *Albatros* has in the past been chartered by British tour companies such as Arena Travel, Equity Cruises and The Cruise Collection; offering cruises exclusively to British passengers to the Baltic Capitals, Scandinavia, the Atlantic Islands and the Mediterranean. She was sold to be scrapped in Alang, India in 2004.

*Albatros*, once Cunard's *Sylvania*, entering Lisbon.

# Polish Ocean Line

## *Batory*

14,287grt
526ft length overall
71ft breadth
76 first-class and 740 tourist-class passengers (800 cruise passengers)
Built in 1936 by Cantieri Riuniti dell Adriatico, Monfalcone
Powered by twin-screw Sulzer diesel engines

*Batory* was one of a pair of ships built for the New York service. Her sister, *Pilsudski*, was sunk at the beginning of the war. Shortly after the war, having returned to the New York service, the *Batory* was blacklisted as a result of the political climate in the United States in the early 1950s. For a time she was moved to a new service between India and Pakistan. Having been made suitable for tropical voyages, *Batory* alternated her long-haul voyages with cruises – often from Southampton – to the Mediterranean, Canary Islands and sometimes to the Norwegian fjords. In 1956, when the Suez Canal was closed, she was taken off the India run and, instead, was returned to the North Atlantic, but this time sailing to the St Lawrence ports. She also continued to operate cruises from Southampton and Tilbury. Having made her final Atlantic voyage, she completed three farewell cruises to the Canaries before being withdrawn from service in 1969. She was then used for a time as a hotel ship in Gdynia before being sold for scrap in Hong Kong in 1971.

*Batory* was sold for scrap in 1971 after a career of almost thirty-five years.

Originally Holland America's *Maasdam*, the *Stefan Batory* was sold to Polish Ocean Line in 1968. Here she is at Oslo in 1986.

## *Stefan Batory*

15,024grt
503ft length overall
69ft breadth
39 first-class and 734 tourist-class passengers (779 in one class from 1976)
Built in 1952 by N.V. Wilton, Fijenoord, Schiedam
Powered by single-screw steam turbine engines

*Stefan Batory* was completed as the Holland America Line's *Maasdam*, a mainly tourist-class liner. Along with her sister, *Ryndam*, she revolutionised the look of transatlantic travel with the majority of on-board space being given over to tourist-class passengers. In 1968 she was withdrawn from Holland America service, having been sold to Polish Ocean Line as a replacement for their *Batory*, and was handed over to them that October. She was given an extensive refit at Gdansk, which considerably altered, and modernised, her external appearance. Whilst a fine ship, and one that came to enjoy immense popularity, there were many (apparently especially in Poland) that were disappointed that she had been chosen to replace the former *Batory*. The pre-war flagship was regarded as being a far superior vessel. The *Stefan Batory* maintained the service to Canada from Gdynia, calling at Copenhagen, Cuxhaven and Rotterdam, also calling at Tilbury on her voyages to Canada and Southampton on the return voyage. In later years Cuxhaven was dropped and then Southampton, with calls being made at Tilbury in both directions. Many British passengers used the voyage to Canada as a round-trip cruise, whilst others used the European section of the voyage as a cruise. However, like her predecessor, *Stefan Batory* established herself with British passengers as a very popular cruise ship. Out of the Atlantic season she would regularly sail from Tilbury to the Canaries and North Africa, or on rather longer cruises into the Mediterranean and the Black Sea (in 1979 she undertook one such cruise lasting fifty-two days). She also made regular cruises across the Atlantic to the Caribbean. In August 1986 *Stefan Batory* made her first cruise to the Norwegian fjords, and such was its success that two similar cruises were undertaken the following year. On 7 October 1987 she departed Montreal for the final time, Polish Ocean Lines had decided that it was time to withdraw her from service. However, she undertook two very grand farewell cruises. On 7 November she departed Tilbury for a two-month cruise to Brazil and Argentina, and this was followed by a sixty-three-day Caribbean cruise. She spent a brief time as an accommodation ship in Gothenburg and then a long time idle in lay-up in Greece before being scrapped in 2002.

# Red Star Line

## Belgenland

27,132grt
697ft length overall
78ft breadth
500 first-class, 600 second-class and 1,500 third-class passengers
Built in 1914 by Harland & Wolff, Belfast
Powered by a triple-expansion engine plus low-pressure turbines

The Red Star liner *Belgenland* was a perennial cruising favourite in the late 1920s and early 1930s. Here she is seen in Southampton Water.

*Belgenland* was laid down in 1912 as an Atlantic liner for the Antwerp to New York service, and was launched on 31 December 1914. She was then placed in lay up in an incomplete state due to the war. However, by 1917 she was hurriedly completed as a cargo vessel and in June of that year delivered to White Star Line as the *Belgic*. Then, in 1918 she underwent further work in New York, where she was fitted out as a troop transport with accommodation for approximately 3,000. In 1921, with no further role, she was laid up in Liverpool and it was not until March the following year that she was sent to Harland & Wolff to be completed as per the original plans. The work took one year to complete, and on 17 March 1923 she emerged as an Atlantic liner, once again named *Belgenland*. Whilst employed on the Antwerp–New York service she was also used extensively as a luxury cruise ship, with her passenger capacity reduced to approximately 500, and at the time was the largest liner to be used on round-the-world cruises. By the late 1920s she was employed solely as a cruise ship. However, all these cruising activities were from New York and the Depression had reduced her to operating 'booze cruises' of sometimes just a few hours duration. In March 1933 *Belgenland* was returned to Europe and laid up at Antwerp. That summer she undertook some Mediterranean cruises from London but was again placed in lay-up once they were completed. She remained inactive until early 1935 when she was sold to the Panama Pacific Line and renamed *Columbia* for the New York to California service. This was short lived as it proved not to be profitable, and it appears that the liner also failed to be profitable on a series of Caribbean cruises out of New York. She was therefore withdrawn from service in early 1936, having been sold to be broken up. She left New York in April for Bo'ness, where she was scrapped.

## Lapland

18,866grt
606ft length overall
70ft breadth
481 first-class, 440 second-class and 1,008 third-class passengers
Built in 1909 by Harland & Wolff, Belfast
Powered by twin-screw quadruple-expansion engines

*Lapland* was built for the Antwerp–New York service in 1909 and made her maiden voyage in April of that year. In 1914 she was transferred to British registry and was employed on the White Star Line service to New York, sailing mostly from Liverpool and sometimes from Southampton. She reopened the Antwerp–New York service in 1920 and in 1929 she was transferred to F. Leyland & Co., which was another IMM concern, though neither her livery nor her route were changed. Her last transatlantic voyage from Antwerp was in 1931 and for the following two seasons *Lapland* was used solely as a cruise ship. She did not prove to be very profitable in this role and consequently was sold for scrap. She was broken up by Japanese breakers.

# Royal Mail Lines

The Royal Mail Steam Packet Company was formed in 1839 to operate the mail service to the West Indies and South America. In 1861 the Federal warship USS *San Jacinto* intercepted the company's steamer *Trent*. The American Civil War was in progress and two representatives of the Confederacy, who were proceeding to the UK and then to France in the *Trent*, were forcibly removed. This incident nearly brought Great Britain into the war on the side of the Confederacy. To ensure that both Britain and France remained neutral, the Federal authorities were forced to release the men.

By 1895 the company owned twenty-seven seagoing vessels. In 1903, Owen Philipps, later to become Lord Kylsant became the chairman of the company. Royal Mail purchased the shareholding of the Pacific Steam Navigation Company (PSNC) and Orient Line in 1906, giving it an entry into the Australia and New Zealand trade. This trade lasted until 1909, although the links with PSNC, another Kylsant company, lasted longer. Royal Mail acquired a number of other companies including Thomas Brocklebank, Shire Line and Elder Dempster, all prior to 1914. In 1914 Royal Mail began to operate a UK–Canada service having acquired a government contract.

In 1927 shares of the White Star Line were acquired from International Mercantile Marine of J. Pierpont Morgan but by 1929 the company was in dire financial troubles. The Kylsant empire was broken up and PSNC was separated from the group of companies.

The company was an early entrant into the cruise market using the *Solent* – one of the first purpose-built cruise vessels – and the *Berbice*, to offer Caribbean cruises from the UK. The two ships were stationed in the West Indies and cruise passengers transported from the UK or New York by the regular Royal Mail service – an operation akin to the fly-cruising of today. Between the wars all of the company's 'A'-class liners at one time or another, with the exception of the *Arlanza*, were sent on a cruise.

In addition to specific cruising itineraries there were those who could afford it who used the Royal Mail liner service as a cruise to escape the British winter by taking the ship out from the UK and then returning to the warmer British weather in spring.

The RMSP ship *Araguaya* tendering in a Norwegian fjord.

The most well known and influential of the Royal Mail cruise ships was the *Andes*. Beginning her cruising career in 1960, *Andes* and the TSA/Union-Castle cruise ship *Reina del Mar* introduced many Britons to cruising in the 1960s.

In 1972 the Royal Mail name disappeared, as the company became a part of the Furness Withy Group. The last of the company's cruise ships, the *Andes* was scrapped in 1971.


## *Alcantra*

22,181grt
656ft length overall
78.5ft breadth
410 first-class, 232 second-class and 768 third-class passengers
Built in 1926 by Harland & Wolff, Belfast
Powered by twin diesel engines as built

The largest motor ship in the world when built – her gross registetred tonnage was slightly in excess of that of her sister *Asturias*. A two-funnelled design with the forward funnel being a dummy, she was built for the UK–River Plate service. She undertook some cruising for the UK market both before and after the Second World War. In 1934 she was re-engined with geared turbines at Harland & Wolff.

Refitted as an Armed Merchant Cruiser in 1939, she was in action with the German raider *Thor* on 28 July 1940. Hit on the waterline, her speed was diminished and *Thor* escaped. In 1943 she was converted to a troopship.

She re-entered Royal Mail service with a single funnel in 1948 and gave ten years more service, including cruises to the Mediterranean for the UK market, before being scrapped in Japan in 1958.


## *Andes*

14, 787grt
669ft length overall
83.5ft breadth
480 cruise passengers from 1960
Built in 1939 by Harland & Wolff, Belfast
Powered by single-reduction steam turbines

One of the best-loved British cruise ships and intended as the Royal Mail flagship, *Andes* did not enter commercial service until 1948. On 26 September 1939 (100 years since the formation of the company), instead of her maiden voyage, she sailed from Belfast to Liverpool where she was converted to a troopship. One of her final military duties was to return the Norwegian government to Norway in May 1945.

After trooping duties throughout the world, she was released in 1946 and refurbished in Belfast, entering the South American service in January 1948.

In 1959, with passenger numbers falling, it was decided to convert her into a one-class cruise vessel, together with the almost obligatory white hull. The conversion work was carried out in Flushing in the Netherlands and in 1960 she entered the UK cruising market. Together with the *Reina del Mar*, she introduced many of today's frequent cruise passengers to the joys of a cruise holiday. Always kept to the highest standard, it was a sad day in February 1971 when she was withdrawn from service and sailed to the breaker's

Royal Mail's *Andes* is, after *Canberra* and *QE2*, probably one of the most loved of the older cruise ships.

yard in Belgium. A classic looking, single-funnelled ship, she had sailed over 2,750,000 miles in both war and peace.

### *Arcadian* (1899/1910)

7,945grt
515ft length overall
55ft breadth
320 cruise passengers from 1910
Built in 1899 by Vickers, Sons & Maxim, Barrow in Furness
Powered by twin triple-expansion engines

Built as the three-class *Ortona* for the joint Orient Line/PSNC service from the UK to Australia, in 1906 she was acquired by Royal Mail as part of the financial transfer of PSNC shares to Royal Mail. She remained on the Australia service until 1910 when she was refitted to carry 320 single-class cruise passengers and renamed *Arcadian*.

In 1914 she was requisitioned as a troopship and served as Sir Ian Hamilton's headquarters during the ill-fated Gallipoli campaign in 1915. In 1917 she was torpedoed and sunk in the Eastern Mediterranean with the loss of 279 of the 1,335 on board.

Deck sports on board the *Arcadian* of 1910.

## Avon

11,073grt
535ft length overall
62ft breadth
300 first-class, 140 second-class and 1,200 third-class passengers
Built in 1907 by Harland & Wolff, Belfast
Powered by quadruple-expansion engines, twin-screw

The first voyage of the *Avon* was in June 1907 from Southampton to Argentina. In August 1914 she was converted to a troop transport and the following year she became an auxiliary cruiser and was renamed *Avoca*. She reverted to the name *Avon* in 1917 and in November 1919 she was returned to service sailing to South America. During the 1920s she was often used as a cruise ship and in 1927 she was given an all-white livery that further enhanced this role. In September 1929 she was laid up at Southampton and the following January was sold to T.W. Ward at Briton Ferry to be broken up.

## Araguaya

10,537grt
532ft length overall
61ft breadth
285 first-class, 100 second-class and 800 third-class passengers
Built in 1906 by Workman Clark & Co., Belfast
Powered by quadruple-expansion engines, twin screw

*Araguaya* entered service on the South America run in September 1906, and was regarded as being a particularly fine vessel. During the First World War she saw service as a hospital ship, returning to Royal Mail in 1920. In 1926 she was withdrawn from the South American run and was rebuilt as a cruise ship with accommodation for just 365 passengers. Her time as a cruise ship was short lived, being by this time somewhat outdated. So Royal Mail sold her at the end of 1930 to Jugoslavenski Lloyd of Dubrovnik. Renamed *Kraljica Marija*, she was employed on Mediterranean and Black Sea routes. In 1940 she was sold to the French Government and was operated by CGT as *Savoie*. She was sunk off Casablanca in 1942 during the Allied landings in North Africa.

## Arcadian (1907/1923)

12,105grt
520ft length overall
62ft breadth
300 first-class, 140 second-class and 1,200 steerage-class passengers
Built in 1907 by Harland & Wolff, Belfast
Powered by twin quadruple-expansion engines

Built as the *Asturias* for the UK–River Plate service (although her maiden voyage was to Australia), she was requisitioned in 1914 to serve as a hospital ship. Despite her hospital-ship markings she was torpedoed in March 1917. She did not sink, however, and was towed to Plymouth and used as an ammunition hulk, ownership passing to the Admiralty.

In 1919 she was re-purchased by Royal Mail and in 1923 she emerged from a refit at Harland & Wolff, Belfast, with a rebuilt interior as the cruising liner *Arcadian*. She was laid up in 1930 as uneconomic and scrapped in Japan in 1933.

## Asturias

22,048grt
656ft length overall
78.5ft breadth
432 first-class, 223 second-class and 453 third-class passengers
Built in 1925 by Harland & Wolff, Belfast
Powered by twin diesel engines

The largest motor ship in the world when built, a statistic she lost to her sister *Alcantara* of 1926, she was a two-funnelled design, with the forward funnel being a dummy. She was built for the UK–River Plate service and undertook cruises to New York from the UK in 1927. In 1934 she was re-engined with geared turbines.

Converted into an Armed Merchant Cruiser in 1939, she was torpedoed in the South Atlantic in July 1943 but was towed the 500 miles to Freetown. Royal Mail abandoned its interest in her and at the war's end she was converted to an emigrant ship and finally, in 1954 a troopship.

In 1957 she was sold for breaking but, before broken up at Faslane, Scotland she was used as a prop in the film *A Night to Remember* about the sinking of the *Titanic*.

The motor-ship *Asturius* leaving Jamaica, *c.*1932.

*Atlantis* and Blue Star's *Arandora Star* at Copenhagen.

## Atlantis

15,620grt
590ft length overall
65ft breadth
450 cruise passengers from 1929
Built in 1913 by Harland & Wolff, Belfast
Powered by triple-screw, triple-expansion engines

Originally intended for the PSNC, she was transferred to Royal Mail whilst building and named *Andes*. She traded to South America until 1915 when she was converted into an Armed Merchant Cruiser, her last passenger voyage being from Valparaiso, Chile in March of that year for PSNC. Together with her sister, *Arlanza*, she engaged the German raider *Greif* on 29 February 1916. Both *Greif* and *Arlanza* were sunk in the exchange. *Andes* returned to the South America service in 1919.

In 1929 she was refitted in Liverpool as a full-time cruise liner and renamed *Atlantis*. With a white hull and accommodation for 450 cruise passengers, she became a very popular vessel in the years before the Second World War.

During the conflict she served as a hospital ship before being chartered to carry emigrants from the UK to Australia and New Zealand. At the end of her four-year charter, in 1952 she was laid up in Scotland where she was broken up later in the same year.

## Berbice

2,379grt
300.5ft length overall
38ft breadth
100 first-class and 50 second-class passengers
Built in 1909 by Harland & Wolff, Belfast
Powered by a quadruple-expansion engine

Following the success of the *Solent* as a cruise ship and within the inter-island trade in the West Indies, *Berbice* was built as a replacement. Larger than *Solent* she served from 1909 until the outbreak of war in 1914. Cruise passengers travelled to the West Indies in the regular Royal Mail steamers from the UK and the USA and then cruised in *Berbice*.

   *Berbice* served as a hospital ship between 1914 and 1918 and was sold in 1920 to Michael Cotts of London, for whom she became *Suntemple*. She was broken up in 1924.

## Caribbean

See the entry for *Dunottar Castle* (1890) under the Union-Castle heading.

## La Plata

4,464grt
420.5ft length overall
45.75ft breadth
120 first-class, 90 second-class and 50 third-class passengers
Built in 1882 by J&G Thomson, Glasgow
Powered by a single triple-expansion engine

Built as the *Moor* for the Union Line, she was merged into the Union-Castle fleet in 1900. In 1901 she was sold to Royal Mail, renamed *La Plata*, given a white hull, and used for cruising. She was sold to the Polytechnic Touring Association, who renamed her *The Viking*, for cruising to the Norwegian fjords. She was broken up in 1913.

## Solent

1,908grt
321.5ft length overall
35ft breadth
Approximately 80 cruise passengers
Built in 1878 by Oswald Mordaunt & Co., Southampton
Powered by a single screw, coal-fired compound steam engine

Designed for the inter-island services in the West Indies, *Solent* was transformed into the company's first cruise ship in 1905. Cruise passengers were brought from the UK or New York by regular steamer to join the ship, making the operation the forerunner of today's Caribbean fly cruises. She was broken up in 1909, being replaced by the larger *Berbice*.

## Saga

In 1951 Sidney De Haan realised that retired people would appreciate the opportunity to take lower-cost seaside holidays outside of the main vacation periods. Many in the holiday business scoffed at De Haan's decision to target a particular niche market. However, his company, Saga, grew and grew. In the 1960s De Haan pioneered tourism in the Algarve, it being an ideal holiday destination for the older person.

In 1996 Saga surprised the cruise industry with a bold development – cruises that were solely for the over-50s (they can take a partner aged 40+ with them). Believing that there was a large enough market for a cruise ship for the over-50s, Saga acquired the 24,500grt *Sagafjord* from Cunard in 1996 and renamed the vessel *Saga Rose*. Saga offers a door-to-door holiday service, something that is appreciated by their clientele. Saga also sells places on other cruise ships and provides a representative on board to look after the interest of its customers.

Saga's cruise business grew to the degree that in 2002 it was announced that they were to increase capacity by chartering the 12,500grt *Minerva* (built on the hull of an incomplete ex-Soviet spy ship) with accommodation for 352 passengers for a trial period in 2003. The ship was renamed *Saga Pearl*. Having aquired the *Caronia* from Cunard, she is due to enter Saga service in March 2005 as Saga Ruby.

### Saga Pearl

See entry for *Minerva* under Swan Hellenic.

### Saga Rose

24,474grt
619.5ft length overall
80ft breadth
620 cruise passengers
Built in 1965 by Forges et Chantiers de la Mediteranee, France
Powered by diesel engines

Built as the *Sagafjord* for Norwegian America to such a high standard that the shipyard had major financial problems following her completion, she served with her near sister *Vistafjord*, later to be renamed *Caronia*. Both ships passed to Cunard when they acquired Norwegian America and *Sagafjord* continued in Cunard service until 1997 when, after briefly being renamed *Gripsholm* for a charter to the German company Transocean Tours, she was sold to Saga as the *Saga Rose*.

Saga's requirements were for a ship with sufficient range to undertake an annual world cruise (retired people can afford to take the 100 days required to circumnavigate the globe), larger cabins than the industry norm and a good proportion of single cabins.

The on board entertainment is designed to appeal to an older age range and includes not only singers and comedians but also a number of specialist lecturers.

## Shaw, Savill & Albion

Shaw, Savill & Co. was founded by Robert Ewart Shaw and Walter Savill in 1858 and was particularly important in UK–New Zealand trade.

Prior to the end of the Second World War, most of the Shaw, Savill & Albion (as the company was then titled) fleet comprised of cargo or cargo/passenger vessels. In 1934, however, with the merger of White Star and Cunard, the company acquired the 18,481grt passenger steamer *Ceramic* (which was sunk during the war with the loss of almost everyone on board, bar one man lucky enough to be picked up by a U-boat) and in 1939 added the quadruple-screw 27,000grt *Dominion Monarch* to the fleet. Post-war the company operated the *New Australia*, a reconstruction of the *Monarch of Bermuda*, originally built in 1931. *New Australia* operated as an emigrant ship for UK citizens going to live in Australia between 1950 and 1957 on the Assisted Passage scheme. The ship was then sold to become the *Arkadia* of the Greek Line.

In 1955 the passenger-only *Southern Cross* was built to operate a round-the-world service from the UK via New Zealand and Australia and she was followed by a near sister called *Northern Star* in 1962. Both ships were revolutionary in that the engines and funnel were aft, giving a large amount of deck space. Neither carried any cargo. As the liner trade diminished both ships began to cruise out of UK ports, using both Southampton and Liverpool. The cruise fleet was increased in 1970 when the company acquired the *Empress of England* from Canadian Pacific.

The effects of industrial action by seamen and the huge rise in oil prices of the 1970s saw the company leave the cruise business with the sale of *Southern Cross* in 1973 and the scrapping of *Ocean Monarch* and *Northern Star* in 1975 – the former after only five years with the company. Thus ended over a hundred years of passenger services.

## Northern Star

24,756grt
650ft length overall
83.5ft breadth
1,437 passengers
Built in 1962 by Vickers Armstrong, Newcastle-upon-Tyne
Powered by twin-screw steam turbines

Built as a passenger-only single-class vessel for the UK–New Zealand round-the-world service, she was slightly larger than *Southern Cross*. She had her machinery aft, thus freeing up deck space for passengers and avoiding funnel trunkings in her public rooms. As the liner trade decreased she was switched to cruising but was sold for scrapping in Taiwan in 1975.

## Ocean Monarch

25,971grt after 1970–71 refit
640ft length overall
85ft breadth
1,068 cruise passengers from 1971
Built in 1957 by Vickers Armstrong, Newcastle-upon-Tyne
Powered by twin-screw steam turbines

For the earlier career of this vessel see the entry for *Empress of England* under the Canadian Pacific heading.

She was acquired by Shaw Savill in 1970 and introduced to the company's cruise service in 1971 having cost £1.5 million to refit. She was only in service until 1975 when Shaw Savill left the passenger shipping and cruise industries. She was scrapped in Taiwan

*Southern Cross* at Southampton, *c.*1970. She has recently gone to the breaker's yard at Alang, India.

in 1975, another victim of the industrial unrest in the British Merchant Navy at the time and the rises in the price of fuel oil.

## Southern Cross

20,204grt
560ft length overall
78ft breadth
Built in 1955 by Harland & Wolff, Belfast
1,100 one-class passengers
Powered by twin-screw steam turbines

Built as a passenger-only single-class vessel for the UK–New Zealand round-the-world service, she was one of the first liners to have all of her machinery aft. As the liner trade decreased she was switched to cruising but was sold in 1973 to become the *Calypso* of the Ulysses Line. As *Calypso* she re-entered the UK cruise market as a result of a charter to Thomson – the UK holiday company (see the entry under Thomson). She became the *Azure Seas* in 1980, and the *Ocean Breeze* in 1992 when she sailed on Caribbean cruises based in Aruba. Owned since 2000 under that name by Imperial Majesty Cruises she undertook short cruises to the Bahamas – see the entry under Thomson Cruises for more details – until withdrawn from service in 2003 and scrapped in 2004.

# Sitmar Line

The Sitmar company was an Italian concern founded in 1938 and operated by Alexandre Vlasov (the V on the funnel of the Sitmar ships referring to his surname). After the Second World War the company entered both the emigrant trade and the North Atlantic liner run. In 1965 the company commenced a cruise operation out of Australia, later expanding into the lucrative US cruise market. The company was sold to P&O in 1988 (for $210 million) and absorbed into the Princess Cruises brand. The senior management of Sitmar later went on to found Silversea Cruises.

### Fairstar

23,764grt
609ft length overall
78ft breadth
1,280 cruise passengers
Built in 1957 by Fairfield Shipbuilding & Engineering Co., Glasgow
Powered by twin-screw geared turbine engines

*Fairstar* was built as the Bibby Line troopship, *Oxfordshire*. Following the British government's decision to end troop movements by sea, *Oxfordshire* and her near sister, British India's *Nevasa*, were withdrawn from service. Initially *Oxfordshire* was chartered to Sitmar Line for a period of six years, and they had her converted into a one-class liner capable of accommodating 1,910 passengers, to be employed on their service between northern Europe and Australia. The conversion work was carried out by the Wilton-Fjienoord yard at Schiedam, Holland. As the conversion proved more difficult, costly and time-consuming than initially anticipated, to speed things up Sitmar bought the ship outright, and had the conversion work finished by Harland & Wolff in Southampton. She made her first voyage as *Fairstair* to Australia in May 1964, and maintained this service for almost nine years before undertaking a cruise, from Australia. It was not until 1974, when Sitmar were seeking new markets, that they positioned *Fairstar* at Southampton to operate a season of summer cruises to the Mediterranean and the Atlantic Islands. The experiment was not a success, *Fairstar* not attracting the level of interest that Sitmar had hoped. She was returned to Australia, never to return, and instead became a cruising legend in the South Pacific. She was ultimately withdrawn from service in January 1997 and scrapped in India.

# Southern Ferries

### Eagle

11,500grt
465ft length overall
72ft breadth
450 cruise passengers
Built in 1971 by Dubigeon-Normandie SA, Nantes
Powered by twin-screw Pielstick diesel engines

*Eagle* was built primarily for a ferry service between Southampton, Lisbon and Tangier. The company had sometimes operated their older, smaller ferries, *Dragon* and *Leopard* to

Sailing on the Southampton–Tangier via Lisbon route, *Eagle* often catered for mini-cruises too.

both Lisbon and Casablanca with considerable success and emboldened by this the company took the opportunity to design a very much bigger and faster ship, which alone would be able to maintain a frequent service to Lisbon, with every third voyage extended to Tangier. This step made it possible to provide much more spacious accommodation, which would make the ship suitable for extended cruises in tropical climates. It appears that consideration was given to the possibility of operating her for at least part of the year in the West Indies, offering fly cruises. *Eagle* was truly a dual-purpose vessel, being fully suited to either role of ferry or tropical cruise ship. She was generously provided with public rooms, two restaurants and swimming pool. Her cabin accommodation was in three standard sizes (and when in ferry service could accommodate 700). While Southern Ferries never sent *Eagle* out to the West Indies to undertake cruise duties, there were those passengers that did take her extended Lisbon–Tangier voyage as a mini-cruise, the round-trip taking just under a week. *Eagle* was, however, a far from successful ship on the service and after barely four years she was sold to Nouvelle Cie de Paquebots for Mediterranean cruising, and renamed *Azur*. In this role she proved herself to be far more successful. Her car decks were rebuilt in 1981, increasing her passenger accommodation to 1,039. In 1987 she was sold to Chandris and her name changed to *The Azur*. In 1994 she was sold to Festival Cruises, retaining the same name and was still operating in 2003.

With the collapse of Festival in early 2004, *The Azur* was sold to become the *Royal Iris*, operating out of Israel.

## Sovereign Cruises

The UK entrepreneur Ted Langton started Sovereign Cruises in the early 1970s. The operation was based on using charter aircraft to fly the cruise passengers from the then small airport at Gatwick south of London. A seven-day cruise cost less than £45! The first ship chartered was the *Queen Frederica*, followed by the *Galaxy Queen*. The operation only lasted a few years as the oil price increases of the 1970s made operating such vessels uneconomic. Nevertheless, many Britons were introduced to fly cruises by the Sovereign operation.

## Queen Frederica

See Chandris Line.

## Galaxy Queen

14,708grt
492ft length overall
69ft breadth
790 passengers (approximately)
Built in 1942 by Western Pipe & Steel Co., San Francisco
Powered by single-shaft, geared turbines

Built as an escort aircraft carrier, HMS *Fencer*, on a standard US Government C3-type cargo ship hull, after the war she was sold, along with her sister ship HMS *Atheling*, to Flotta Lauro. Totally rebuilt in Genoa, the ships were transformed into passenger liners for the Mediterranean to Australia service. *Fencer* being renamed *Sydney*, and *Atheling* became *Roma*. When Lauro introduced the larger, and far superior *Angelina Lauro* and

*Galaxy Queen* was originally an escort aircraft carrier. She was broken in 1974.

*Achille Lauro* onto their Australian service *Sydney* and *Roma* were transferred to the Naples to Venezuela run. They remained on this service only briefly, and in 1967 *Roma* was withdrawn and sold for scrap. Lauro placed the *Sydney* in Mediterranean cruise service, renaming her *Roma*. This was not a successful venture and in 1969 she was sold to Aretusa SpA. She sailed for them for just one season and then was laid up in October 1970. She was then acquired by Sovereign Cruises and was given the name *Galaxy Queen*. She entered service operating Mediterranean cruises for the British market in March 1971. Despite having undergone a major refit she suffered various mechanical problems and received a great deal of bad publicity. Withdrawn from service she was sold in 1972 and renamed *Lady Dina*, however she remained laid up. In 1973 she was chartered to Siosa Line and given the name *Caribia 2*. Her poor condition meant that she again received a great deal of bad publicity. Her cruises were being marketed in the UK and with low take-up rates she was sold to be broken up the following year.

# Swan Hellenic

In 1930 W.F. Swan, the owner of the Swan Travel Bureau set up a new company, Swan Hellenic, to provide cultural cruises around Greece and its islands.

In 1954 the company began to offer cruises under its own name. The first ship chartered was the *Miaoulis* and over the years a number of vessels were used, including the Turkish *Ankara*. For a number of years between 1974 and 1995 the company chartered the *Orpheus* from Epirotiki Lines before being replaced by *Minerva*. Swan Hellenic was acquired by P&O in 1983 but is still operated as a distinct brand. For the 2003 season the company acquired the use of *Minerva II*, a much larger ship, reflecting the growth in this type of cruising.

Swan Hellenic cruises are for those interested in the culture of the areas they are visiting – areas that span a much greater part of the globe than the Hellenic world – the original destination for the company. Swan Hellenic does not have casinos but the cruises are accompanied by leading authorities – archaeologists, historians, art critics, politicians, statesmen and women and religious figures, including archbishops. A large number of shore excursions led by acknowledged experts are included in the price of the cruise. A Swan Hellenic cruise has been described as 'cruising country house style'.

## *Ankara*

6,178grt
409ft length overall
62ft breadth
407 cruise passengers
Built in 1927 by Newport News Shipbuilding & Dry Dock Co., Virginia
Powered by twin geared turbines

She was built in 1927 as the two-funnelled *Iroquois* for the New York–Florida–Cuba service in winter and in the summer the New York–Maine and Nova Scotia services of Clyde Mallory Lines. Redundant after the Second World War, she was purchased by Turkish Maritime Lines and converted to a single-funnelled cruise ship.

First chartered by Swan Hellenic for one cruise, in 1959, a further two cruises were operated by the ship in 1960 and three in 1961. Then, for the twelve years from 1962 to 1974 *Ankara* became the principal Swan Hellenic cruise ship, sailing on ninety-nine cruises for the company.

*Aegaeon* of Typaldis Line and *Ankara* of Turkish Maritime Lines, both of which were operated by Swan Hellenic. Taken at Rhodes, the Chandris *Fantasia* is on the left.

Regular stalwart for Swan Hellenic was the *Ankara*, broken up in the mid-1970s.

Running on fuel oil rather than diesel made her expensive to operate and the *Orpheus* replaced her as the Swan Hellenic ship in 1975.

On 26 September 1975, whilst on a cruise for Turkish Maritime Lines, she was damaged entering Ajaccio Harbour. On her return to Turkey she was laid up for some time before being broken up.

## *Orpheus*

5,092grt
375ft length overall
50ft breadth
318 cruise passengers
Built in 1948 by Harland & Wolff, Belfast
Powered by twin diesel engines

She was built as the *Munster* for the Irish Sea service of the British & Irish Steam Packet Co. as a post-war replacement for a ship of the same name that had been lost during the war. As an Irish Sea ferry she could accommodate 1,500 passengers. In 1948 the demand for car transportation between Britain and Ireland was not foreseen, although the ship had accommodation for up to 484 head of cattle!

By 1967 the ferry customers required drive on–drive off car ferries and the *Munster* and her sister *Leinster* were put up for sale. *Munster* was bought by the Epirotiki Company of Greece in 1968 and refitted as a cruise ship. She was to have been named *Theseus* but, during the refit, the name was changed to *Orpheus*.

*Ankara's* replacement was *Orpheus,* a converted Irish Sea ferry.

She undertook both Mediterranean, Alaskan and Caribbean cruises for her new owners but in 1974 Swan Hellenic chartered her. Although she undertook some other charters, from then until 1995 she became a much loved cultural haven for the 'Loyal Swans' as the company's repeat passengers are known.

Swans chartered Orpheus for the 1975 season and it was the beginning of a long association between the company and the ship. Her simple décor and unpretentious charm earned her a very loyal following, and Swan Hellenic chartered her for the next twenty years. Whilst the focus of Swan Hellenic cruises was in the Mediterranean, Aegean and Black Sea, in 1980 they extended their cruise programme to include Spain, Portugal, France and the British Isles. It was a successful experiment and in later years *Orpheus* included other Northern European and Scandinavian ports to her itineraries. In 1984 the ship was modernised and was given a more stylish appearance with a new raked bow. When P&O took control of Swan Hellenic, in 1983, consideration was given to replacing *Orpheus* but she remained with the company until 1995. She had by this time operated 327 cruises for Swan Hellenic.

A merger of Greek cruise operators, including Epirotiki, led to the formation of Royal Olympic Cruises and *Orpheus* sailed under the new brand until she was laid up in 2001 and sold for scrap in 2002.


## Miaoulis

1,714grt
268ft length overall
42ft breadth
Number of passengers unknown but 128 Swan Hellenic passengers were on board for the company's first cruise
Built in 1952 by Cantieri Runiti dell'Adriatico
Powered by twin-screw Fiat Diesels

*Miaoulis* was owned by the Greek company Nomikos Lines, sailing between Italy and the Greek Islands. In August 1954 Swan Hellenic was able to book 128 passengers aboard the ship. They travelled by train from England to Venice, boarding the ship there. This was the beginning of the Swan Hellenic tradition of cultural cruising.


## Aegaeon

2,040grt
291ft length overall
46ft breadth
Passenger capacity unknown
Built in 1911 by Swan, Hunter & Wigham Richardson Ltd, Newcastle
Powered by triple-expansion engines, single screw

*Aegaeon* was built as the *Princess Alice* for the Canadian Pacific Railway Co. for their Victoria–Vancouver night boat service. In 1949 she was sold to the Greek company Typaldos Lines for service in the Mediterranean. On 31 March 1955 Swan Hellenic was able to charter the ship outright and 268 passengers took the company's second cruise, which included Turkish as well as Greek ports. Although the Swan Hellenic passengers had admired the ship's period charm the company never chartered her again. However, the ship remained in Typaldos service until being destroyed by fire in 1966.

## Mediterranean

3,925grt
330ft length overall
47ft breadth
Passenger capacity unknown
Built in 1908 by Fairfield & Co., Glasgow
Powered by two triple-expansion engines, twin screw

*Mediterranean* began life as the *Princess Charlotte* for the Canadian Pacific Railway Co.,
sailing between Victoria and Vancouver. In 1949 she was sold to Typaldos Lines and after
some rebuilding entered their service in 1950 as *Mediterranean*. Swan Hellenic chartered
her for two cruises in 1956, two in 1957 and one in 1958. The ship remained in service
until 1965, when she was sold to be broken up.

## Philippos

1,941grt
282ft length overall
38ft breadth
122 first-class and 184 second-class passengers
Built in 1940 by Ailsa Shipbuilding Co., Troon
Powered by twin-screw steam turbines (replaced in 1959 by Crossley diesels)

Built as the coastal steamer *Empress Queen*, for P&A Campbell, she was sold to the
Kavounides Shipping Co. Ltd of Piraeus in March 1955, being renamed *Philippos* before
she departed Britain for Greece. She was extensively rebuilt to enable her to undertake
cruises of up to fourteen-days duration. Swan Hellenic chartered her for just one cruise,
during 1956. She was further rebuilt in 1959 and continued in Greek islands cruise
service throughout the 1960s but never again sailing for Swans. The ship was destroyed
by fire in February 1972 whilst undergoing repairs.

## Adriatiki

2,040grt
300ft length overall
36ft breadth
263 passengers
Built in 1943 by Canadian Vickers Ltd, Montreal
Powered by triple-expansion engines, single screw

Built as the 'River-class' frigate HMS *Lossie* she was acquired by Typaldos Lines in 1955
from G. Sigalas of Piraeus who had already begun to convert the ship to passenger use.
Typaldos spent a considerable sum completing the work creating several attractive public
rooms and a swimming pool. Several of her cabins had private bathrooms (quite a luxury
for the times). She proved to be quite a popular ship with Swan Hellenic and was
chartered by them for two cruises in 1957 and two in 1958. In 1959 she undertook a
further three cruises for the company and again three more cruises in 1961.

## Tarsus

9,451grt
475ft length overall
62ft breadth
189 first-class, 66 second-class and 210 third-class passengers
Built in 1931 by the New York Shipbuilding Co., Camden
Powered by steam single-reduction geared turbines, single screw

*Tarsus* was built as the American Export Lines' *Exochora* for their United States–Mediterranean service. She served during the war as an Attack Transport Vessel and during this time was named *Harry Lee*. Her three sister ships were all lost in action. She was bought by Turkish Maritime Lines in 1948 and was used on various routes in the Mediterranean and occasionally operated cruises. In 1960 she was chartered by Swan Hellenic to undertake two cruises. *Tarsus* was destroyed by fire in December that year while at anchor in the Bosphorus, having been hit by a drifting ship following a collision between two tankers.

## Neptune

For details of the ship see under *Meteor*, Bergen Line.

In the spring of 1989 *Orpheus* suffered from engine problems. While she was undergoing repairs, Epirotiki Line chartered to Swan Hellenic her fleet mate, *Neptune*. During April and May *Neptune* undertook four cruises for Swan Hellenic.

## Aurora II

3,300grt
270ft length overall
46ft breadth
80 passengers
Built in 1992 by Flender Werft, Germany
Powered by twin-screw diesels

*Aurora II* was built as the *Lady Sarah* for a company called Windsor Cruise Line. However, the company folded before the ship, and her identical sister vessel, *Lady Diana*, entered service. Both ships were very luxuriously appointed, somewhat in the style of private yachts. The vessels remained inactive for about two years after they were completed. Swan Hellenic chartered the ship in May 1993 (by this time she had been given the name *Aurora II*) for a British Isles cruise. This was the only cruise she operated for the company. In 1995 she was acquired by Star Cruises, was re-named *MegaStar Taurus*, and operates short cruises in Malaysian waters.

## St Helena

6.767 grt
344 ft length overall
63 ft breadth
128 passengers
Built in 1990 by A&P Appledore, Scotland
Powered by twin-screw diesels

The RMS *St Helena* is a cargo/passenger vessel built to maintain the liner service between Britain and the islands of St Helena (and occasionally Ascension Island and Tristan Da Cunha) and Cape Town. Whilst she was not designed with a cruising role in mind, Swan Hellenic chartered her in July 1995 to operate a British Isles cruise. She remains in service but is operated solely on the St Helena–Cape Town route.

## Clipper Adventurer

5,750 grt
330 ft length overall
54 ft breadth
122 passengers
Built in 1976 by Brodgradiliste Uljanik, Yugoslavia
Powered by two Mann B&W diesels, twin screw

She was built for the USSR as the *Alla Tarasova* to operate with five identical sister vessels on their passenger services in Arctic waters. *Alla Tarasova* was based in Murmansk. This was a short-lived operation as she was transferred to the Yugoslavian Navy for a time. In 1997/98 she was totally rebuilt and brought up to western cruise ship standards and renamed *Clipper Adventurer* for her new operators, Clipper Cruise Line. Whilst ideally suited to operating 'soft adventure' cruises to Arctic and Antarctic waters, *Clipper Adventurer* also cruises the Mediterranean, Baltic and Northern Europe. Swan Hellenic has chartered the ship on several occasions: in October 1998 to operate cruises along the coast of Brazil and up the Amazon; in September 2000 on a Greenland and Arctic Circle cruise, in October a Caribbean cruise and in November a repeat of the Brazil and Amazon cruise; in September 2001 on a Maritime America cruise and in October 2002 on an Inca Gold cruise. *Clipper Adventurer* remains in service and has also been used by Noble Caledonia.

## Clipper Odyssey

5,218 grt
337 ft length overall
50 ft breadth
128 passengers
Built in 1989 by the NKK Tsu Shipyard, Japan
Powered by twin-screw Wartsila diesels

She was built as the *Oceanic Grace* for a single-ship operation, Oceanic Cruises, operating cruises out of Japan to various ports in China and Korea as well as Japanese coastal cruises. She was and is a very luxurious vessel, built in the style of a private yacht. She was later transferred to another Japanese operator, NKK Line and at this time renamed *Oceanic*

*Odyssey*. In 1999 she was acquired by Clipper Cruise Line and again underwent another name change, this time to *Clipper Odyssey*. Swan Hellenic used her in May 2001 for a cruise to ports in Japan and China.


## Minerva

12,000grt
436ft length overall
65.5ft breadth
456 cruise passengers
Built in 1996 by Marriotti (see note below)
Powered by twin diesel engines

*Minerva* was laid down as the *Okean* – a spy ship for the Soviet Navy. The incomplete hull was purchased by the V Ships concern (V Ships had connections to Sitmar Line in the past and also to Silversea Cruises) and the ship was completed in Italy, being especially tailored to the needs of Swan Hellenic. She gained a reputation for elegance and culture. Her library was one of the best afloat. So popular was the ship that the need for a larger vessel became apparent and in 2002 it was announced that she was to be chartered by Saga Cruises for six months per annum as the *Saga Pearl*.


## Minerva II

30,277grt
594ft length overall
83.5ft breadth
838 cruise passengers
Built in 2001 by Chantiers de l'Atlantique, France
Powered by twin diesel engines

The replacement for *Minerva* is *Minerva II*. Built as the *R Eight*, she was the last of the identical 'R' ships built for Renaissance Cruises between 1998 and 2001. Renaissance Cruises suffered heavily after 11 September 2001 and with the company in dire financial straights all of the ships were placed on the market. In addition to *R Eight*, P&O also acquired two more of these vessels for operating under the Princess brand in the Pacific. With a large number of balcony cabins *Minerva II* brings the traditions of fine cruising and culture for which Swan Hellenic is rightly known into an extremely modern and elegant vessel.


# Swedish Lloyd

## Saga

6,458grt
421ft length overall
55ft breadth
340 passengers in three classes in North Sea service, capacity reduced to 240 in one class when in cruise service
Built in 1940 by Lindholmen A/B and completed in 1946 by Gotaverken A/B, Gothenburg
Powered by single-screw Gotaverken diesels

*Saga* was often used for cruising, making her first trip in 1946.

Whilst the *Saga* was built for Swedish Lloyd's London–Gothenburg service, she was also designed with cruising in mind. Very soon after she entered service, on 20 May 1946, she undertook a Whitsun cruise to Bergen and Hardangerfjord from London. In October of that year she undertook a month-long cruise to the Canary Islands, Morocco, Spain and Portugal, and a similar cruise was undertaken each winter for several years. However, these cruises were not always of a month in duration. On 15 October 1951, *Saga* departed Tilbury on a fourteen-day cruise to Lisbon, Cadiz, Malaga, Tangier and Casablanca. At the end of 1956 Swedish Lloyd sold the *Saga* to Compagnie Generale Transatlantique, and she was renamed *Ville de Bordeaux*. In 1964 she was sold again, this time to the Bulgarian company, Navigation Maritime Bulgare, and was given the name *Nessebar*, and was used in Black Sea–Mediterranean services. She was scrapped in 1975 in Yugoslavia.

## Patricia

7,775grt
454ft length overall
58ft breadth
344 passengers in three classes when on North Sea service, capacity reduced to approximately 250 when in cruise service
Built in 1951 by Swan Hunter & Wigham Richardson, Tyneside
Powered by single-screw geared turbines

*Patricia* was a refinement of the design of her near sister, *Saga*. She was also designed to serve both the London–Gothenburg route during the summer months and to operate as

*Patricia*, another Swedish Lloyd vessel, was built in 1967.

a cruise ship during the winter. Her first cruise began from Gothenburg on 13 September 1951, but included a call at Tilbury to embark British passengers, before continuing to the Mediterranean. Her second cruise was from Tilbury on 8 October 1951, and again was into the Mediterranean and lasted for twenty-six days. However, her days serving the British market as either a cruise ship or on her North Sea service were brief. In the winter of 1952 she had been sent on an experimental cruise to Bermuda, but following that she was chartered to operate cruises from America to the Caribbean. In 1955 she was chartered to Hapag Lloyd and in 1957 she was sold to them, and was renamed *Ariadne*. She was sold again in 1960 and from then on, under the ownership of several companies, she operated successfully in the Caribbean. In 1973 she came under the ownership of Chandris, as *Bon Vivant*. By the mid-1970s she was returned to the Mediterranean, and again was marketed in the UK – but not exclusively so. She was eventually scrapped in India in 1997, after several years of inactivity in the Far East.

## *Patricia, Hispania* and *Saga*

8,000grt approximately
460ft length overall
68ft breadth
750 passengers approximately
Built in 1966/67 by Lindholmens Varv, Gothenburg
Powered by twin-screw Pielstick diesel engines

In May 1967 Swedish Lloyd took delivery of the *Patricia*, the third of a series of passenger/car/cargo ferries. She was virtually identical to the England–Sweden Line's

*Saga* and Svea Line's *Svea*. All three ships carried the Swedish Lloyd Line's funnel markings of a gold star on a blue disk. *Svea* was initially used on the Hull–Gothenburg route while *Saga* sailed on the Gothenburg service from Tilbury. *Patricia* sailed on the company's new service, from Southampton–Bilbao. *Svea* was later renamed *Hispania* and also operated on the Bilbao run. Whilst none of the ships were built with a cruising role in mind, during the 'off-peak' months passengers were able to book the round trip as a mini-cruise. Each of the ships was furnished to a very high standard and they functioned very well as part-time cruise ships, attracting many passengers on their four-day voyages. By the mid-1970s, however, the ships were withdrawn from Swedish Lloyd service and since then have found employment on a variety of other routes.

## Thomson Cruises

Thomson is one of the largest UK holiday companies. In addition to selling places on the ships of other cruise lines, Thomson began to offer cruises solely for its customers on vessels it had chartered. In recent years Thomson has chartered its vessels from Louis Cruise Lines and has, like My Travel, moved away from the more resort type of cruise towards a more traditional cruise product. Thomson, again like My Travel and First Choice, has the advantage of its own airline – in the case of Thomson it is Britannia – and can offer flights from UK regional airports. Many of the Thomson Cruises can be linked to a resort stay either before or after the cruise. Until 2003 Thomson Cruises had operated mainly in the Mediterranean and the Caribbean.

### *Calypso*

20,204grt
604ft length overall
78ft breadth
950 passengers
Built in 1955 by Harland & Wolff, Belfast
Powered by twin-screw geared turbines

After a sixteen-year career sailing successfully as both a long-haul liner to Australia and New Zealand, and as a cruise ship, for Shaw Savill, the *Southern Cross* was withdrawn from service and made available for sale. Shaw Savill believed that she was unsuitable for further trading as a cruise ship. In January 1973 she was sold, for what amounted to little more than scrap value, to Cia de Vap Cerulea SA, Ithaka (they actually traded as Ulysses Line). She was given an extensive internal rebuild, which involved total reconstruction of all her cabin accommodation, as well as refurbishment of her public rooms. She emerged from the refit in April 1975 with her original profile little changed but internally a virtually new ship. *Calypso* entered service for the first time with Thomson Cruises in June that year, sailing from Tilbury to Scandinavia. She also undertook cruises from Southampton to Spain, Portugal, the Atlantic Islands, North Africa and the Mediterranean. A similar programme of cruises was repeated during 1976 and 1977. Thomson's then withdrew from the cruise market until 1996.

*Calypso* was then operated by her owners, Ulysses Line, during 1978, out of Tilbury to Norway, the North Cape and Spitzbergen, and into the Baltic. She also operated a programme of eastern Mediterranean cruises from Venice, all of which were targeted at the British market, capitalising on the popularity she had already generated with Thomson Cruises. This was a short-lived venture, however, and in 1980 she was sold to

*Southern Cross* became *Calypso* after ending her Shaw Savill career.

Eastern Steamship Lines and, under the name *Azure Seas*, she operated from American ports. She continued to sail very successfully for various owners, including Dolphin Cruises and Premier Cruises under the name *Ocean Breeze*. She sailed from Florida on short cruises to the Bahamas as *Imperial Majesty* for Imperial Majesty Cruises, until withdrawn in 2003.

Details of this vessel chartered by Thomson for a number of cruises between 1975 and 1980 can be found under *Southern Cross* in the section on Shaw, Savill & Albion.

## Ithaca

8,977grt after conversion to a cruise ship in 1972
501ft length overall
65ft breadth
780 cruise passengers after conversion to a cruise ship in 1972
Built in 1956 by Deutsche Weft AG, Hamburg
Powered by single-screw, twin sets of geared turbines

Chartered by Thomson between 1973 and 1977 as the *Ithica*, she was built in 1956 as the *Zion*, a combination cargo/passenger vessel. She was designed for the Israel–New York service of the Zim Israel Navigation Company, the national shipping line of Israel. The ship and her three sisters were built in Germany as reparation to Israel after the Second World War.

In 1966, following the decline in the transatlantic liner trade, she was sold to the Portuguese company Sociedade Geral de Commercio Industria e Transportes. Renamed

*Amelia De Mello*, she operated on the service from Lisbon to the Azores. As this trade also declined she was laid up in 1971 and, in 1972, sold to the Vlasspoulos concern and renamed *Ithaca* for a major conversion into a cruise ship. The conversion was carried out in conjunction with Thomson following the decision by the UK holiday company to charter the ship for four years.

The conversion was very sympathetic and produced a good-looking modern cruise ship. She sailed for Thomson for the four years of the charter but rising oil prices brought about a decision by Thomson to withdraw from the cruise market.

After charters to other companies the ship was transferred to another Vlasspoulos concern and placed on three–four-day cruises out of Florida under the name *Dolphin IV*. Towards the end of her service she was running day cruises out of Miami and was withdrawn in late 2002 when she was sold for breaking in India.

## Island Breeze

31,793grt
760ft length overall
90ft breadth
1,464 cruise passengers from 1996
Built in 1961by John Brown & Co., Clydebank
Powered by steam turbines

Chartered by Thomson during the summer season in the late 1990s this classic ocean liner was by then owned by Premier Cruises. Built in 1961 as the single-class *Transvaal Castle* for the Union-Castle UK–South Africa mail service, she was transferred to the

Originally *Transvaal Castle*, *Island Breeze* ended her life as *Big Red Boat III*.

South African Marine Corporation (a company linked to Union-Castle) as the *SA Vaal*. In 1977 she was withdrawn and sold to Carnival Cruises for whom she entered service in 1978 as their second vessel in the fleet. She was given the name *Festivale*. Refitted with increased accommodation in 1987, she was acquired by Premier Cruises in 1996 and renamed *Big Red Boat III*. Following the failure of Premier in 2002 she was laid up and then sent to the breaker's yard in Alang, India, in 2003.

## Sapphire

12,183grt
491.5ft length overall
71ft breadth
650 cruise passengers
Built in 1967 by Cantieri Navale Felszegi, Italy
Powered by diesel engines

Built as the *Italia* for Sunsarda SpA of Trieste as a cruise ship, she was sold in her first year of operation to Crocieri d'Oltremare of Cagliari and placed on the US west coast on charter to Princess Cruises marketed but not operated under the name *Princess Italia*.

In 1974 she was acquired by Costa and operated cruises in the Mediterranean, Caribbean and South American areas. In 1983 she became the *Ocean Princess* of Ocean Cruise Lines operating in South America in winter and in Northern Europe in summer. After a serious grounding in the River Amazon, she was sold in 1990 to Croisières Paquet and then in 1996, after a series of name changes (*Sea Prince*, *Sea Prince V* and *Princesa Oceanica*), she was acquired by Louis Cruise Lines and given the name *Sapphire*. Louis Cruise Lines chartered her to Thomson and she gained a good reputation as a value-for-money cruise ship.

Long and low, she presents an unusual yet not displeasing profile. She sailed for Thomson until 2000 at which time she reverted to the Louis Cruise Line fleet and was still in service in 2004.

## The Emerald

26,431grt as converted 1993
599ft length overall as converted 1993
84ft breadth
1,198 cruise passengers
Built in 1958 by Newport News Shipbuilding, USA
Powered by twin steam turbines

*The Emerald* was built as the 11,353grt combination passenger/cargo liner *Santa Rosa* for the New York–Central America service of Grace Lines (New York). In this role she carried 300 passengers. Laid up in 1971 she saw no further service until 1993 when, after massive conversion to a cruise ship, she entered service as the *Regent Rainbow* for Regency Cruises. In 1997 she was acquired by Louis Cruise Lines and renamed *The Emerald*. By 1999 she was under charter to Thomson and was still in their service in 2003 as the running mate to the *Thomson Spirit*.

*The Topaz*, formerly Canadian Pacific's *Empress of Britain*, remained in Thomson service until 2003.

## The Topaz

For early details of this vessel see the entry for *Empress of Britain* under Canadian Pacific.

With her accommodation increased to 1,386 and at 31,500grt the ex-*Empress of Britain* was sold by Royal Olympic (in whose service she was named *Olympic*) to Louis Cruise Lines in 1994. In 1998 she began to operate all-inclusive cruises for Thomson, i.e. cruises in which many of the drinks, etc., were included as part of the cruise price. No other Thomson ships operated this system. A classic liner, she remained in Thomson service until 2003 when she was chartered for three years to operate round-the-world cruises as the Japanese Peace Boat. She is owned by Topaz International, a company belonging to Captain Katsoufis.

## Thomson Spirit

33,930grt
704ft length overall
89ft breadth
1,350 cruise passengers
Built in1983 by Chantiers de l'Atlantique, France
Powered by diesel engines

In the spring of 2002 Thomson announced that a new ship was to be introduced to their cruise operation in 2003. Although chartered by Louis Cruise Lines and sub-chartered to Thomson, the vessel was to carry the company's name in its name – *Thomson Spirit*.

*The Topaz* at Madeira, February 2002, after Thompson was absorbed into the German travel company TUI.

Once Holland America's *Nieuw Amsterdam*, *Thomson Spirit* is shown here at Agadir.

Built as the *Nieuw Amsterdam* for Holland America Cruises and designed for the US market the ship was one of a pair of stylish vessels.

In 2000 it was the intention of the newly formed United States Lines (a company that had acquired the name of the prime US operator on the North Atlantic in the days of the liner trade) to acquire the ship and rename her *Patriot*. The ship operated under this name for a brief period.

United States Lines were a victim of the 11 September 2001 terrorist attacks and the subsequent downturn in cruise bookings The ship reverted to the name *Nieuw Amsterdam* for a short while until she was placed on long-term charter by Holland America's parent company, the Carnival Group, in 2002 and given the *Thomson Spirit* name by her charterers, Louis Cruise Lines, to reflect the Thomson sub-charter. *Nieuw Amsterdam's* sister *Noordam* has become *Thomson Celebration*

### Thomson Destiny

See Sunbird under Airtours/My Travel. Sold to Louis Cruise Lines for charter to Thomson effective 2005.

# Union-Castle

Union-Castle was the best-known name on the UK–South Africa run, operating a series of mail ships that provided a high-quality, regular service. Formed by the merger of the Union Steam Ship Company and the Castle Line in 1900, the lilac-hulled vessels were a frequent sight in London, Southampton and Cape Town. In 1911 the company became part of the Royal Mail Group under the chairmanship of Lord Kyslant; the Kyslant empire suffering financial failure in the mid-1930s. In 1936 the shares of Union-Castle were placed back in the public market.

In 1956 Union-Castle, Clan Line and the Bullard King Groups were merged to form British & Commonwealth Shipping. In 1973 British & Commonwealth (Cayzer, Irvine & Co. – the major shareholder), Clan Line and the South African Marine Corporation (Saf Marine) combined their operations as International Liner Services. By 1982 air travel had decimated the liner trade and the final Union-Castle ships, both freighters, were sold.

Union-Castle was never a major player in the cruise market until the mid-1960s, although a number of its ships did cruise when not required for the company's core business – the mail service between the UK and South Africa.

Although not strictly UK market cruises it should be noted that the 11,951grt *Llangibby Castle* of 1929 and the *Durban Castle* and *Warwick Castle* of 1938 operated a series of 'round Africa' cruises during their careers. The passengers on many of these cruises were either British or British ex-pats.

The Union-Castle name became known to a wider audience of cruise passengers through the company's management and then ownership of the *Reina del Mar*.

In 1964 the ex-PSNC ship was chartered to the Travel Savings Association – TSA (owned jointly by Union-Castle, Canadian Pacific and Royal Mail Lines) and managed by the entrepreneur Max Wilson.

TSA became wholly owned by Union-Castle in late 1964 but the ship remained in the ownership of PSNC and charted to Union-Castle for five years. *Reina Del Mar* was painted in Union-Castle colours (lilac hull, red and black funnel) from November 1964. In 1973, prior to the expiry of the charter, the vessel was purchased outright by Union-Castle.

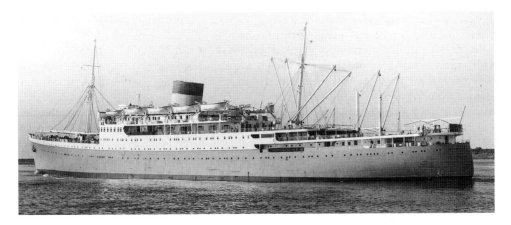

Union-Castle's *Braemar Castle* cruised from the UK in 1965.

## Braemar Castle

17,029grt
594.5ft length overall
76.5ft breadth
556 one-class passengers
Built in 1952 by Harland & Wolff, Belfast
Powered by steam turbines

*Braemar Castle* was one of four similar vessels (the others being *Kenya Castle*, *Rhodesia Castle* and their near sister *Bloemfontein Castle*). A combined cargo/passenger liner, she spent 1965 cruising out of the UK before being scrapped in Faslane, Scotland in 1966.

## Dunnottar Castle (1936)

15,002grt
560ft length overall
72ft breadth
258 first and 250 second-class passengers
Built in 1936 by Harland & Wolff, Belfast
Powered by two nine-cylinder engines

Note the different spelling to the *Dunottar Castle* of 1890.

Designed for the UK–South Africa mail service, *Dunnottar Castle* undertook seasonal UK market cruises both before and after the Second World War. During the war, she served as both an Armed Merchant Cruiser and a troopship.

In 1958 she was withdrawn and replaced by the *Rhodesia Castle*. She was sold in 1959 and completely reconstructed and re-engined in the Netherlands. When she emerged as the US market cruise ship *Victoria* for Incres Lines she was unrecognisable as the *Dunnottar Castle*. Despite a number of changes of owner and renaming as *The Victoria* (not be confused with the *Victoria* of P&O) she was still cruising in 2003 as the *Princesa Victoria* for Louis Cruise Lines – over sixty-seven years since she was laid down in Belfast. She was sold to be broken up in India in 2004.

## Dunottar Castle (1890)

5,625grt
433ft length overall
50ft breadth
160 first, 90 second and 100 third-class passengers
Built in 1890 by Fairfield Shipbuilding & Engineering Co., Govan, Scotland
Powered by triple-expansion steam engines driving a single screw

Note the different spelling to the *Dunnottar Castle* of 1936.

Designed as a fast mail steamer for the Castle Line, she joined the merged Union-Castle fleet in 1900 and served on the UK–South Africa route until she was laid up in Southampton Water between 1904 and 1907. She could also serve as a troopship for 1,000 troops. As built, she carried sails on her foremast but these were removed in 1897. In 1907 Sir Henry Lunn Ltd chartered her for cruises to the Mediterranean and the Norwegian fjords. *Dunottar Castle* also performed cruises in the Mediterranean. She was sold to Royal Mail in 1913 and renamed *Caribbean* but was requisitioned firstly as a troopship and then as an Armed Merchant Cruiser in 1914. Found to be unsuitable as an auxiliary warship she was converted into a dockyard accommodation ship. En route to Scapa Flow she foundered in heavy seas off Cape Wrath with the loss of fifteen lives.

## Dunvegan Castle

5,958grt
450.5ft length overall
51ft breadth
200 first and 400 third-class passengers
Built in 1896 by Fairfield Shipbuilding & Engineering Co., Govan, Scotland
Powered by triple-expansion steam engines driving a single screw

Built for the Castle Line mail service to South Africa she originally carried sails on her foremast but these were removed in 1900 when she was included in the merged Union-Castle fleet. In 1904 she spent a summer season operating cruises out of Southampton before being laid up until 1910. She was brought into service again but laid up once more in 1914 soon to be requisitioned as a troopship. In 1915 she was used to operate a wartime mail service to South Africa before her conversion to a hospital ship later that year. She was returned to her owners in 1916 but remained at the service of the Government. After the war she undertook brief charters to Cunard and the French Government before being laid up in 1921 and broken up in Germany in 1923.

## Reina del Mar

20,750grt
601ft length overall
78ft breadth
1,047 cruise passengers in one class
Built in 1956 by Harland and Wolff, Belfast
Powered by twin-screw geared turbines

The TSA *Reina del Mar* in Union-Castle livery.

She was built to join the *Reina Del Pacifico* of 1931 on the UK–South America service of the Pacific Steam Navigation Company (PSNC) – a subsidiary of Royal Mail Lines. As built the ship had a gross tonnage of 20,263 and carried 766 passengers in three classes.

In 1964 the ship was chartered to the Travel Savings Association and managed by the entrepreneur Max Wilson (as described above). Prior to the charter, the ship was given extra lido space and a cinema that was underneath the large, enclosed sundeck forward of the funnel. The forward cargo spaces were converted to passenger cabins. She entered cruising service at the time of the UK currency restrictions.

TSA became wholly owned by Union-Castle in late 1964 but the ship remained in the ownership of PSNC and chartered to Union-Castle for five years – eventually being purchased outright two years before her withdrawal.

Union-Castle used her for spring–autumn cruises out of the UK and for cruising in South American waters during the winter.

*Reina Del Mar* was positioned below Royal Mail's *Andes* but above the Greek operators in the British market and gave many middle-class Britons their first taste of cruising, as well as allowing them to have foreign holidays without the currency restrictions then in place. The cabins added to the ship later were plain and functional but many of her A-deck outside cabins retained the wonderful wooden murals fitted by PSNC. The ship was reputed to have the longest bar afloat.

The removal of currency restrictions, the competition from land-based package holidays, industrial unrest in the shipping industry and rises in the price of oil led to Union-Castle leaving the cruise market in 1975 and the *Reina Del Mar* was sold for scrapping in Taiwan where she arrived in July of that year.

In 1982 Union-Castle withdrew from the shipping industry altogether and the name disappeared. In 1999 the name and some of the company's memorabilia were acquired for use on a round-Africa Millennium cruise using P&O's *Victoria*, whose funnel was painted in the red and black of Union-Castle, albeit with her white hull.

## Rhodesia Castle

17,041grt
576.5ft length overall
74ft breadth
530 one-class passengers
Built in 1951 by Harland & Wolff, Belfast
Powered by steam turbines

*Rhodesia Castle* was one of three similar vessels, the others being *Braemar Castle* and *Kenya Castle*. It is interesting to note that there never was a real Rhodesia Castle or Kenya Castle, Union-Castle used the names of colonies they served together with their usual 'Castle' suffix. A combined cargo/passenger liner she undertook some UK market cruises in addition to her mail service to South Africa. She was laid up in 1967 and scrapped in Taiwan in the same year.

# Vacation Liners

The aim of Vacation Liners was to offer a totally 'no-frills' cruise operation; no cabin service (passengers made their own beds), buffet meals and minimal entertainment. The ship operated with a crew of just twenty-nine. Although Vacation Liners was a Dutch company, the *Vacationer* was initially aimed at the British market, being sold through Cadogan Travel, and began cruising in March 1982. However, the no-frills idea was a flawed concept, and in 1987 the ship was placed in lay-up in Curacao and the idea was abandoned.

## Vacationer

2,446grt
251ft length overall
43ft breadth
176 passengers
Built in 1971 by De Merwede, Hardinxveld
Powered by a single-screw diesel engine

*Vacationer* began life as the short-sea container vessel *Craigavon*. In 1981, Vacation Liners acquired her with a revolutionary plan for her conversion into a cruise ship. The work was undertaken by the Scheepswerft Welgelegen yard in The Netherlands, and resulted in a most ungainly looking vessel, with the unimaginative name, *Vacationer*. She was usually based in Gibraltar, and cruised to ports along the southern Spanish coast. During the winter of 1983/84 she was positioned in the Caribbean, and in 1986 was renamed *Carib Vacationer*. During the summer months she still operated cruises in the Mediterranean. Whilst there have been several attempts to return her to service, the ship has remained idle since 1992.

# Voyages of Discovery

In 1984, a Sussex-based company, Schools Abroad, chartered or arranged educational cruises on a large number of vessels. Latterly, the *Ocean Majesty* (see Page & Moy), *Funchal* and *Arion* (see Classic International), and *Aegean 1* have been used by the company – now known as Voyages of Discovery. A number of berths for independent travellers are offered in addition to the accommodation and activities for school children.

The company are also offering cruises on the newly named 19,907grt *Discovery*, ex-*Island Princess*, ex-*Island Venture* of 1971 – one of the two original 'Love Boats®' from the television series. The vessel was refurbished to a high standard for the 2003 season. Since moving into the adult cruise market in the late 1980s the company has found that there is a ready market for cruises that are informative and which have an intellectual content.

Since 1984 the company has provided nearly 200 cruises accommodating some 90,000 students, teachers and adult passengers on destination-intensive cruises designed to bring geography and history to life.

## Aegean 1

11,563grt
461ft length overall
67ft breadth
682 (maximum) cruise passengers
Built in 1972 by Santierul Naval Galatz, Galatz, Romania as *Narcis*
Powered by twin diesel engines

Built in 1972 as the ro–ro carrier *Narcis* for Zim Navigation of Israel she was sold in 1985 to Dolphin Hellas Shipping and given the temporary name of *Alkyon* whilst undergoing conversion to a cruise ship. She emerged in 1988 as the *Aegean Dolphin*. She has also been named just *Dolphin* (1989–90), *Aegean Dolphin* again (1990–98) before becoming the *Aegean 1* of Golden Star Cruises in 1999. Often chartered to travel operators she has been used by Voyages of Discovery for some of the company's educational cruises.

## Discovery

19,907grt
553ft length overall
81ft breadth
717 (maximum) cruise passengers
Built in 1972 by Rheinstahl Nordseewerk, Germany
Powered by twin diesel engines

Built as the *Island Venture* for Flagship Cruises, the ship and her sister *Sea Venture* entered service in 1972 and 1971, respectively. They became the *Island Princess* and *Pacific Princess* of Princess Cruises in September 1972. Princess cruises was acquired by P&O in 1974 and in 1975 the ships became the stars of the US (and later UK) television series 'The Love Boat'. Island Princess left the P&O/Princess fleet in 2000 to become the *Hyundai Pungak* for what turned out to be an unsuccessful venture operating cruises between South and North Korea. In 2003, however, she was purchased by the shipping entrepreneur Gerry Herrod (and was briefly named *Platinum*) and now operates for Voyages of Discovery as the *Discovery*.

# White Star

Up to the 1930s, the White Star Line was one of the best known of British shipping companies. Operating on the North Atlantic the company was known for its large, luxurious steamers. Whilst the name of the White Star liner *Titanic* is recognised worldwide, the company had a series of very luxurious liners where the concentration was on size and luxury rather than speed. White Star ceased to compete for the Blue Riband at the turn of the twentieth century, allowing Cunard to uphold the British name for fast crossings.

Owned by J.P. Morgan International Mercantile Marine combine of the US until after the First World War, White Star became part of the Royal Mail Group in 1929. Royal Mail became bankrupt as a result of financial irregularities aggravated by the Depression and the British Government forced a merger in 1934 between White Star and its rival Cunard as a condition of a subsidy for the construction of the *Queen Mary* and the *Queen Elizabeth*. The new company was known as Cunard White Star. Even in 2004, the Cunard cruise liner *Caronia* had a special White Star menu one night on longer cruises and Cunard have trademarked the phrase 'White Star Service'.

In the Depression years of the 1920s and early 1930s, even the *Titanic*'s surviving sister *Olympic* undertook short bank holiday cruises out of the UK to raise revenue.

White Star did not enter the cruise market to the same extent as Cunard but the company did employ the *Baltic* and *Homeric* on a series of UK market cruises. In 1927 White Star purchased the *Orca*, a PSNC vessel that had been transferred to Royal Mail and renamed her *Calgaric*. Laid up in 1931, she was made available for a single cruise to the Baltic that year when her passengers were boy scouts.

## Baltic

23,884grt
726ft length overall
75ft breadth
425 first, 450 second and 2,000 steerage-class passengers
Built in 1904 by Harland & Wolff, Belfast
Powered by twin quadruple-expansion engines

The largest ship in the world when launched, the *Baltic* undertook a small number of Mediterranean cruises in the early 1900s. Carrying cruise passengers only in her first and second-class accommodation did not make for an economic operation and the ship was soon employed full-time on the North Atlantic run for which she was built.

## Doric

16,484grt
601ft length overall
67ft breadth
600 cabin-class and 1,700 third-class passengers
Built 1923 by Harland & Wolff, Belfast
Powered by twin screw, geared turbines

*Doric* entered service on 8 June 1923 on the Liverpool–Montreal service. As a result of the Depression *Doric* was taken off the Canadian service at the end of 1932 and was refitted as a full-time cruise ship. Along with fleet mates *Homeric* and *Laurentic*, she

*Baltic*, one of White Star's Big Four, was used for cruising early in her career here at Monte Carlo.

Showing the damage from *Formigny, Doric* is lowering her lifeboats as crew inspect the damage to her side directly under the Bridge on her last cruise before scrapping.

operated cruises from Southampton and Liverpool, and sometimes these ships were wholly chartered to travel agencies to operate the cruises under their own names. In September 1935, whilst returning from a Mediterranean cruise, she collided with the French cargo ship, *Formigny*, off the Portuguese coast, and was seriously damaged. Temporary repairs were made at Vigo but once the ship arrived back at Tilbury it was decided that she was beyond economic repair and was sold for scrap at Newport, Wales.

*Laurentic*, which had entered service in 1927, was also used during the early Depression years as a cruise ship, and in 1932 she was used as an exhibition ship for British goods, visiting major Canadian Atlantic coast ports. After a serious collision in August 1935, most of the following four years were spent in lay-up. She briefly served as an Armed Merchant Cruiser and was sunk by a torpedo in November 1940.

The 1907-built *Adriatic*, which had been converted into a cabin-class ship in 1928, was used in 1933 – her final year of service – operating a series of cruises out of Liverpool.

*Homeric*

34,351grt
775ft length overall
83ft breadth
Approx 1,200 cruise passengers
Built in 1913 by F.Schichau, Danzig
Powered by twin-screw triple-expansion engines

*Homeric* was laid down as the *Columbus* for Norddeutscher Lloyd's North Atlantic service. She was launched in 1913 but in 1918 she remained uncompleted and was handed over to Britain in 1920, being bought by White Star the following year. Her construction and fitting out was completed at Danzig, and she entered service on the Southampton–New York service in February 1922. Although her modest speed did not allow her to maintain fully the regular three-ship Atlantic service with *Majestic* and *Olympic* that White Star wanted, she remained on the run for ten years. In 1932 White Star decided to withdraw her from the North Atlantic and convert her into a cruise ship. *Homeric* was as luxurious as any of the major liners on the Atlantic service and the company made a great deal of this in promoting her for her new role. While *Homeric* operated several cruises from New York, she also undertook cruises from both Southampton and Liverpool to the Atlantic Islands, West Africa and the Mediterranean. Her role as a cruise ship was, however, to be short lived. When Cunard and White Star merged, in 1934, *Homeric* was one of the first ships to be disposed of. She was laid-up off the Isle of Wight in September 1935 after having returned from a cruise. The following February she was sold to T.W. Ward at Inverkeithing to be scrapped.

   White Star Line also operated their 15,801grt liner *Arabic* as a cruise ship. In 1905 she made the first of several annual spring cruises to the Mediterranean.


# Yeoward Line

Yeoward Line began life as fruit importers, and purchased their first ships in 1900, trading between Liverpool and Portugal, Spain and the Canary Islands. The limited passenger accommodation on their first ships proved to be so popular that in 1903 they placed an order with the Caledon yard for the *Ardeola*, with a maximum passenger capacity of

White Star's *Homeric* at Funchal, 1933 with the Booth Line's *Hilary*.

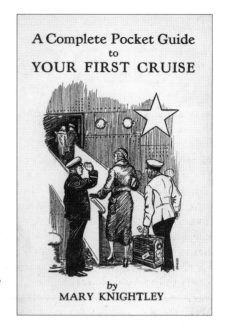

A Complete Pocket Guide
to
YOUR FIRST CRUISE

by
MARY KNIGHTLEY

A pocket guide to your first White Star Line cruise – the contents of which have much information still relevant to today's cruiser.

thirty-six. Three further ships were built, each with a further increase in passenger accommodation, and with these ships Yeoward developed a very popular cruise service, from Liverpool down to the Canary Islands, Madeira and Portugal. In fact, the 'Yowas', as they were known in the Canaries, probably initiated the Canaries cruise call, carrying at least seventy passengers there every week. The company suffered severe losses during the Second World War but returned to the service in 1946. In 1959 the contract to carry Canary Islands produce was lost to Aznar Line, with Yeoward acting as their Liverpool agents.

## Andorinha

2,548grt
290ft length o.a.
Built by Caledon Shipbuilding & Engineering Co. Ltd, in 1911
115 passengers

*Andorinha* sailed in Yeoward service until 1929 when sold to the Pacific Steam Navigation Co. for whom she sailed as *Champerico*. She was later sold to Chilean owners and sailed until 1960 as the *Vina Del Mar*.

## Ardeola

3,140grt
310ft length o.a.
Built by Caledon Shipbuilding & Engineering Co. Ltd in 1912
110 passengers (approximately)

*Ardeola* was the last ship to be delivered to the company before the outbreak of the First World War. She returned to Yeoward's Canary Islands service after the war and remained thus until requisitioned for service at Aden as a result of Italy's invasion of Abyssinia in

1935. Although returned to Yeoward the following year she no longer carried passengers. She was sunk in 1943, after being captured by Vichy forces off Tunisia.

## Aguila

3,255grt
315ft length o.a.
Built by Caledon Shipbuilding & Engineering Co. in 1917
110 passengers (approximately)

*Aguila*'s launch had to be delayed until September 1916 and she was not completed until the following November. She operated on the company's passenger/cargo service to the Canaries up until the outbreak of the Second World War. She was sunk in a torpedo attack in August 1941.

## Alondra

3,445grt
319ft length o.a.
Built by Caledon Shipbuilding & Engineering Co. in 1922
110 passengers (approximately)

*Alondra* sailed for the company until 1938 when she was sold to the Chilean State Railways. She remained in their service until 1959 when she was broken up.

## Avoceta

3,442grt
319ft length o.a.
Built by Caledon Shipbuilding & Engineering Co. in 1923

*Avoceta* entered Yeoward service in early 1923 on the Canaries run but by the 1930s the company also sent her on other cruises. It was planned for her to sail on two cruises into the Baltic in the summer of 1939. The second of these cruises was hurriedly cut short while the ship was at Stockholm in late August. *Avoceta* was sunk in September 1941 while in a convoy heading for Britain.

## Alca

3.712grt
319ft length o.a.
Built by Caledon Shipbuilding & Engineering Co. in 1927
110 passengers (approximately)

*Alca* entered service in August 1927 on the Canaries run. *Alca* was the only Yeoward ship to survive the war: during this time she had operated as a minelayer base ship. She underwent an extensive renovation and rebuild and returned to Yeoward's passenger/cargo service in 1946. She remained in this service until May 1954, which was the end of the Yeoward passenger operation; from then until 1959 they operated cargo only vessels. *Alca* briefly sailed under a charter between Denmark and Greenland before being sold for scrap. She was broken up at Preston in 1955.

# BIBLIOGRAPHY

## Books

Cartwright, Roger and Baird, Carolyn, *The Development and Growth of the Cruise Industry*, Butterworth–Heinemann, 1999.

Cooke, Anthony, *Liners and Cruise Ships – Some Notable Smaller Vessels*, Carmania Press, 1996.

Cooke, Anthony, *Liners and Cruise Ships – 2 – Some More Notable Smaller Vessels*, Carmania Press, 2000.

Cooke, Anthony, *Liners and Cruise Ships – 3 – Further Notable Smaller Vessels*, Carmania Press, 2003.

Dawson, Philip, *Canberra – in the Wake of a Legend*, Conway, 1997.

Dawson, Philip, *Cruise Ships – an Evolution in Design*, Conway, 2000.

De Kerbrech, Richard P., *Shaw Savill Line*, Ship Pictorial Publications, 1992.

Fox, Robert (with Harvey, Clive – consultant), *Liners – the Golden Age*, Könemann, 1999.

Kludas, Arnold, *Great Passenger Ships of the World Today*, Patrick Stephens, 1976.

Harvey, Clive, *Saxonia Sisters*, Carmania Press, 2001.

Harvey, Clive, *The Last White Empresses*, Carmania Press, 2004.

Haws, Duncan, *Merchant Fleets – Royal Mail and Nelson Line*, TCL Publications, 1982.

Haws, Duncan, *Merchant Fleets No 11 – British India S N Co.*, TCL Publications, 1987.

Haws, Duncan, *Merchant Fleets No 18 – Union, Castle and Union-Castle Lines*, TCL Publications, 1990.

Howarth, David and Howarth, Stephen, *The Story of P&O*, revised edition, Weidenfeld & Nicolson, 1994.

Ingall, Carola, *The P&O Line*, Ship Pictorial Publications, 1997.

Louden-Brown, Paul, *The White Star Line*, Ship Pictorial Publications, 1992.

Mallett, Alan S., *The Union-Castle Line*, Ship Pictorial Publications, 1990.

Maxton-Graham, John, *Liners to the Sun*, Macmillan, 1985.

Maxton-Graham, John, *Crossing and Cruising*, Scribers, 1992.

McAuley, Rob, *The Liners*, Boxtree, 1997.

McCart, Neil, *Passenger Ships of the Orient Line*, Patrick Stephens, 1987.

Miller, William, *The Great Luxury Liners, 1927–1954*, Dover, 1981.

Miller, William, *The First Great Ocean Liners, 1897–1927*, Dover, 1984.

Miller, William, *Great Cruise Ships and Ocean Liners from 1954 to 1986*, Dover, 1988.

Miller, William, *Picture History of the Cunard Line*, Dover, 1991.

Miller, William, *Modern Cruise Ships, 1965–1990*, Dover, 1992.

Miller, William, *Pictorial Encyclopaedia of Ocean Liners, 1860–1994*, Dover, 1995.

Miller, William, *Ocean Liner Chronicles*, Carmania press, 2001.

Miller, William, *Picture History of British Ocean Liners, 1900 to the Present*, Dover, 2001.

Newall, Peter, *Union-Castle Line: a Fleet History*, Carmania Press, 1999.

P&O, *Oriana – from Dream to Reality*, P&O, 1995.

P&O, *Aurora – Dawn of a New Era*, P&O, 2000.

Williams, David L., *Glory Days: Cunard*, Ian Allan, 1998.

Williams, David L., *Glory Days: P&O*, Ian Allan, 1998.

Wooley, Peter W. and Moore, Terry, *The Cunard Line*, Ship Pictorial Publications, 1990.

## Magazines

*Fairplay – the International Shipping Weekly*
*Marine News – World Ship Society*
*Sea Breezes*
*Sea Lines – the Magazine of the Ocean Liner Society*
*Ships Monthly*

# INDEX OF SHIPS